Free Stuff From the Internet is a great way to learn about what the Internet can do for you.
—*MacDigest*

What does everybody want? Free Stuff. So if you're a super-highway aficio-nado, take a look at *Free Stuff From the Internet.*
—*PC Magazine*

Free Stuff From the Internet promises that if you're the kind of person who hangs out at Happy Hour for the free food, this book is definitely for you.
—*Online Access* Magazine

I am not sure what got may attention first, the words *Free Stuff* in the title or the bright neon green cover. Whatever it was, I am thankful!
—*Windows User News*

Patrick Vincent

Free Stuff From the Internet offers enough information to be worth 10 times the price!
—*The Reader's Review*

This book is exactly what it claims to be: a huge collection of freebies from the Internet.
—*The Toronto Star*

 CORIOLIS GROUP BOOKS

D1304680

Publisher	Keith Weiskamp
Editor	Ron Pronk
Proofreader	Jenni Aloi
Interior Design	Rob Mauhar
Cover Design	Keith Weiskamp and Bradley O. Grannis
Layout Production	Rob Mauhar and Anthony Stock
Publicist	Shannon Bounds
Indexer	Lenity Mauhar

Library of Congress Cataloging-in-Publication Data

Vincent, Patrick 1963-
    Free Stuff From the Internet / Patrick Vincent
        p. cm.
    Includes Index
    ISBN 1-883577-11-x : $19.99

Printed in the United States of America

10 9 8 7 6

Contents

Computers and Software   *71*

Education and Teaching Tools 109

The Environment and Nature 121

Food and Cooking   129

Games   139

Government and Politics   149

Health and Nutrition 161

History 181

Household and Consumer Finance   *191*

Humor   *207*

International Affairs 217

Internet Resources 229

Kid Stuff 241

Language and Linguistics   253

Law   263

Movies and Videotapes   273

FREE $TUFF from the Internet

Shopping   *323*

Space and Astronomy   *333*

FREE $TUFF *from the Internet*

The Tightwad's Guide To Mosaic　　　*379*

The Poor Man's Passport to Cyberville   *429*

Preface

Psst. Can we let you in on a little secret? You're making history. Right now.

"Who, *me*?" you say?

You may not realize it, but by the simple act of reading this book you're making history. You're becoming an accomplice to the greatest revolution mankind has ever realized. Bigger than the French Revolution. Bigger than the Russian, American, and Chinese revolutions combined.

Times 10. Times 100. And not a shot has been fired.

A revolution in communication is raging around the world, and it's called the Internet. And whether you realize it or not, you are now on your way to being the latest foot soldier in this latter-day Information Crusade. Welcome to the Internet.

This might be your first Internet book (if so, it likely will not be your last), or you may have a shelf full at home. It doesn't really matter. *FREE $TUFF* is for *anyone* interested in learning about the latest treasures available on the Internet, many free for the taking. And it's for people interested in saving money.

Whether you're a student, teacher, doctor, lawyer, business executive, priest, rabbi, full-time parent, or full-time kid—this book has something for you: games, business and personal finance software, sports, pictures, self-help guides, and more, more, more. But this list only scratches the surface. Browse through some of the topics in the book and you'll be amazed at the huge variety of freebies, bargains, and timesavers offered here. It's simple to get started, so hop aboard and start saving money!

Getting Started

If you've never cruised the Internet superhighway, you'll soon see that the Internet doesn't have to be an intimidating mish-mash of high-tech cryptic jargon. As you'll learn, a few simple commands will take you a long way, and in just a few hours, you'll have mastered the basics and will be heading down the road to full-fledged Internet guru status.

Experienced Internauts know that the sheer vastness of Cyberspace makes it impossible to discover all the best freebies on their own. With this book, you'll pick up the tricks and tips that will get you pointed to parts of the Internet you didn't even know existed so you can start digging up your own hidden treasures.

Cyberspace Evolves

While the actual writing of this book was done in a flurry of several months, its true evolution has taken place over years of exploring, writing about, and teaching others the fundamentals of traveling Cyberspace. A lot of careful checking and rechecking by a lot of talented people went into researching the sites listed in this book. Usually, they remained constant, but sometimes—just enough to cause headaches throughout production—an address would change, a file would no longer be found, or an entire site would be swallowed up overnight, vanishing without a trace, an electronic Atlantis. These mishaps served as a constant reminder that the Internet is a work in progress, an expanding universe of ideas and knowledge, growing and changing.

Shareware

Many of the "freebies" you'll find in this book are a result of a software marketing strategy known as *shareware*. Shareware programs are ones you can download for free, try out for free, and if you don't care for them, toss out for free—sort of a "try before you buy, drive it around the block" approach to selling software. But if you decide you like a program, most programmers ask that you send them a little something for the effort they put into developing the programs, an electronic "passing of the hat" if you will. Once you've registered your software, most programmers will send you upgraded programs with more bells and whistles than the hobbled version you're using. Look for registration information when you load the programs.

Acknowledgments

Although this book has only one name on the cover, it would never have gotten out of the idea stage were it not for the help and dedication of a core of highly talented sadists, whip-crackers, gluttons for punishment, and obsessive compulsives:

- My wife, Lisa, for her constant help, encouragement, and support through every phase of this book's development. Lisa's love helped keep me sane through the often insane process of writing.

- Ron Pronk for his patience, leadership, motivation, and dedication from conception to final production. Ron was able to take my random acts of raving and turn them into coherent bits of information.

- Keith Weiskamp for his original vision of what this book could be. I appreciate his confidence in me and for actually paying me to write a book that was a true labor of love.

- Jeff Duntemann for his input on all things Mosaic. Jeff has been a sounding board and troubleshooter for the duration of this project.

- Jenni Aloi for her indefatigable editing and proofreading, which always improved the quality of the manuscript. There are few professions in which obsession is such an overriding prerequisite, and Jenni has found her niche.

- Shannon Bounds for constantly feeding me with new ideas and information for inclusion in the book. Her tireless efforts in tracking down leads and breaking through the brick walls I banged my head against were always appreciated.

- Rob Mauhar, whose talent for layout made the manuscript come to life with its pictures and artwork. Through Rob's efforts, the sum has truly been made greater than the parts.

- Special thanks to PageMaker™ gurus Anthony Stock and Brad Grannis for their general good cheer and willingness to make a seemingly endless stream of last minute changes to the page proofs. Never once did they grumble (at least not to *my* face).
- The publisher would like to thank John Kilcullen of IDG Books for his great encouragement and Vince Emery for his fantastic suggestions and advice.

Finally, thank you to all the faceless personalities and characters I've exchanged E-mail with throughout this project. I wish I had the room to thank each of them here. Their encouragement and help in providing lists and pointers to their favorite sites throughout Cyberspace proved an invaluable resource that never went unnoticed nor unappreciated.

Send Me Your Comments

The development of a book is like an experiment performed in the sterility of a laboratory. Final input on its contents was determined by a small group based on their personal tastes, as well as their opinions of what others would like or dislike. But all of this is just guessing. Nothing is certain until we hear back from the ones whose opinions mean the most: the readers. Let us know what you liked about *FREE $TUFF from the Internet*. Let us know what you disliked, as well. I would appreciate any suggestions or comments you may have. I can be reached at:

pvincent@coriolis.com

Patrick Vincent
Phoenix, Arizona
October 1994

 # FREE $TUFF

Get your motor running
Head out on the highway
Lookin' for adventure
In whatever comes our way . . .

BORN TO BE WILD, Steppenwolf

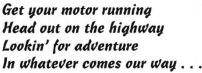

Getting
the Goods

1

Truth Is Stranger than Science Fiction

It sounds like the plot to a low-budget science fiction movie: Government scientists working on a secret military project devise a weapon designed to protect the United States during the Cold War. Their experiment is a success, but it has some unexpected consequences, consequences that none of them could have foreseen. Their creation grows and grows, slowly at first, but then its size increases almost exponentially, until it's bigger than anyone would ever have imagined. Soon its effects are felt around the globe, a computer-generated monster that no one can control.

Okay, enough of the melodrama. But read between the Saturday matinee story lines and what I said is true. The Internet's beginnings can be traced back to the late 1960s when the Advanced Research Projects Agency— part of the United States Department of Defense—created ARPANET, a computer network designed to safeguard military data stored on computers around the country. Four computers, located in universities in California and Utah and used to conduct military research, were strategically linked through ARPANET so that if one link in the network failed (or, more accurately, was destroyed as a casualty of the impending nuclear war), the remaining computers in the network would continue to communicate with one another.

It worked, and computers at universities and military research sites around the country started linking up to this fledgling network. Soon, other networks were created. Like drops of water that join to form a pool, these networks began linking together into networks of networks. Thousands of networks later, this huge intertwining of phone lines, cables, monitors, and keyboards has become the Granddaddy of all networks: the Internet.

The Freebies Center of the Universe

If you're a bargain hunter, you're going to love the Internet. Every corner of it is packed with free goodies: newsletters, software, photos, art, video clips, music, catalogs, coupons, product samples, and lots more! It's a tightwad's gold mine; a shopaholic's dream come true!

But one thing the Internet lacks is organization, and it's easy to spend hours looking for your diamond in the rough if you're not sure where to look. It would be like burning ten dollars of gasoline driving around town hoping to save five dollars on a sale item. That's not exactly our idea of a good deal. *FREE $TUFF from the Internet* points you right to the bargains, and helps you to find your own bargains along the way. With this book, you'll find great freebies for your:

- Business

- Vacation

- Health

- Funny bone

- Sports fetish

And that's just a small sampling of the subjects you'll find in *FREE $TUFF from the Internet.*

Let Me Talk to the Guy In Charge

While there are several groups who help guide the Internet (the Internet Society and Electronic Frontier Foundation, among others) no one owns it—yet everyone owns it. It's a computer-age cooperative maintained and operated by the multitude of networks—universities, non-profit organizations, government agencies, large corporations, and more—of which it's comprised.

And it's growing . . . . From those first four computers and a couple hundred users just over 20 years ago, the Internet now links over 25 million users on three million computers in more than 150 countries!

And growing . . . . The Internet doubles in size every year.

And growing . . . . By the year 2000, estimates Vint Cerf, one of the original developers of the Internet and president of the Internet Society,

there will be as many as 500 million people hooked into the Internet on 100 million computers worldwide.

Many corporations are already conducting business on the Internet. Customers can use it to order products, request samples, and order or download catalogs. Just as mail order and the use of toll-free numbers exploded over the last several years, the Internet is fast emerging as the tool of choice by many businesses to keep in touch with their customers. As this trend continues, just think of all the great freebies you'll be able to get your hands on! And we'll be telling you how to get them just as fast as we can.

Who Uses It

Before the Internet and other networks were available to the masses, working at your computer meant, in essence, shutting the rest of the world out. Sure, you could load programs and files onto it, but that's the proverbial equivalent of the mountain coming to you. What if you wanted to look something up at the Library of Congress? Are you going to load all their data on floppy disks and put them on your computer? There ain't that many floppy disks available, folks.

What if you wanted the latest information on AIDS research? You could subscribe to the leading medical and scientific journals, then wait by your mail box in hopes they have just the information you want. It's the information age, but information doesn't do you much good unless it's available *when* you need it, *where* you need it.

But now through your computer you can go to the mountain—instantly. When you connect to the Internet, you travel through Cyberspace to Croatia where you're given first-hand accounts of the latest fighting-truce-fighting. You jump to Washington, D.C. to find out word-for-word what the President said about health care today. In Germany you heatedly debate the pros and cons of sending U.S. troops to Haiti. And maybe you relax by challenging someone in the U.K. to a game of backgammon. The possibilities are endless, limited only by your imagination. You can even access a company's computer, such as Apple, and download free upgrade software.

Who's Out There?

Who uses the Internet? Really, the question is who *doesn't* use it. Once jealously guarded by scientists and techno-nerds, today the Internet is open to anyone:

- Researchers (the life-blood of the Internet). Today scientists communicate world wide, exchanging ideas and data in minutes where it used to take weeks.

- Students. Many colleges and universities offer free access to students and faculty, and some courses are even going "paperless," with all handouts and tests distributed by computer.

- Parents. Moms and dads keep in touch with their college-bound children.

- The police. The FBI is using the Internet to try to find leads to unsolved crimes.

- World leaders. Even the White House is getting in on the act. (you can send notes to the President by using the special address: president@whitehouse.gov.)

- Executives. Business men, while in flight, are hooking up their laptops to the telephones installed on passenger planes so they can read their mail and transfer files back to the home office.

- Sports fans. There are discussion groups and team schedules available for every sport imaginable.

- Shoppers. Virtual "malls" are popping up everywhere as bargain hunters and shopaholics look for everything from gourmet coffees to new automobiles.

- Terrorists. Iraqi troops used the Internet to communicate with each other after their military communication lines were decimated during the Gulf War, ironically proving that the Internet's original purpose had been realized.

Joining the party is simple. All you need is a computer (nearly any kind will do), a modem, a phone line, and a way to connect. See the *Computers* section later in this book for details about online providers, what they offer, and where to go for more information. Most will even provide you with *free* airtime to let you test out their services (something I strongly recommend).

Some Internet Providers Are More Equal than Others

It's important to note that while all of the online services mentioned in this book provide Internet access, many of them offer only *limited* access. If you want to get the most out of this book, you'll need all the bells and whistles. Read *Tools of the Trade* later in this chapter to see what tools you'll need to get to the far corners of Cyberspace.

Is This Book for You?

FREE $TUFF from the Internet is written for Internet users and Internet wannabe's around the world. It shows you some of the best freebies the Internet has to offer. It's for those who witness with excitement the information explosion we're experiencing, and who comprehend that the future of communications technology is incomprehensible. It's for those who understand that the flood gates holding back a revolution in information technology have opened, but that we're nowhere near the high water mark.

- If you're looking for adventure, knowledge, great bargains, and cool freebies, *FREE $TUFF from the Internet* is for you.

- If you enjoy the thrill of the chase as much as the kill, *FREE $TUFF from the Internet* is for you.

- If you want to learn how to get the best the Internet has to offer— newsletters, software, photos, art, video clips, music, catalogs, product samples, and even free Internet access time, *FREE $TUFF from the Internet* is for you.

- If you're the kind of person who hangs out at Happy Hour for the free food, *FREE $TUFF from the Internet* is *definitely* for you.

Getting Connected

FREE $TUFF from the Internet is a book about the Internet. An obvious statement, true, but necessary nonetheless. Too many books containing thousands of entries about all the great places you can visit in Cyberspace and all the great things you can find there are crammed onto already crowded shelves. But think before you buy: One book may point you to all the great stuff available on America Online, and then show you all the hot software on CompuServe. But what it won't say is that unless you belong to more than one online service, only a fraction of the "thousands" of listings you read about will be available to you.

If you subscribe to Delphi, for instance, you're not getting past the front door at America Online. If you're on Prodigy, those listings for CompuServe won't do you any good.

This book was written with one purpose: If you have full Internet access, *everything* you read about is yours free for the taking. There are many commercial full-service Internet providers you can choose from, several of which are discussed next.

Online Access Providers

Getting hooked up to the Internet doesn't have to be complicated. There are many online providers that will even give you several free hours to try out their services—sort of a "try-before-you-buy" approach before you make a choice. The ones listed below are the most popular online services (in no particular order), and they all have different degrees of Internet access—from basic E-mail to all the bells and whistles. Try them all so you can compare their different features.

One Free Month of CompuServe

You'll get free, easy-to-use software and a free month of unlimited online time for basic services and e-mail access to the Internet.

Dial

(800) 848-8990

Ask For

Free trial subscription

Free DELPHI Trial Membership

Explore the Internet with five hours of free access time. DELPHI offers you *full* access to the Internet: FTP, Gopher, Telnet, and more.

Dial

(800) 695-4005

Ask For

Free trial subscription

BIX Trial Offer

Five hours of free online time for new members. BIX allows *full* Internet access: Usenet news, Gopher, FTP, Archie, and more. An easy-to-use graphical interface for Windows makes it easy to navigate the Internet.

Dial

(800) 695-4775

Ask For

Free trial subscription

America Online—For Free

Ten free hours to explore what America Online has to offer. You'll get access to the Internet, including Gopher, FTP, newsgroups, and E-mail. AOL expects to offer World Wide Web access and 28,800 baud modem access by mid 1995. AOL also offers Time magazine online before it hits the newsstands, "real-time" conversations with other AOL members on dozens of different topics, online shopping, encyclopedias, and more.

Dial

(800) 827-6364

Ask For

Free trial subscription

Online with Prodigy

Ten hours of free Prodigy airtime will get you connected to Internet E-mail and World Wide Web, online shopping, games, encyclopedias, and much more. Great for kids.

Dial

(800) PRODIGY

Ask For

Free trial subscription

These are just the leading online service providers, though there are dozens of others. While many providers offer complete Internet access, not all offer you free online time to explore their services. Prices, though, are generally pretty reasonable. For a list of Internet providers you may want to check out, see the *Internet Service Providers* section at the back of this book.

Also, many universities provide full Internet access to students for free, as do many companies for their employees. You may already have a free link giving you full access to the Internet without even being aware of it!

Free-Nets

A new phenomena—*free-nets*—are also starting to appear. Free-nets are community-run computer networks that offer lots of information of local interest. Many also provide links to the Internet. Turn to the Free-net section at the back of this book, or check with your local public library to see if your community has a free-net you can access.

Tools of the Trade

To take advantage of all the Internet has to offer, you first need to familiarize yourself with some of the tools you'll be using on it. While you can still surf Cyberspace without access to all of these tools, you'll be limited as to what you can do. As I said earlier, not all online services offer the same tools. Those who tout *complete* Internet access offer all of the bells and whistles listed next and then some, while others may offer only one or two. Be sure of what you're getting *before* you sign up with any of these services and you won't be disappointed later.

E-mail

E-mail (electronic mail) is the basic foundation tool for communicating on the Internet. Any online service that offers even the barest of connections to the Internet offers E-mail.

If you work in a mid-size or larger office, you're probably already familiar with E-mail. It's been used in the business world for years to inform employees of meeting schedules, policy changes, and, of course, the latest gossip. On the Internet, E-mail is probably used more than any other tool. Its appeal lies in the fact that it's so fast and easy to use. For just pennies, you can instantly send a contract to a business partner or receive a cookie recipe from Aunt Fern across the country—or around the world. Just try that through conventional postal services. You can also use it to subscribe to online magazines and newsletters, access thousands of discussion groups, and send and receive computer files. To use E-mail:

1. Start your E-mail program (usually by typing **email** or clicking on an E-mail button, depending on your Internet provider).

2. At the To prompt, type the Internet address of the person or site you're sending mail to (**pvincent@delphi.com**, for example), then press **Enter**.

3. At the Subject prompt, type a brief description of the message you're sending (**Meeting Canceled**, for example), then press **Enter**.

4. Now you can type the note you wish to send. When you're finished, press **Ctrl+Z** or click on Send (again, depending on your Internet provider).

Know Your Name and Address ...

Conceptually, Internet addresses are very much like postal addresses or telephone numbers. Each is unique so that the only one who gets your messages is you (though like with the phone, you'll get the occasional wrong number, and as with the postal service, you'll get your share of junk mail). Internet addresses are made up of a person's user ID, an @ (at) symbol, the person's online service provider, and the type of site (such as *com* for commercial Internet providers, *edu* for educational institutions like colleges and universities, and *mil* for military sites). Each of these pieces is then connected by "dots" (periods) that collectively make up your address.

If you look at the address earlier in this section (pvincent@delphi.com), you'll see that the user's ID is pvincent, he's located *at* (@) Delphi (the company that links him to the Internet), and that Delphi is a commercial Internet provider (com). Simple.

FTP

File Transfer Protocol, or *FTP*, is a program you use to copy files stored on computers around the globe. Games, software upgrades, pictures, and documents are yours to download by using FTP. To FTP a file:

1. Start your FTP program (either from an FTP menu or from a command prompt by typing **FTP**), then enter the name of the FTP site you wish to access (**ftp ftp.nevada.edu**, for example).

   This FTP site at the University of Nevada is very popular. It contains all kinds of free sheet music for guitar players that you can copy and download to your own computer.

2. Once you've connected, you'll be prompted to enter a username. Press **Enter** or type **anonymous**.

3. When prompted for a password, enter your username and address (**pvincent@delphi.com**, for example). While this isn't always necessary, it's good "netiquette" to let those running the site you're accessing know who's using it. (On the Internet, "anonymous" is a matter of courtesy . . .)

4. Go to the appropriate directory (**cd pub/guitar**, for example).

Read the documentation your online provider has about how to use FTP. Not all FTP programs work exactly the same way, so it would be impossible to cover all the differences here.

5. To go back up a directory, type **cdup** (no space).

6. Once you've located the freebie you want, you need to download it. Type **ascii** if the file extension is .TXT, otherwise type **binary**.

7. Type **get** *filename* where *filename* is the name of the file you're down-loading. For instance, to download a file called game.zip, you would type **get "game.zip"**.

8. To leave the FTP program, type **quit**.

Just the FAQs, Ma'am

Each Internet tool has its own FAQ (*frequently asked questions*) file that provides instructions on using that particular tool that you can read online or download and print. As the name suggests, FAQs give you the answers to the questions most often asked by new users. I highly recommend printing the FAQs so you have an easily accessible document that you can refer to as you wander the Internet.

Telnet

You use *Telnet* to "beam" to other computers anywhere in the world, and control them as though they were on your desk in front of you. Telnet differs from FTP because when you FTP to another computer you're only allowed to browse directories and download files. These are important and critical functions to be sure, but with Telnet you're actually hooked directly into the remote computer as though you're sitting in front of it. When you Telnet to the Library of Congress, for instance, it's like you're standing in its lobby, looking up the information you need. With Telnet, you can download files, play games against other people, read and leave messages, link to other computers, and much more. To Telnet:

1. Start your Telnet program (usually by typing **telnet**), then key in the name of the Telnet site you wish to access (**telnet fraggel65.**

mdstud.chalmers.se 4321, for example). This Telnet site, located in Sweden, let's you play backgammon against other Telnetters around the world.

2. Once you've connected, follow the instructions that appear (most Telnet sites will have you choose a login name and password, and may have you enter some other information).

If you're familiar with accessing bulletin boards, (or especially accessing remote Unix systems) you'll have no trouble using Telnet. It's really no different, you're merely using the Internet to link up with the remote computer instead of dialing to it direct (and paying the toll charges).

Telnetting to FedWorld and the CIC BBS

FedWorld, a huge government bulletin board, has links set up that allow you to connect to many other bulletin boards. One of the most popular and valuable links is to the Consumer Information Center's Bulletin Board Service (CIC BBS). Several entries in this book are for government publications of interest to consumers, and are downloadable from CIC. The following steps will help guide you to the files you're looking for:

1. Follow the login instructions (if it's your first time on FedWorld, you'll need to enter your name, address, and some other information, then choose a password).

2. Type **Q** to get to FedWorld's main menu.

3. Type **/GO GATEWAY**, then press **Enter** to go directly to FedWorld's Gateway System to Government BBSs.

4. Type **D**, then press **Enter** to connect to the Government system/ database.

5. At this point, there are over a hundred different bulletin boards for you to choose from. Type **6**, then press **Enter** to connect to the Consumer Information Center's BBS. (Press **?** for a listing of all the bulletin boards.)

6. Follow the login instructions (if it's your first time on CIC, you'll need to enter your name, address, and some other information, then choose a password).

7. Press **Enter** several times until you're at CIC's main menu.

8. Press **F**, then press **Enter**.

9. Type **D**.

10. Enter the filename you're downloading.

11. Press **Enter** to begin downloading the file.

12. Press **Y** if you'd like to automatically log off the CIC bulletin board and return to FedWorld after your file is downloaded.

Downloading files is really pretty simple, but it might seem a little intimidating the first couple of times, especially if you don't have much experience roaming around bulletin boards. Once you get the hang of it, though, you won't even need to refer to these steps.

Gopher

Gopher is one of the easiest Internet tools you can use to search for, view, and download documents, files, and other freebies. Because of its menu-driven simplicity, it's become one of the most popular ways to surf through Cyberspace. Often, the Gopher site you're accessing is connected to many other Gopher sites and utilities (such as FTP and Telnet) that you can shamelessly access.

The nice thing about Gopher is that you need very little technical knowledge to browse a site's directories and subdirectories; you just enter the number that corresponds to your selection or point and click. To use Gopher:

1. Start your Gopher program (usually by typing **gopher**).

2. Enter the item number you wish to access from the menu that appears or the name of the Gopher site you want to access (**gopher.gsfc.nasa.gov**, for example).

This Gopher site at the Goddard Space Flight Center is loaded with fun and interesting documents, files, and links to other Gophers. Suppose, for instance, you wanted to get information about your Congressional representatives, including their Washington addresses, phone numbers, and fax numbers. Once you've entered this Gopher site, follow these menu items down until you get to the Congressional member directory:

US Government

Congress

Congressional Directories

House Directory (from House Gopher)

Member Directory

3. You can then view the document online or download it to your computer and view it with any word processor or text editor.

World Wide Web (Mosaic)

The *World Wide Web (Mosaic)* is a collection of documents, graphics, videos, and other files scattered throughout the internet and linked together into hypertext documents on every concievable subject (and many that are inconcievable) for you to browse through.

One of the best tools for trolling through the WWW is a Windows-based interface called Mosaic, which itself is a freebie. Whenever you see the Mosaic icon that appears next to the previous heading, you'll know that the item is easily accessible via Mosaic. For more information on using Mosaic, please refer to *The Tightwad's Guide to Mosaic* near the back of the book.

Finger

You use the *Finger* command primarily to find out information about other users and computers. You can also modify what information is displayed about you when someone uses the Finger command with your user ID.

College instructors might display their office hours and reminders about upcoming tests, an office worker might post where she can be reached in an emergency, and some public information offices put up-to-the-minute postings about important events. If you type in the command **finger nasanews@space.mit.edu**, for instance, you'll get the latest news from NASA, including shuttle schedules, upcoming events, and other highlights. It's a very simple and handy way to get information without having to FTP or Telnet.

Usenet

Usenet is a collection of literally *thousands* of special interest newsgroups that you can access to read and discuss *thousands* of different topics. If you are into bike racing, try rec.bicycles.racing for racing tips, rules, and results. Have a question about nutrition? Post it to sci.med.nutrition. Maybe you'd like to put your two cents in about gun control. Send your argument to talk.politics.guns. With Usenet, there's literally something for everybody.

Usenet can be broken down into these eight basic areas:

news   News and information about Usenet

soc   Sociology-related news and issues

sci   Science-related news and issues

comp   Computer-related news and issues

rec   Sports, hobbies, and recreational topics

talk   Talk radio on the Internet, with discussions and debates on different topics of interest (you'll need a sound card and *a lot* of free disk space for this one)

alt   Discussions on alternative, bizarre, and often (by most people's standards) offensive subjects

misc   The catchall for odds and ends

To use Usenet:

1. Start your Usenet or newsgroup program (usually by typing **usenet**). Usually, you'll be given several options to choose from. For instance, you can display a list of available newsgroups or (if you know it) you can type in the name of the newsgroup you wish to access.

2. Enter the name of the newsgroup you want. A list of current subjects is displayed, as well as the number of posted messages available for you to read. The more popular newsgroups may have hundreds or even thousands of messages waiting for you to wade through.

3. You can either start at the top and start reading every message, or scan the subjects for the ones you're most interested in.

When you're done reading a message, you'll be asked if you want to read the next one, reply to the message you read, or post a message with a new subject.

Think before You Speak

Anyone can post messages, but it's a good idea to read a newsgroup for a week or two before you start participating in the discussions. This will give you a feel for the people who use that newsgroup and what topics have already been covered.

Mailing Lists (Listservers)

Mailing lists are very similar to newsgroups, except instead of you going to them, they come to you. In other words, when you subscribe to a mailing list, messages are sent to your Internet address as soon as they're posted, 24 hours a day, rather than being posted to a newsgroup. This way, you're constantly sent the latest information about whatever topic the mailing list covers.

Also, mailing lists generally are not the journalistic free-for-alls that newsgroups tend to be. Most have moderators who decide whether your message should be posted. Censorship to be certain, but without it, many intelligent debates quickly digress into sophomoric *flame wars* that almost everyone hates

Turning Up the Heat

A *flame* is an E-mail message that's sole intention is to insult, embarrass, harass, degrade, humiliate, and incite the person it was sent to (sounds like your typical Rush Limbaugh broadcast).

Rarely are flames sent confidentially. Instead, they're most often posted to a newsgroup for thousands to read. Naturally, someone who's been flamed is not likely to take it lying down, but will instead turn up the heat himself with a flame even nastier. The result is a full-blown *flame war* that can often take weeks and dozens or hundreds of messages to die down.

Some mailing lists are rather exclusive (that is, *snobby*) and won't let just *anyone* join, but most are pretty open. You just need to send E-mail to the mailing list's administrator or to the computer that automatically processes subscription requests and ask that you be added to the list.

Viewers

GIF and JPEG files are photographs, drawings, or other types of pictures that have been converted to electronic files. GIFs and JPEGs can be found all over the Internet, usually as files with the extensions .GIF or .JPG. You can download these files just as you would any other file, but in order to view them, you first need to download a viewer program, many of which are available on the Internet for all types of operating systems. See the *Computers* section of this book to find out where you can find a viewer to download. (Note also that you need a viewer to play sound files you get off the Internet.)

Archives

Some files available for downloading from the Internet have been compressed, so that they take up less space when stored on disk. Taking up less storage space also means that such files will take less time to download. A side benefit of most common compression schemes is that multiple files can be combined into a single compressed "archive" file that is smaller in size than the total size of the component files in the archive.

Archive files like this have file extensions of .ZIP, .Z, .GZ, .LZH, and others. There are numerous schemes for archive compression and decompression, and just as many different utilities for doing it. The most popular (especially for PC platforms) is the "ZIP" format created by PKWare and implemented in their PKZIP and PKUNZIP utilities. These are the files with the .ZIP extensions. SIT (StuffIt) is the most common format for Macintoshes. Regardless of the compression format used, you can uncompress the file(s) by downloading some of the many uncompressing utilities mentioned in the *Computers and Software* section of the book.

The PKUNZIP.EXE utility will "de-archive" .ZIP files and extract the contained files into separate files on your hard disk. Using PKUNZIP is simplicity itself: Simply execute the command PKUNZIP followed by the name of the .ZIP file you want to open, for instance **pkunzip carpix.zip**. This command will extract all files from the .ZIP file CARPIX.ZIP.

There are many options and other features of PKUNZIP, and you can display a brief help screen by entering the command **pkunzip** without any parameters.

The PKZIP and PKUNZIP utilities are shareware, and may be obtained on the Internet using Gopher or FTP. See the *Computers* section of this book for information on where to download your copy.

Encoding

Many newsgroups are little more than libraries for collections of pictures on a particular subject, such as fine art, cartoons, or even erotica. Since newsgroups can only be used to store and transmit *text* files, and since most pictures are *binary*, UUENCODE was developed. With UUENCODE, binary files are converted to text files, which can then be posted to newsgroups or sent through E-mail. Once you've downloaded the file you want, you convert it back to its original form using UUDECODE and view it with a GIF or JPEG viewer (which we discussed earlier). See the *Computers* section of this book to find out where you can get a copy of UUENCODE and UUDECODE to download.

Tips for Finding Your Own FREE $TUFF

We've never known anyone, no matter how much money they had in their pocket, who wouldn't stop to pick up a dollar bill lying on the sidewalk. It's ingrained in our "shop-till-you-drop, operators-are-standing-by, only-200-shopping-days-left-before-Christmas" mentalities never to pass up a good deal.

You might think you can't get something for nothing, but maybe you're just not looking in the right places. *FREE $TUFF from the Internet* will go a long way to helping you find loads of bargains floating through Cyberspace, and with a little ingenuity and common sense, you can dig up a few of your own, too. Here are some simple tips to help you get started.

Make Some Phone Calls Companies around the world are just starting to discover the PR potential the Internet offers for keeping in touch with customers. In addition to getting instant feedback about their products and services, these companies get a good demographic profile of their customers. Take advantage of the toll-free numbers used by the makers of your favorite products and call them to see if they're wired into the Internet. If they are, send them E-mail requesting some samples, coupons, and more information about their products.

Many sports clubs are jumping on the bandwagon as well, offering free schedules, team profiles, and memorabilia. Call them up and find out what they offer.

Scan the Newsgroups You'll be amazed at how many freebies you can locate just by reading the postings in some of the different newsgroups. Check out **alt.consumer.free-stuff** for postings about where to find products and promotional materials, some of which are available right on the Internet.

Read the Fine Print A lot of businesses are starting to place E-mail addresses in their advertisements. Computer and software manufacturers have been doing this for years, but it's now hitting the mainstream. Before long, seeing E-mail addresses will be as common as 800-numbers are today.

Ask Around Go to newsgroups that are similar to the kind of freebies you're looking for and request information. If you're looking for a program that will help you keep track of business expenses, post a message in **comp.binaries.ibm.pc.wanted** asking if anyone knows where you can find one. Do you collect sports cards? There's software out there to help you index your collection, if you know where to look (find out in **rec.collecting.cards**).

Think Like an Internet Old Timer Those who've been around the Internet for awhile know that a few sites are always good for several freebies on a particular topic or area of interest. As you read through this book, take note of some of the sites that are mentioned repeatedly. They're listed frequently not because we were lazy in our efforts to find material, but because they are genuinely great sources for information, software, and other gimmies. It's a good idea to take some time to surf these sites. There's nothing like the feeling you'll get from discovering something great on your own.

Binary and Text Files

A *text* file is a file that contains no special codes or commands—such as bold, italics, or graphics—only text. Text files can be viewed without any special software, such as word processors or image viewers. A *binary* file, on the other hand, *does* contain special codes that you can only read with some special software. Files with graphics, bold or underlined text, or computer programs are all examples of binary files.

There are many other tools you can use to explore the Internet besides those we've discussed so far, and the more you experiment online the more of them you'll discover. I've only covered the tools you'll use in this book. Get a feel for these first, then you'll be ready to go off on your own to see what else is out there. Happy exploring!

He Who Hesitates . . .

It's important to point out that the Internet is far from stagnant. It is a living, growing, thing that is in a constant state of evolution. Since it is always changing, some of the locations and addresses mentioned in this book may also change. Sometimes housekeepers at the different sites are kind enough to leave forwarding addresses for the data that has been moved, but this isn't always the case. But keep your eyes open. Often, one site loaded with data will be "mirrored" at another site to help alleviate traffic jams on the Information Highway. Mirrors are sites that are exact duplicates of popular Internet sites. The point is, if you find that one site has disappeared, you may be able to find the same files in several other places in Cyberspace.

Just to Make a Point

Here's a good case in point. You're reading a third or later printing of *FREE $TUFF from the Internet.* In February 1995, an important Gopher server basically crashed and burned, leaving a lot of Internauts scratching their heads. The site is **quartz.rutgers.edu**, and its caretakers have set up a temporary FTP site in its place until the original server is back up and running, which could be the case by the time you read this. However, if you want to download software or other information from **quartz.rutgers.edu** and you get a message indicating that the site can't be found, try this location instead:

How
FTP

Where
ftp.etext.org

Go To
pub/Quartz

FREE $TUFF

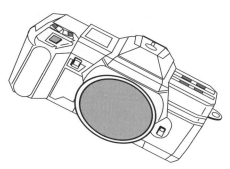

It's not hard to understand modern art. If it hangs on a wall it's a painting, and if you can walk around it it's a sculpture.

Joshua Reynolds

Arts and Culture

New York City Museums

Planning a trip to the Big Apple soon? It's an understatement to say that some of the greatest museums in the world are located in New York City. Of course, you can find plenty of guidebooks on New York City's public museums in bookstores and newsstands. But is the information up to date and, more important, is it *free*? You get both on the Internet. The Metropolitan Museum of Art, the Museums of Modern Art, the Whitney Museum, and many other public art collections are listed here, along with brief descriptions and other information about them.

How

Gopher

Where

echonyc.com

Go To

Arts and Cultural Resources
List of New York City Museums

New York City Galleries

Whether you just feel like browsing New York's art galleries or you're eager to shell out a few thousand for an original mural, watercolor, or sculpture, this is the Cyberspace place to start. Here you'll find a listing of public and commercial art galleries in and around New York city. From the mainstream to the eclectic, you'll find something to satisfy everyone's tastes. There are also brief descriptions and other important timely information to keep you on track.

How

Gopher

Where

echonyc.com

Go To

Arts and Cultural Resources
List of New York City Galleries

Art Criticism

Here's a group devoted to in-depth discussions on "real art subjects," focusing on criticism and theory in the visual arts. If you want to express your views on postmodernism or funding for the arts, give this mailing list a try. You'll find that it has a scholarly flavor, but the forum will be of interest to all visual artists, critics, museum curators and docents, and just about any serious art patron who would like to learn more today's art world.

How

E-mail

Where

listserv@vm1.yorku.ca

Ask For

subscribe ARTCRIT *<name>*

Photography

Are you interested in being more than "just" a shutterbug? How about learning more about the history of photography, including the pioneers of this art form? Ever wonder why nobody in those nineteenth-century photos ever smiled? *You* try smiling while standing perfectly still for several minutes while the photographer prepares his plate. This fascinating newsletter is devoted to the origins of photography, tracing the roots of photography, and examining its evolution.

How

E-mail

Where

listserv@asuvm.inre.asu.edu

Ask For

subscribe PHOTOST <name>

The OTIS Project

You'll see "OTIS" splattered in many places throughout the Internet and elsewhere. Well, let's decipher the letters now. Specifically, the OTIS acronym stands for the"Operative Term Is Stimulate." So, go stimulate yourself with this electronic art gallery of original artwork in a variety of media. All types of media are represented, from scanned pencil drawings to graphics generated entirely on computer. You'll find photos, scribblings, etchings, animations, and lots more.

OTIS also includes several up-to-date files that provide more information about the project and its participants. Read the file NEW for a list of recently uploaded artwork, OLD for a list of artwork that has recently been deleted, replaced, or moved, OTISNEWS.TXT for a description of goings-on within the OTIS community, and ARTISTS for bios and other information about participating artists. The file OTISINFO.TXT provides additional information about the OTIS project itself.

How

FTP

Where

sunsite.unc.edu

Go To

pub/multimedia/pictures/OTIS

Pssst...Ya Wanna Buy a Paintin'?

Every year, American consumers lose millions of dollars purchasing counterfeit prints of artists such as Dali, Picasso, Chagall, Miro, and hundreds of lesser known yet reputable artists. To help protect you, the Federal Trade Commission has published *Art Fraud*, a free booklet that will teach you how these "con artists" work and how to protect yourself.

How

Telnet

Where

fedworld.gov (see page 13 for instructions on how to download files from the Consumer Information Center)

Go To

ARTFRAUD.TXT

ArtNet

ArtNet might be described as the avant garde avenue for Internet art users who are ready to travel a route less travelled by the mainstream. This location provides a forum for artists, art administrators, writers, theorists, students, and teachers who want to stretch the existing boundaries of art. It's open to anyone interested in "network, installation, project, communication, temporary, ad-hoc, transient, mobile, time-based, formless, de-centered art," and encompasses:

- Projects
- New work
- Events
- Collaboration

- Funding
- Technology
- Shows
- Jobs
- Conferences
- Proposals
- Organizations
- Information
- Publications
- Education
- Wild speculation

Although ArtNet is open to anybody interested in these topics, you should be aware that much of the focus of this group is to serve the avant-garde art community in the United Kingdom.

How

E-mail

Where

mailbase@newcastle.ac.uk

Ask For

subscribe ARTNET *<name>*

Smithsonian Collections

Many people don't realize that the Smithsonian Institution (SI) in Washington, D.C. is much more than a collection of museums. Established in 1846 by James Smithson as "an establishment for the increase and diffusion of knowledge," the Smithsonian actually includes several research laboratories, collections, and exhibits in a wide range of fields in the arts and sciences. It even encompasses the National Zoo (now known as a "BioPark" because it incorporates plants and animals into a single environment) in Rock Creek Park, Washington, D.C.; SI also sponsors scientific expeditions and publishes their results.

Now you can download hundreds of Smithsonian GIFs of fascinating artifacts, artwork, animals, vegetation, dinosaurs, and other national treasures. For instance, you can download a photo of an Asian Elephant crushing aluminum cans for recycling, an artist's drawing of the Hubble Space Telescope, a model of the John Bull locomotive, or even photographs of ancient mummies.

Be sure to download the file CHAPMAN.TXT, which provides a wealth of descriptive information about each image available here.

How
FTP

Where
sunsite.unc.edu

Go To
pub/multimedia/pictures/smithsonian/*

FineArt Forum Newsletter

FineArt Forum is the free newsletter of the Art, Science, and Technology Network (ASTN), a virtual organization whose board members "meet" in Cyberspace. The newsletter serves the interests of all artists and other creative people interested in the application of technology of many kinds to the arts, including but not limited to literature, the visual arts, and music. Founded in 1987, FineArt Forum is one of the oldest network newsletters for the arts. The bulk of this newsletter contains announcements and news items sent in by readers.

You can subscribe to the newsletter or read and download the current issue and back issues. An Online Directory provides a list of all conferencing lists, from a discussion of Quebecois literature to a discussion of fiction writing to a discussion of electronic music. There are currently more than 60 conferencing lists available. The Directory also identifies more than 20 other arts newsletters that you can subscribe to. As you can see, FineArt Forum is the Cyberspace meeting house of choice for artists of all stripes and preferences.

How
=====

E-mail

Where
=====

fast@garnet.berkeley.edu

Ask For
=======

subscribe FINEART *<name>*
Also include your postal address, telephone and fax number, and E-mail address

Origami Online

If you're into the fine Japanese art of paper folding, here's a great place to go for new folding techniques, display ideas, descriptions of new folds, and ideas on creativity, materials, and organizations. This group even provides computer representations of folds.

How
=====

E-mail

Where
=====

listserver@nstn.ns.ca

Ask For
=======

subscribe ORIGAMI-L *<name>*

Wap! Bam! Pow!

Back in school, was your idea of literature limited to Superman, Archie and Jughead, or Richie Rich? When it comes to comic books, some people never grow up. If you're longing for those good ol' days, sign up to this mailing list to get the latest comic book industry info. If you're a comic book illustrator, collector, writer, or enthusiast, this mailing list might have information that you can follow up on.

How

E-mail

Where

listserv@unlvm.unl.edu

Ask For

subscribe COMIC-L *<name>*

A Gallery of Information

Looking for a clearinghouse for information about virtually any art topic? Check out ArtSource, a repository of electronic information concerned with art and architecture. Files stored here include such diverse items as guides for electronic resources, bibliographic instruction materials, primary source materials available in an electronic format, network tips for art scholars, directories, and much more.

How

FTP

Where

convex.cc.uky.edu

Go To

pub/artsource/*

ASCII Art for Artless Computers

We weren't sure whether to put this under "Visual Arts" or "Computers," but, well, it *is* art, if not always artistic. This site provides more than 500 pictures you can download. The trick is that all of the graphics were created using ASCII characters, so the "images" can be displayed and printed from *any* computer, especially computers that don't support "real" graphic formats like GIF or JPEG.

There are a few tips to keep in mind when viewing these graphics. Many of them were recreated from photos or published illustrations, so they can be quite sophisticated. If you view some of the images at their created size, usually about 12 point, they often look like nothing more than a jumble of characters. However, if you size the images down to the equivalent of 6-point type or smaller, they'll take shape, often with impressive clarity. Make sure you use a monospace font, like Courier, to view or print the images. If you use a proportional font, you'll just get a mess.

How

Gopher

Where

Art and Images
ASCII Clipart Collection

Go To

/pub/asciiart (for FTP); otherwise:
Animations
ANSI Color Art
Drawings
Illustrated Stories
Logos
Maps
Nudes
Photo-ASCII Images
Three-D Art (and many more)

```
                          ,?)'
                        =:J |
                      ,*-. ?&
                     WP) Y9P
                    YP   ,W'
                   ,W)  ,WW.'
                  WW)  ,WWW)
                 7W),WWWW'
                 'WWWWWW'
                  9-W)
           ,,-WPL=YXW===
          (P),CY:,I/X'F9P
          WUT===-/===9)
          -HP+--Y(C=9W)
          '9Y3'-'-OWPT-
           'WWLUIECW
           (:7L7C7'
          ,P-=YWFL
         Y-=:9)UW:L
        3-'9=WU/.7
        ,WP9HTFUW'()
        9W7W))UF 9)
       7WYW))PW W
        7WH)),WC)
        7L-/XY)
        9=-,KY7)
       W9-Y3+7)
       W'=9WI7)
      ,W  '-YY)
      W    ::W                ,
     ,T     :X)              ()
     ()     '9W  'L.         ()        ,-
     (C     =:9  '9L         ()       ,T
     ()    ,,-7)   7WL      WW     ,F'
     ()     ,T9)   '9WL     -     ,YF
     ()     '-/(W      ===+PE9P7===O)         -,
    'W, ,   T+/WX=L-. ,WP+(+3L3,),=WL   ===-T-
     7)     -,YW '-=9WPL+PT- ':-L/=9WP=-'
     'W-,.-,++W.   WWWHP    ,,-/ .9CP3)
      W  -':-9:7=9W-T ,-=FT''=++,(TFYW=====-,
      W   .=*'/. 7W-,WE=-,,=-:9H=9W*'-~~~~'
     ()    ':'/Y, (L-9PXWWW,YWWX,(U3C
     9' ,,:-:/Y,/, 7LW+'-'7)()-'(MWW)
    ,,-/:',T,'-:',) ,3WWW, .Y=W'.(+WPW)
   ,F=T:9/:':C' /W),WMW9PO),m-+-9+WYW)
  ,3Y:/-.'-,',F=FHWWWE/LMWU.'-X3CWW(WL
  YP:/:' -/'-Y-,W-T)9X,WCWWWX=WWWW39/OW
  7WF=,/:-:P:,P(-'))PWWHYT79WWWHPWOW7W'
 'WU7C-:==-C9'WF,):):H7L   '7C17WEXP'
 7L-,Y=3F::,=,:-/,'P=.,  :79UWEW)
 'WEW9P=/,)/ -:,P: / L7:'=-,+YMWWW)
 'W)=+T,T()/-,F,.,) ',.-+(L=W9WW.
 '+C/:I''',P:''/ '  ''9. == '-'7-
 (W-+'. ,YF )/:'      ')-. ,:-FX-L
 'WM/'/,/CP /,:'     ..:) ,T',/:' 'W,
 W-,YXT /''),   ,P=-/,P' '(:' 'W,
 (WEXWF Y',)  ,/'-,,YT    ///,,'.W.
 ,WWWWWT,.' .Y:/.',,,=',- ,YY(). +3,W)
 WFXF:,'P ,,)/  ,'.,P',-,FI,))) I3'W)
 -HP,X'',/' ',//,'',/',P3'I(:) W) W)      /=+=,
 9WY),.,/'  ,/'-'  ,=-9-/'Y'((',W) PW    /' '-==L,
 'WY,'  ,/,P  ,YP- C/',',)( (W'(WW.  /'     '7==L.
 ()'   /:/',,WT' 3F','/)W (W (K() /'  .    '7X
 ()  ,P,P',)T=:- ,WP'.' ,P,T (W (-9L ,Y)' ,X//,  Y:P
 ,F  ,F,',-,/:' ,+P' ' Y):) (E' YHWLWT)-''-9/',-' ,,WF
 ,P.,P),-3- ,-,' ,WF.   ,Y (' (L-WCTWEW3OV-/',:'=/P+E7WF
 W- Y,P/C)',Y',' ,WT   Y) : (P-=Y:UW9CX)3-=- .W:9/PXXW.
 /T./:P/)' ,P',' YW-   ,P' :, 9M).()WTHW3,C' 9C9=9'W3WW)
 ,EPOP/YR. /F ,',/W)   /' : (W)'W979WO0=WC:,,9LPXWWP-
 3H:WL-R' /' /'/WF   ,) ,,   (U'(HW=WWXO:-:,:'(W=WWF'
,WLWWWI:,F' /-'3WF '   Y ),   (),T(O)WO9YPL.' ,WP==='
 -YWX-F Y',WWT' :': (' ()7) (MT: WP)3C)-'' 3C'
   WF /' YW-, , Y  W (),YM+C' 9+I3UV:' .YP'
   (T  3',H3-., ,,. .,) ,) )F-=T-. (0,9L,' /P'
  ,W Y' 33P . / Y Y) (Y' R,: 7)Y+-),,=W'
  /'.F.,W)      ,,.',) ,W) +) 3), (WT9XW=3P'
  /F:T.:WF. '..:' ' (W. 7) '=', 'WT7WWP '
  ,P,F'WF . ,-': ,) YC.,/) 'HY.  WPOWC'
  ,P:9::YP ' '(' :, W) .W) +3) 9TLWC
 (P/Y(,P' ... ''; ,.) ,W) :3) X+. WFUW)
 'WW),I',' ..,, = ': ,O+',W' )9, 99U()
 7W,=',,' ' :.'. . ' ,W) =3 )+. ,OH:O)
 'L,F,: ' .:C::' ' (W) 9W 7+  'H,:L
 7W'++: .. ,':' ' YT Y). :- XU:W
 (T':,''','',' 3' ,-) ,-' 77XW
 (W),J.-:/-:))' P )9) :,Y .T,9)
 (WUI:TY:,,,:,  /' ,- W) YC: 9/7)
```

Miscellaneous Art

Literally thousands of GIF, JPEG, and other image formats are part of this collection available through Washington University at St. Louis and through other mirror sites. This is one of the largest collections of GIF and JPEG files available on the Internet. Once you get into the pubs/pics directory, you're on your own—there are dozens upon dozens of subdirectories of photos and art available.

How
FTP

Where
wuarchive.wustl.edu

Go To
pub/pics/<numerous subdirectories>

EAGLE.GIF downloaded from pub/pics/animals

Silicon Graphics Online

Silicon Graphics sponsors an electronic magazine called *IRIS-On-Line* that specializes in 3-dimensional computer art and graphics. You'll find lots of cool articles about computer graphics, animation, and multimedia. The magazine also distributes freeware to subscribers.

How

E-mail

Where

list-manager@sgi.com

Ask For

Subscribe <Name> iris-on-line

Where to Find More Goodies

You'll find lots of GIF, JPEG, and other computer graphics in the *Computers and Software* section. Other arts-related and cultural topics are available in the *Languages and Linguistics*, *Books and Literature*, *Movies*, and *Music* sections.

FREE $TUFF

A book is like a garden
carried in the pocket.

Chinese proverb

Books and
Literature

Catalog of Electronic Texts

We've come a long way since the invention of moveable type. One of the great successes of the Internet has been the efforts of several groups to make books available for the masses to download. As this wealth of words has mushroomed, however, it has become increasingly difficult to keep track of just what's available and where. *Alex,* a catalog of electronic texts on the Internet, is helping to change that by organizing Cyberspace. *Alex* allows users to find and retrieve the full text of over 700 books and essays scattered around the globe. Included are publications from Project Gutenberg, Wiretap, the On-line Book Initiative, and more.

How
Gopher

Where
rsl.ox.ac.uk

Go To
The World

Gopherspace

Alex

> 🗋 Carroll, Lewis, 1832-1898/Jabberwocky
> 🗋 Carroll, Lewis, 1832-1898/Jabberwocky/1k
> 🗋 Carroll, Lewis, 1832-1898/Through the looking glas...
> 🗀 Carroll, Lewis, 1832-1898/Through the looking glas...
> 🗋 Carroll, Lewis, 1832-1898/Through the looking glas...
> 🗋 Carroll, Lewis, 1832-1898/Through the looking glas...
> 🗋 Cather, Willa, 1873-1947/Alexander's bridge/PG 94
> 🗋 Cather, Willa, 1873-1947/Alexander's bridge/155k/P...
> 🗋 Cather, Willa, 1873-1947/O pioneers!/308k/PG 24
> 🗀 Cather, Willa, 1873-1947/O pioneers!/1992/PG 24
> 🗋 Cather, Willa, 1873-1947/O pioneers!
> 🗋 Cather, Willa, 1873-1947/The song of the lark/1915...
> 🗋 Catullus, Gaius Valerius/Iuuentius cycle/2k
> 🗋 Cervantes Saavedra, Miguel de, 1547-1616/Don Quixo...
> 🗋 Cervantes Saavedra, Miguel de, 1547-1616/Don Quixo...
> 🗋 Chaucer, Geoffrey, d. 1400/Canterbury tales/1993/6...

A partial listing of works for "C" authors

Electronic Newsstand

Articles from periodicals have long been available on various bulletin board services—for a fee. At the Electronic Newsstand, you have *free* access to current and past articles from over 80 of the world's leading magazines, including *Discover*, *Inc.*, *Internet World*, *Outside Magazine*, *Maclean's*, and many more. Find what you need by title or subject. There's also information on how to subscribe, with special rates for "internauts" like yourself.

How

Gopher

Where

internet.com

Go To

Introduction to the Electronic Newsstand

- 🗀 AI in Finance
- 🗀 American Demographics
- 🗀 American Journal of International Law
- 🗀 American Quarterly
- 🗀 Animals
- 🗀 Arthritis Today
- 🗀 Automatic I.D. News
- 🗀 Bass Player
- 🗀 Best Friends
- 🗀 Bio/Technology
- 🗀 Blue & Gold Illustrated - Notre Dame Football
- 🗀 Body Politic
- 🗀 Broadband Networking News
- 🗀 Business Communications Review
- 🗀 Business Week
- 🗀 CADENCE Magazine

Partial list of periodicals available on the Internet

Wherefor Art Thou, Shakespeare?

"Sup them well and look unto them all. To-morrow I intend to hunt the Internet again!" Some quotes are timeless, and easily ruined by mischievous authors of computer books. Alas. Anyway, William Shakespeare, England's unrivaled dramatist until his death in 1616, is still considered the greatest English playwright, and perhaps the greatest playwright ever. Discover the genius of Shakespeare through his many plays and sonnets. You'll find comedies like *Much Ado about Nothing* and *Taming of the Shrew*, as well as such tragedies as *Hamlet* and *Macbeth*.

How
Gopher

Where
etext.archive.umich.edu

Go To
Fiction
Shakespeare

New York Times Best Sellers

If you want to find out what's a good read, or if you're just wondering what everyone *else* thinks is a good read, check this list. Updated weekly, this site lists the hot fiction, nonfiction, and advice/how-to listings from the *New York Times* Bestsellers List in both hardback and paperback. See what's moving up, as well as what's heading for the remainder bins (hopefully, not *this* book).

How
Telnet

Where
ucsdbkst.ucsd.edu

Login
ult

Russian Humanities

"Death is finished," he said to himself. *"It is no more!"* (Name that novella.) Gone, too, are the Russian authors who have given humanity some of its most admirable masterpieces, although the literature lives on. Humanities students and anyone interested in Russian culture will enjoy reading these works of Chekhov, Dudintsev, Kuznetsov, and others.

How

FTP

Where

sunsite.unc.edu

Go To

pub/academic/russian-studies

Moe's Books

Moe's Books, located in Berkeley, California, is a used bookstore specializing in rare, antique, remaindered, and imported books. With over half a million titles to choose from, there's sure to be something for you, as well as everybody on your Christmas list. Send for a free catalog that covers children's books, photography, art, and more.

How

E-mail

Where

moesbooks@delphi.com

Message

Free catalogs

Get Published!

If you're a writer looking for magazines to print your work, you'll be happy to know that the Internet has all sorts of resources for writers—and this site should be your first stop. Download this list of publications—both paper and electronic—that accept online submissions. There are also loads of tips on how to write a query letter (online), how to submit your articles and in what format, and lists of other electronic resources for writers.

How
Gopher

Where
quartz.rutgers.edu

Go To
Internet Information and Documentation

Internet Education Resources

Writers Resources

Move Over Strunk and White

Here's a great addition to the collection of reference books you keep at the office. *Elements of E-text Style*, is a writer's manual for the 21st century. It explores how electronic communication has changed the rules of writing and how "E-text" differs from traditional print media. With E-mail becoming the communication tool of choice in the workplace, you'll want (or maybe even need) to learn how to use this style guide to communicate more effectively.

How
Gopher

Where
quartz.rutgers.edu

Go To

Internet Information and Documentation

Miscellaneous Internet Material

Elements of E-text Style

Ode to the Internet

I think that I shall never see/A poem that downloads for free. Hundreds of poems are available here, from Auden to Yeats. Click on the name of your favorite poet (Shakespeare, Tennyson, Keats, Seuss) or poem to make your choice. For ye that are verse challenged, just start at the top and scroll down until you find something you recognize.

How

Gopher

Where

wiretap.spies.com

Go To

Wiretap Online
Library
Classics
Poetry

Academic Journals and Newsletters Galore!

The Internet began as a tool for exchanging research information. Over the past 25 years, that original purpose has not been lost. Here's a comprehensive listing of electronic journals and academic newsletters compiled from colleges and universities around the world. This is a great source for researchers!

How

Gopher

Where

gopher.unc.edu

Go To

SunSITE Archives
Internet Dog-Eared Pages
Guides to the Internet
Directory of Electronic Journals and Newsletters

Cyber-Sleaze

It's like "MTV meets *The National Enquirer*."
Subscribe to this mailing list and you'll get lots
of gossip and news about the music and entertainment business, brought to you by former MTV
veejay Adam Curry.

How

E-mail

Where

cyber-sleaze-request@mtv.com

Message

Subscribe CYBER-SLEAZE *<name>*

Voices from the Internet

Subscribe to this mailing list to read about the Internet's movers and
shakers. You'll get fascinating articles and essays about the creators of
the Internet and the people trying to improve it.

How

E-mail

Where

mgardbe@andy.bgsu.edu

Subject

Voices from the Net

Message

Subscribe

Electronic Publications

Regardless of your taste in reading material, this site will definitely have something for you. There are hundreds of electronic publications, from *Australian Football League Magazine* to *Z*Net Magazine*, for you to read and download.

How

Gopher

Where

gopher.cic.net

Go To

Electronic Serials
Alphabetic List

🗀 Canadian Microelectronics Corporation News
🗀 Capital (Civil Air Patrol Information Transfer Ali...
🗀 Carolina (Elektronicky tydennik FSVUK)
🗀 Catharsis (Chronic Fatigue and Immune Dysfunction ...
🗀 Center for Economic Policy Research Bulletin
🗀 Central America News
🗀 Central Hockey League Newsletter
🗀 Chalisti
🗀 Chaos Computer Club (CCC)
🗀 Chaos Corner
🗀 Chaos Digest
🗀 Chemical Engineering Digest
🗀 Chess in the Press
🗀 Chilean Information Project News (CHIP)
🗀 China Spring
🗀 Chinese Professionals Club News

Partial listing of "C" electronic serials (that's British for "periodicals")

USA Today

As Paul Harvey likes to say, "Have you seen *USA Today* today?" Once called "McNewspaper" by some critics because of its condensed, "fast-food" style of journalism, *USA Today* has become the most widely circulated newspaper in America. Read it online when you register at this Telnet site and get the latest headlines, sports, and more.

How
Telnet

Where
yfn2.ysu.edu

Login
visitor

Go To
Follow the login instructions

E-Mail to U.S. News

"Dear Bozo . . . ." Let off some steam with a letter to the editors at *U.S. News and World Report*. Many of the letters published in the magazine are from E-mail submissions, so start scribbling. You'll sleep much better tonight having said your piece.

How
E-mail

Where
71154.1006@compuserve.com

Message
Letter to the editor

Inc. Magazine No-Risk Trial Subscription

Tired of punching the clock or feeling obligated to laugh at the boss's bad jokes? Get a risk-free trial issue of *Inc.* Magazine, the premier publication for entrepreneurs and small-business owners and managers. A one-year subscription is only $14 and your satisfaction is guaranteed. If you're not satisfied for any reason, simply mark "Cancel" on your first bill and the free issue is yours to keep.

How

E-mail

Where

inc_magazine@enews.com

Message

Please send me a risk-free trial subscription to *Inc.* magazine (include your name and postal address)

'Twas a Dark and Stormy Night

"Evermore! Quoth the Internet raven." Ever more indeed, and more's the better. Through the Online Book Initiative (OBI), you can download many of the world's great classic works of literature. You'll find copies of *Moby Dick*, *Tom Sawyer*, short stories by Poe, and much, much more.

How

FTP

Where

ftp.ste.com

Go To

obi

Sci-Fi Info

"Beam me down *there*, Scotty!" Science-fiction lovers, this site's for you. All things sci-fi are covered, including book and movie reviews, television shows, convention information and other upcoming events, and much more.

How

E-mail

Where

sf-lovers-request@rutgers.edu

Message

Subscription to SF-Lovers

Where to Find More Goodies

The *Religion and New Age* section includes sites for downloading all or selected text from *The Bible, The Koran,* and many other religious texts.

The *Language and Linguistics* section includes several resources that will be of interest to readers of international texts.

The *Music* section includes several sites that provide lyrics for hundreds of songs, including folksongs and lyrics in musicals and films.

The *Kids Stuff, Games,* and *Education* and *Teaching Tools* sections all include resources for helping children to read, write, and better comprehend literature.

FREE $TUFF

I don't want any yes-men around me.
I want everybody to tell me the truth
even if it costs them their jobs.

Samuel Goldwyn

Business and
Career

Stay Ahead of the Competition

To not only succeed but to excel in business, you need every advantage you can get. Part of gaining that advantage is to know more about your market *and* your competition than the other guy. HeadsUp is a personalized, interactive news service delivered daily to your Internet address. Based on your personal profile, HeadsUp scans over 12,000 articles a day from more than 300 domestic and international sources to deliver to you each morning the news that you want most. Use it for 30 days free to track competitors, identify sales opportunities, uncover partnerships, evaluate vendors, monitor industry trends, and stay on top of the market.

How
E-mail

Where
headsup@enews.com

Ask For
Information on a free trial subscription

Economic Indicators

Econ 101 teaches you the principles of supply and demand, but school's out and it's sink or swim time in the real business world. Stay afloat with these up-to-the-minute statistics on the leading economic indicators, including housing starts, durable goods shipments, personal income, and more.

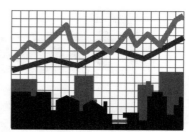

How
Gopher

Where
gopher.gsfc.nasa.gov

Go To

Virtual Reference Shelf

Economic Bulletin Board and Exchange Rates

Economic Indicators

Rules and Regulations

When it comes to the Federal government R&R doesn't stand for rest and relaxation, but for rules and regulations. If you own your own business, R&R means read and remember these important laws and notices from all government agencies that affect your company.

How

Gopher

Where

gopher.gsfc.nasa.gov

Go To

US Government

US Federal Register

Overseas Jobs

If you've always wanted to see the world, but your Great Uncle Lester didn't leave you a fortune to travel first class, why not work your way abroad? The United States and Foreign Commercial Service (FCS) has over 1250 American and foreign employees stationed in nearly 70 countries and 134 cities worldwide filling jobs of all types. Try this source for a listing of available overseas jobs with the U.S. Government and the FCS.

How

Gopher

Where

gopher.gsfc.nasa.gov

Go To

Virtual Reference Shelf

Economic Bulletin Board and Exchange Rates

General Information Files

Overseas Job Vacancies with US & FCS

Federal Government Job Postings

Uncle Sam wants you! Hundreds of government jobs are available to the right people. Start your job search here for positions open with the U.S. government and its agencies. Information is organized by city and by federal department. Be sure to read the file *Information Useful to Federal Job Applicants* to learn more.

How

Gopher

Where

esusda.gov

Go To

Extension Service USDA Information

USDA and Other Federal Agency Information

Job Openings in the Federal Government

```
VACANCY ANNOUNCEMENT
Patent & Trademark Office
Up to 10 Patent Examiner positions will be filled on a Term basis, not-to-exceed 2 years.  Upon
completion of the Term, employees may be given an opportunity to compete for a permanent position.
TERM APPOINTMENTS DO NOT CONFER COMPETITIVE STATUS FOR FEDERAL POSITIONS.
TITLE, SERIES, AND GRADE
Patent Examiner
(Computer Science)
GS-1224-5/7/9
Up to 10 positions may be filled
If filled at the GS-5 level, the promotion potential is GS-9.  If filled at the GS-7 or GS-9, the
promotion potential is GS-11.
VACANCY LOCATION
Patent Examining Corps
Arlington, Virginia
```

An excerpt from the Department of Commerce jobs listing

You're Hired!

Although this one technically should be in the *Computers and Software* section, it's just too ideal for this section to put it anywhere else. You're Hired! Is a job interview simulator that provides you with interactive training and experience in preparing for a job interview. The program asks you common, challenging interview questions and records elapsed times as you verbally respond. The program provides help and advice for answering questions, plus you can customize the questions and interview format to build yourself into an outstanding job candidate.

How

FTP

Where

garbo.uwasa.fi

Go To

pc/database/yh132.zip

Put Your Finger on the Market Pulse

Want a quick yet thorough (and, of course, free) overview of the performance of the financial markets today, but don't have the *Wall Street Journal* handy? The Daily Market Report provides a good overview of the activities of several financial markets, including the day's major activities, current interest and foreign exchange rates, and other economic data.

How

Telnet

Where

a2i.rahul.net

Login

guest

Go To

Current System Information

Market Report

Internetworking

Networking today means more than Tuesday morning breakfast clubs, shaking hands, and passing out business cards. Today's business is global, and that means a whole new way of networking. Stay on top by making those all-important contacts through the Internet. Check out the loads of job postings and helpful tips in beginning your job search.

How

Gopher

Where

info.umd.edu

Go To

Resources

Student Information and Resources

Jobs, Community Service & Career Information

North America Free Trade Agreement

Will NAFTA be an economic boon to thousands of businesses throughout Canada, the U.S., and Mexico or, as Ross Perot warned, should we start listening for the giant sucking sound of American jobs going south? Read the full text of NAFTA and decide for yourself.

How

Gopher

Where

wiretap.spies.com

Go To

Government Docs

North America Free Trade Agreement

Incorporate Online

Is incorporating for you? It's a good idea to do some research first—before you decide. There are a lot of variables involved that can mean the difference between saving you money or making incorporation more trouble than it's worth. If you're thinking about incorporating your small business, talk to Company Corporation first, the largest online incorporation service in the world. They'll answer all your questions and help you decide what's best for you and your business.

How
Gopher

Where
incorporate.com

Go To
The Company Corporation

Bears versus Bulls

There are more exciting ways of investing your money than in the stock market: You can let it all ride on double zero, learn to play the ponies, or put it all into commodities ala Hillary Clinton. (Personally, I think you'll have better luck with the ponies.) But if it's money you're after, not excitement, the stock market is still your best bet. Bears and bulls alike, here's where you'll find the most current quotes from Wall Street.

How
Telnet

Where
a2i.rahul.net

Go To

Login: guest
N
Current System Information
Market Report

The Number You Have Dialed...

From Argentina to Zimbabwe, Aachen to Zwolle, here's a database of telephone area codes from around the world. Just enter the city you want and let the search begin. You'll never dial a wrong number (or, at least, area code) again!

How

Gopher

Where

gopher.aecom.yu.edu

Go To

Internet Resources
Miscellaneous
World Telephone Code Info

ZIP-a-Dee Doo Dah

Do you ever have trouble falling asleep at night because you can't remember the ZIP code for Pascagoula, Mississippi? Well, then you need professional help. Of course, hunting for ZIP codes *can* be annoying and time consuming. And if you don't use the correct codes, the Postal Service just might take all the ZIP out of your mail delivery. Here's a database *guaranteed* to solve that problem. Type in the name of any U.S. city to get the corresponding ZIP code.

How

Gopher

Where

gopher.aecom.yu.edu

Go To

Internet Resources

Miscellaneous

Search the USA Zip Code Database

Resources for Economists

Use the Internet to access huge amounts of economic data about businesses, industries, cities, and countries. And it's all right at your fingertips. This site contains information on many gophers, bulletin boards, newsgroups, and graduate programs devoted to economists or anyone interested in economics.

How

E-mail

Where

bgoffe@whale.st.usm.edu

Ask For

Resources for Economists on the Internet

Surfin' on Silicon

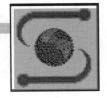

Silicon Graphics (SGI) is a leading developer of applications to create three-dimensional graphics, and is a major corporate booster of and participant on the Internet. Now you can download *Silicon Surf*, SGI's online industry newsletter. Read the latest SGI news, learn about training courses, see videos, and get free software.

How

Mosaic

Where

http://www.sgi.com/silicon_surf.html

Academia This Week

Find jobs listings from the current edition of *The Chronicle of Higher Education* listed here on the day of publication. You can search for position listings by geographic location, through the Chronicle's list of job terms, or by keyword. This is one of the best sources for finding positions with colleges and universities in the U.S., as well as international institutions and research companies.

How

Gopher

Where

chronicle.merit.edu

Go To

Jobs

Coping with Unemployment

Other than the death of a family member or a divorce, few situations cause more stress than unemployment. When you lose your job, you're deprived of more than just a steady income. The familiar routines, structures, and work relationships that made up your day are gone as well. *Coping with Unemployment*, published by the National Institute of Mental Health and the Department of Labor, will help you manage the difficulties you might face if you find yourself out of work.

How

Telnet

Where

fedworld.gov (see page 13 for instructions on how to download files from the Consumer Information Center)

Go To

NFCUNEMP.TXT

Career Connection's Online Information

Find the job you've always wanted with Career Connection's Online Information service. This menu-driven, job-hunting tool lets you search for positions by geographic location or job title. You can even apply for jobs online! (Be sure to have your resume on hand so you can enter the necessary info.)

How

Telnet

Where

career.com

Go To

Follow the registration instructions

Online Career Center

Ready for a career change? Make your first step a trip to the Online Career Center, which posts openings within industrial, corporate, institutional, health care, governmental, and educational organizations. Postings from the Help Wanted USA database found on America Online are also listed. If you're an employer looking for qualified employees, check out the '94 College & University Resume section of the database, which provides separate directories for each university, with resumes provided from dozens or hundreds of qualified graduates or near-grads from each institution.

How

Gopher

Where

msen.com

Go To

The Msen Career Center

1994 Online College & University Resume Books/Diskettes (to examine resume books submitted by leading universities and other academic institutions worldwide)

Note: You may also enter your ASCII-formatted resume into the OCC Internet database for free via E-mail. Resumes posted by 5 p.m. EST usually are listed the following day. Your resume remains in the database for 90 days, and you may re-enter it any time.

How

E-mail

Where

occ-resumes@msen.com

Subject

The Subject line will be your resume's title, so be specific

```
How To Enter Your Resume
Make your resume available to thousands of employers across the country through
OCC on Internet.  The OCC online keyword searchable database is available to
all employers who have Internet access. There are no charges for employers to
access your resume, and no charge to you if you enter your own resume online.
--------------------- ATTENTION ------------------------
| IF YOU POST YOUR RESUME BY 5:00 P.M. EST, YOU MAY SEE IT   |
| IN THE OCC DATABASE AFTER 7:00 A.M. EST THE FOLLOWING DAY. |
|          THIS IS A PUBLIC ACCESS DATABASE                  |
|        AND MAY BE ACCESSED BY ANY INTERNET USER.           |
------------------------------------------------------------
1) You may, at no cost, enter your full-text resume
   into the OCC Internet database via email.
   - Email your resume to:  occ-resumes@msen.com
   - *** Your resume must be in ASCII format.  ***
   - THE EMAIL "SUBJECT:" LINE SERVES AS YOUR RESUME "TITLE" -- and will be
     the first information seen by employers when viewing your resume.
   - Your resume will stay in the OCC database for 90 days.  To extend your
     resume beyond 90 days,  you may re-enter it at any time.
   - Each email account number is permitted only one resume at any given time.
     Therefore, the most recent resume uploaded will be displayed.
   - To change or update your resume, simply re-enter it, and the previous one
     will disappear.
```

Tips for entering your resume into the OCC database

Information Researchers

Information Researchers is a full-service, professional information broker offering custom research, online database searching, and document delivery. This service is great for businesses that are highly information oriented. With quick and convenient document delivery from a wide variety of sources, Information Researchers provides a broad range of custom research on any topic, including:

- Retrieval of specific facts and statistics
- Literature and online database searches
- Custom bibliographies
- Company and industry profiles
- Written reports, from brief summaries to extensive papers
- Custom mailing lists
- Custom-designed projects

For over 18 years, Information Researchers has served individuals and organizations in business, government, manufacturing, law, health sciences, and more to meet their researching needs. E-mail them for details about a free consultation.

How
E-mail

Where
info@uiuc.edu

Ask For
Information on custom research

Are You Keeping Up with the Joneses?

Incomes differ dramatically throughout the U.S. for identical jobs, depending on where you live. While $30,000 may seem like a good salary in one, city, state or region, it might not even be enough to pay for rent in another. Find out how your income compares with incomes in other parts of the country with these personal and disposable income statistics broken down by state, region, and metropolitan areas throughout the U.S.

How

Gopher

Where

gopher.gsfc.nasa.gov

Go To

Virtual Reference Shelf

Economic Bulletin Board and Exchange Rates

Regional Economic Statistics

	PER CAPITA PERSONAL INCOME							
	Total Personal Income		Percent of National Average		Percent Change Rank		Percent Change Dollars	
	1980	1990	1980	1990	1980	1990	1980-90	1980-90
U.S.	9,919	18,696	100.0	100.0	88.5	106.9		
Abilene, TX	9,840	16,021	99.2	85.7	124	211	62.8	74.4
Akron, OH	9,836	18,029	99.2	96.4	125	120	83.3	82.8
Albany, GA	7,543	14,695	76.0	78.6	293	281	94.8	94.1
Albany-Schenectady-Troy, NY	9,618	19,404	97.0	103.8	148	69	101.7	111.2
Albuquerque	9,238	17,518	93.1	93.7	185	137	89.6	116.9
Alexandria,LA	7,500	14,615	75.6	78.2	299	283	94.9	88.7
Allentown-Bethlehem, PA-NJ	10,420	19,131	105.1	102.3	85	78	83.6	98.7
Altoona, PA	8,193	14,779	82.6	79.0	265	275	80.4	72.5
Amarillo, TX	9,888	16,961	99.7	90.7	120	158	71.5	84.5
Anaheim-Santa Ana,CA	13,057	24,400	131.6	130.5	7	17	86.9	133.0
Anchorage,AK	15,017	25,035	151.4	133.9	1	13	66.7	113.6

A portion of the personal income for cities ("A" listing)

Consumer News

Here's important information for savvy consumers. Hundreds of tips are available here to help you get the best buys on the best products. Find out how to get the best deals when buying a computer, how to obtain and read a credit report, how to get the best airfares, what to do when you're asked for your Social Security number, and many other valuable, cost-saving, and practical consumer tips.

How
Gopher

Where
gopher.gsfc.nasa.gov

Go To
Virtual Reference Shelf

Consumer News

Grant Proposals Workshop

Have an idea for a serious research project for your business, school, or even just for yourself? Ideas are good, but funding is even better. Grant proposal writers and grant administrators will benefit from Internet Works, Inc.'s online interactive workshops. Although these workshops focus on winning government grants, most of the material is general enough to apply to any type of grant. The content of the workshops is tailored to the interests and background of the participants as much as possible. Topics covered include:

- Developing a strategic plan for funding through proposal writing
- Using the Internet to enhance proposal planning and writing effectiveness
- Identifying realistic funding sources
- Using funding agency guidelines effectively
- Choosing and winning partners
- The most important elements to include in the proposal
- Tips on effective proposal writing
- The mechanics of proposal review
- Tricks of the trade

How
E-mail

Where

hwylen@access.digex.net

Ask For

Information on grant proposals and consulting services

Inventory Tracking

Still trying to manage your inventory by traditional manual stock-picking techniques? Here's a good way to ease into a more automated approach. This simple little program does a good job at tracking inventory and producing reports based on sales histories. By default, it's set up to track auto parts, but you can change the inventory categories and inventory items to anything you want.

How

FTP

Where

oak.oakland.edu

Go To

SimTel/msdos/database/cjpos133.zip

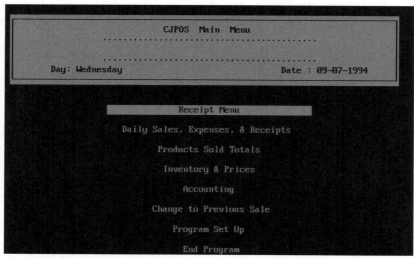

The CJPOS Main Menu

Help for Doing Business in Asia

Advances in transportation and telecommunication technology have linked a large part of our society with those of Asia and the Pacific region. The resulting increase in international, intercultural, and interlingual relationships has created a need for professional competence in context-sensitive international communication. Find out more about the business communication skills you need to compete in the competitive and emerging Asian markets.

How
Gopher

Where
hoshi.cic.sfu.ca

Go To
David See-Chai Lam Centre for International Communication

Get with the Flow

There are dozens of flowchart programs on the market, as well as dozens of packages for creating business presentations. But they all cost money, and probably most of the commercial packages have more features than you'll ever need. So, as Thoreau said, "Simplify, simplify." (So why didn't he just say it once?) This source has only a few flowcharting programs, but most of them are highly specialized. There are programs to make:

- GANTT charts (gantt.zip and ganttman.zip)
- PERT charts
- Nassi-Shneiderman diagrams (psdldemo.zip—demo only)
- Organizational charts (fdrw225a.zip and fdrw225b.zip)

How
FTP

Where

oak.oakland.edu

Go To

SimTel/msdos/flowchrt/*

Market Yourself!

Have yourself or your business listed free in the *NetPages* Internet directory. To get listed, send the following information via E-mail, preferably in this order:

- Your last name
- Your first name and middle initial
- Your E-mail address
- Your company name
- Your job title
- City
- State
- Country
- Indicate whether your E-mail account is for business, personal, or both.

How

E-mail

Where

np-add@aldea.com

Accounting for Taste

Here's a full-featured, DOS-based business accounting package, complete with general ledger, accounts receivable, accounts payable, payroll, and invoice applications. The software also provides some good reports and prints mailing labels.

The user interface to this package is quite good. However, each application is treated as an independent module; there's no menu to tie them together. So, if you want to, say, exit the A/R application and start the A/P application, you have to exit to DOS and load the A/P program separately. If you're running Windows, you could give each application its own PIF. Of course, if you're running Windows, you probably would prefer a true Windows accounting package. But this collection is a good starter package.

How

FTP

Where

oak.oakland.edu

Go To

SimTel/msdos/database/medlin.zip

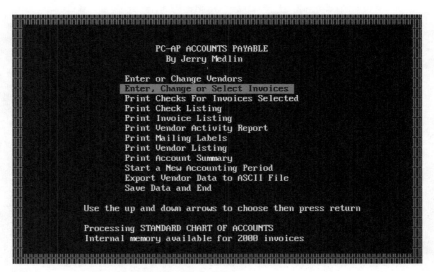

PC-AP Accounts Payable Module: Main Menu

Forms over Function

Sometimes it seems like software developers believe printers are limited to blank 8-1/2" by 11" paper and standard 6" margins, and that all users ever need to create are standard text documents and reports. So what about tax forms, invoices and POs, mailing labels (including standard Federal Express forms), and custom business forms? Most of the programs at this site are forms generators, which allow you to create and/or print on custom forms of virtually any oddball size.

How

FTP

Where

oak.oakland.edu

Go To

SimTel/msdos/formgen/*

Filename	Description
drform31.zip	Powerful, yet easy to use form designer
ezff-10b.zip	EZ-Forms First: Free program to create forms
ezfl-e20.zip	EZ-Forms LT: Makes custom forms, easy to use
ezfx-v24.zip	EZ-Forms EX: Makes custom forms, easy to use
fe-v10.zip	Create/fill forms. Features math and auto-entry
fedex13.zip	Filling out Federal Express forms made easy!
Fmgen40a.zip	FormGen v4.0a, a form generator/editor
form300.zip	Form generator (ver. 3.0)
forms4ez.zip	Collection of forms for EZFORMS
frmatn25.zip	Formation v2.5: Make/print/fill-in forms
lrnfrm.zip	'Teach' printer to fill in forms
w-2a.zip	Prints one-wide and two-wide W-2 forms

Complete list of files in SimTel/msdos/formgen/*

Easy Invoicing for Contractors

Here's a good billing and bookkeeping tool for contractors, accountants, and other self-employed individuals who have multiple customer accounts. MODBILL records and tracks individual transactions, maintains customer account information, and provides complete invoicing and accounts receivable facilities. You can also print mailing labels from within the program.

How

FTP

Where

oak.oakland.edu

Go To

SimTel/msdos/database/modbil74.zip

```
In which area would you like to work?

    1 - TRANSACTION FILE SERVICES
        Enter/View/Print/Change Transactions

    2 - CUSTOMER FILE SERVICES
        Setup/Change/Sort Customer Account Information

    3 - ACCOUNTS RECEIVABLE AND TRANSACTION CODE REPORT

    4 - INVOICE/STATEMENT PRINTING - RECORD UPDATING

    5 - REPORT OF MOST RECENT BILLING

    6 - PRINT LABELS

    7 - CONTROL FILE SERVICES
        Setup/Change Statement Information
        Setup/Change Transaction Codes

    8 - TO EXIT SYSTEM

Enter your choice by NUMBER (0 - 8) <8>
```

The MODBILL 7.4 main menu

Tooling Around

Robotics software for operating machine tools and other numerical control devices frequently cost thousands of dollars to design, write, and debug. This source has two files for aiding in NC machine tool operations: cams305.zip is a program that generates control data for machine tools, and cv3d_110.zip is a three-dimensional graphical CNC/CAM control file viewer.

How

FTP

Where

oak.oakland.edu

Go To

SimTel/msdos/mfg

Basic Business Bookkeeping

This is one of the nicest DOS-based business software packages we've seen. It's got an easy-to-use, attractive menu system, and good templates for entering data. The author has even provided an icon in case you want to run the package under Windows. This is truly a basic bookkeeping system, and does not provide full accounting functionality.

How

FTP

Where

oak.oakland.edu

Go To

SimTel/msdos/database/obbk30.zip

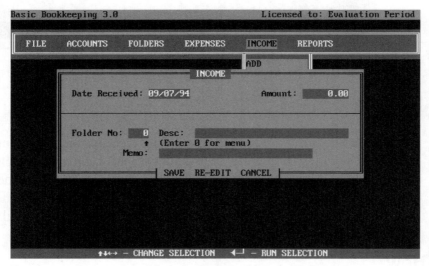

Entering an expense record into the Basic Bookkeeping 3.0 system

Where to Find More Goodies

Check out the *Computers and Software* section for many free programs and utilities that can be used in business.

The Environment and Nature section contains several items that can be useful to business-people, especially the Environmental Protection Agency link that allows you to review EPA regulations and order publications.

The *Household and Consumer Finance* section is mostly devoted to personal finance, but several topics relate directly to business, especially the Gopher site that provides a wealth of information on investment strategies and opportunities.

If you're a human resources manager or other business executive responsible for the welfare of employees, the *Health and Nutrition* section provides several sites where you can go to download free health informational booklets that you can distribute to your employees.

The *Law* section tells you where to find copyright information and important on-the-job information relating to sexual harassment.

FREE $TUFF

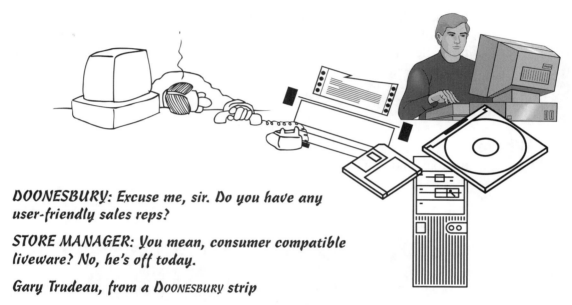

DOONESBURY: Excuse me, sir. Do you have any user-friendly sales reps?

STORE MANAGER: You mean, consumer compatible liveware? No, he's off today.

Gary Trudeau, from a DOONESBURY strip

Computers and Software

A PC User's Miscellany

When you log onto this site, you'll probably feel a little like you've just discovered a cache of valuables in your parents' attic. In fact, this site is basically just that: an Internet "attic" filled with PC-related goodies. There are more than 150 files in this directory, so plan to spend some time browsing here. The following list should give you a pretty good sense for the wide range of software and information that's available here. You'll certainly find at least a few interesting files worthy of your download time. Several files in this collection provide tips and information for shareware authors.

How
FTP

Where
oak.oakland.edu

Go To
SimTel/msdos/info/*

Filename	Description
amirel.zip	Info on AMI BIOS releases, some technical info
asp7901.zip	Association of Shareware Professionals catalog
author29.zip	List of MS-DOS PD & SW author E-mail addresses
authwn07.zip	E-mail addresses of WIN3.x shareware authors
bgi13a.zip	Beginner's Guide to the Internet, Rel. 1.3a
biosdos.zip	List of BIOS error codes and what they mean
copro15a.zip	Article on numeric coprocessors for PCs
dcc9224.zip	List of over 1,000 computer clubs nationwide
dostips1.zip	DOS tips from various magazines - part 1 of 6
ftp-list.zip	List of FTP sites providing Anonymous FTP
geozones.zip	Internet address two-letter country codes list
glosry51.zip	Microcomputer terminology glossary 5.1
hhgdinet.zip	Text: HitchHiker's Guide to the Internet
inter42a.zip	Comprehensive list of interrupt calls - part 1 of 3
legal11.zip	Collection of 150+ legal forms, with index
maxcat.zip	Catalog of over 600 Shareware programs
probdesc.zip	Info about 386/486 external cache flaws

A sampling of files in SimTel/msdos/info

uuencode/uudecode Software

Sending and receiving binary files across the Internet is easy when you have the right software. With uuencode, you can convert binary files, such as graphics, word processor documents, spreadsheets, and so on, into ASCII files and send them through Cyberspace. Want to download and read uuencoded files? Just use uudecode.

How

FTP

Where

ftp.cc.utexas.edu

Go To

gifstuff/*

The Web Crawler Index

One of the problems in locating material on the World-Wide Web is that the Web doesn't lend itself easily to indexing. It was a system created for exploration, but after a certain point you can spend all your time exploring your way past things that are of no conceivable interest to you. The richer the mix on the Web becomes, the more of a problem this will be.

Enter the Web Crawler. This is an experimental server that maintains an index by periodically "crawling" the Web, that is, by visiting every Web page it can find in a breadth-first fashion (to minimize the number of visits to each page) and indexing everything it finds.

The interface is a simple line-editor, into which you enter a word or words for searching. Web Crawler then returns a list of web pages containing the word or words (which can be combined in a search via AND or OR) in a list organized by how close a "hit" Web Crawler thinks each item is.

The Web isn't nearly as mature as Gopherspace, so don't be disappointed if there seem to be huge gaps in Web coverage as revealed by the Web Crawler. We searched for and did not find any mention of Millard Fillmore, for example—but peculiar things like "lawn dart" were well represented.

Sometimes we found the Web Crawler index completely empty—that is, it found nothing at all, even items it had found before—and we suspect that at such times the Web Crawler is re-building its index, which (as you might imagine) can take awhile. At such times you simply have to come back later, preferably the next day.

Give it a try. It's a wonderful way to economize your Mosaic time, once you're a little tired of exploring blindly and want to go straight to the loot.

How

Mosaic

Where

http://webcrawler.cs.washington.edu/WebCrawler/WebQuery.html

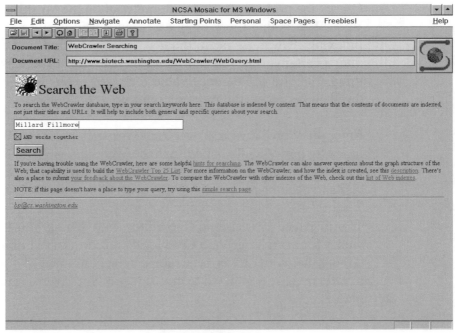

Using Web Crawler to search the World Wide Web

Linux for Your PC—Free!

Linux is a Unix-like operating system that enables users to multitask without the expense, hardware, and software necessary to operate in a Unix environment. Fast and affordable, it's becoming the operating system of choice for many people connecting to the Internet. Now it's yours for free! This site has a lot of software available for you to download, too.

How
FTP

Where
sunsite.unc.edu

Go To
pub/Linux

Exercise Your Right to Assemble

Programming to the metal is getting to be a dying art, but it's definitely an art. If you program in assembly, you'll love this site. There are assemblers for dozens of CPUs, cross-assemblers, and even a few reference manuals. This directory is kept up to date.

How
FTP

Where
oak.oakland.edu

Go To
SimTel/msdos/crossasm/*

Filename	Description
68asmsim.zip	68000 cross-assembler/simulator with C source
as02_103.zip	Optimizing assembler for M6800/6801/6802/6803
embedpc.zip	Tools & source for embedded PC applications
epasm13.zip	Assembler for Intel 8749 & other EPROM chips

A sampling of files in SimTel/msdos/crossasm

Filename	Description
motoasms.zip	Motorola 6800/01/04/05/09/11 cross-assemblers
ps65a12.zip	6502 cross-assembler
ps685a12.zip	6805 cross-assembler
ps68a12.zip	6800-03/08 cross-assembler
psz80a13.zip	8086 Z80 cross-assembler
xasm220.zip	Twelve cross-assemblers (65xx, 68xx, 80xx)

More files in SimTel/msdos/crossasm

Oh No! Pascal!

The Pascal programming language has seen its best days, as the rather skimpy list below illustrates. But Pascal still has its ardent followers, especially in academia where it is well suited to teach good programming habits. This site includes Pascal teaching tools, a few compilers, a few programs with source code, and several informational articles.

How

FTP

Where

oak.oakland.edu

Go To

SimTel/msdos/pascal/*

Filename	Description
mystic.zip	Interactive Pascal compiler
pascsrc.zip	Coronado's Pascal tutor v2.0, (1 of 2)
pasctxt.zip	Coronado's Pascal tutor v2.0, (2 of 2)
pnl001.zip	The Pascal Newsletter: Programming in Pascal
pnl002.zip	The Pascal NewsLetter, issue #2
pnl003.zip	The Pascal Newsletter: Sorting, OOP in Turbo Pascal
pnl004.zip	The Pascal NewsLetter, issue #4
pnl005.zip	The Pascal NewsLetter, issue #5
pnl006.zip	The Pascal NewsLetter, issue #6
pnl010.zip	The Pascal NewsLetter, issue #10

A complete listing of files in SimTel/msdos/pascal/*

Filename	Description
pretypas.zip	Caps and formats reserved words in Pascal code
qp_paint.zip	OOP paint program source in QuickPascal
qparser.zip	Parses 'C' or Pascal
surpas.zip	Shareware Pascal compiler, from Australia
svgadc30.zip	Update for the Digital Crime SVGA driver
where.pas	Locate file on hard disk (ASCII source file)

A complete listing of files in SimTel/msdos/pascal/* (continued)

Microsoft Support and Utilities

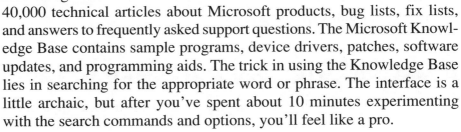

Now you can access the Microsoft Knowledge Base and Microsoft Software Library through the Internet. Ideal for support engineers, the Microsoft Knowledge Base contains more than 40,000 technical articles about Microsoft products, bug lists, fix lists, and answers to frequently asked support questions. The Microsoft Knowledge Base contains sample programs, device drivers, patches, software updates, and programming aids. The trick in using the Knowledge Base lies in searching for the appropriate word or phrase. The interface is a little archaic, but after you've spent about 10 minutes experimenting with the search commands and options, you'll feel like a pro.

If you're a software developer, or just looking for software upgrades and fixes for your MS programs, this is the site for you. In fact, this is the same database that Microsoft's Technical Support staff uses to handle customer problems and questions. So save yourself the time that you would have spent on hold and solve the problem yourself.

How

FTP

Where

ftp.microsoft.com

Go To

pub/*

Bitmaps

Tired of the same old Windows wallpaper? Why not liven things up a bit by hanging some of these bitmaps on your computer screen? Download shots of astronauts walking in space, wild artwork, and lots more.

How

FTP

Where

garbo.uwasa.fi

Go To

windows/bitmaps/*

What Did One Computer Say to the Other?

We're in an age where it's commonplace for computers to communicate across thousands of miles. But if you're not running the right communications software, you might as well be talking through a couple of tin cans and a piece of string. Make your life a little easier by downloading these Windows-based communications programs and utilities. There are programs to help you manage your E-mail, the latest modem software, PC/Unix links, and much more.

How

FTP

Where

garbo.uwasa.fi

Go To

windows/comm/*

Modem Madness

Some of the modem shareware that you'll find here is obsolete by most users' standards, but there are still plenty of communication gems. There are lots of DOS-based utilities for {COMMO}, GT Procomm, US Robotics and other modem programs, and lots of tutorial and informational materials on communications, modems, and protocols.

How

FTP

Where

oak.oakland.edu

Go To

SimTel/msdos/modem/*

Filename	Description
bgdial11.zip	Background autodialer for MS-DOS
bkmail11.zip	BACKMAIL: Background mail/file transfer program
chkmodem.zip	Finds a modem & checks its status, w/source
com2com.zip	Operate PC remotely by modem, like PC Anywhere
commodsz.zip	Zmodem for COMMO communications package
commokey.zip	Commo quick reference, Pop-up for {COMMO} v4.1
emma22.zip	Communications utility for MCI mail users
fonecal2.zip	Modem calls pager when you have phone messages
fsthst22.zip	Set up US Robotics HST modem for fastest speed
haystst.zip	Check Hayes compatibility of your modem
lgring10.zip	Logs time and date of incoming phone calls
modemtxt.zip	Tutorial on operation of Hayes type modems
modmart1.zip	Informative beginner's article about modems
modnoise.zip	Good text files on modem noise fixes
privacc.zip	PC shares phone line with FAX/answer machine
protocol.zip	Discussion of the various protocols available
trm20.zip	Technical reference manual for Hayes modems

A sampling of files in SimTel/msdos/modem/*

Prolific Procomm

Procomm and Procomm Plus have been modem software mainstays for many years. One of the better features of Procomm is its flexible scripting capability for customizing and facilitating communications. This site includes dozens of scripts for Procomm and Procomm Plus, as well as many other utilities.

How

FTP

Where

oak.oakland.edu

Go To

SimTel/msdos/procomm/*

Filename	Description
Aaapcp31.zip	PC Pursuit/Procomm + script package v3.1
add-z.zip	Add Zmodem protocol (DSZ) to Procomm
adl.zip	Automatic download script generator for Procomm
apcp37.zip	Auto PC Pursuit scripts for Procomm +
asp-mdms.zip	ProComm+ scripts optimize modem configurations
autoprcm.zip	Aids in writing Script files for Procomm 2.4
fastpls.zip	Speed up Procomm+ graphics
hostfix.zip	Correct bugs in Procomm host mode
keymail.zip	Procomm+ host mode mail view and editor
pcp_bat2.zip	Automatically start up ProComm in dialing mode
pcplus2.zip	ProComm Plus Utilities (separate directory)
pcpzmod.zip	Beep speaker when external ZMODEM transfer ends

A sampling of files in SimTel/msdos/procomm

Software for Your Mac

If you've got a Mac and are looking for free goodies, you've definitely found the right place. This site has tons of goodies for the Mac, including games, fonts, antivirus programs, graphics, and too much more to list.

How

How

Gopher

Where

sumex-aim.stanford.edu

Go To

info-mac/*

Mac Lite

This site's for Macintosh users only. There aren't very many utilities here, but some of the ones here are quite useful. The unsit30.zip is especially valuable if you use both Macintosh and PC platforms. With this file, you can download a stuffed file (SIT format) on your PC and unstuff it in DOS. If you have PC Exchange, MacLink, or other software that allows your Mac to read DOS disks or DOS files, you can then port the unstuffed files from your PC to your Mac. (Stuff-It normally cannot unstuff a SIT file that was saved to a DOS-formatted disk.) Of course, you'll need PKUNZIP to unzip the unsit30.zip file!

How

FTP

Where

oak.oakland.edu

Go To

SimTel/msdos/mac/*

Filename	Description
binhex13.zip	Encode/decode a Macintosh BinHex 4.0 file
cvtmac.zip	Convert MacPaint pics to PC Paint Plus
d-view.zip	Edit Macintosh MacPaint files with a PC
macbest1.zip	BEST MACPictures #1
macbest2.zip	BEST MACPictures #2
picmac11.zip	Convert PCPAINT .PIC to .MAC
unpakit.zip	Unpack Macintosh packed (.PIT) files
unsit30.zip	Extract Macintosh STUFFIT (.SIT) files in MS-DOS

A sampling of files in SimTel/msdos/mac

The PowerPC Does Macintosh

The PowerPC has been called a whole new way of computing, and has stirred nearly as much excitement as when PCs and Macs were first introduced. Now, the screamingly fast PowerPC chip technology is in the Macintosh and these computers have a whole new name to reflect the new technology: Power Macintosh, or simply Power Macs.

This site includes more than 50 utilities and other programs, all of which have been optimized to run native on Power Mac systems. However, many of the utilities are fat binaries, so they can run on either Power Macs or Motorola 68000-based Macs. There are plenty of great file compression/uncompression utilities here to help you open virtually any compressed file that you find on the Internet. There are also utilities to view and convert GIF and JPEG files, as well as plenty of utilities for adding capabilities to the Finder and to System 7. Actually, you'll find that just about any category of software, including games, is represented here.

How

FTP or Gopher

Where

mac.archive.umich.edu (FTP) or gopher.itd.umich.edu (Gopher)

Go To

mac/powermac/* (FTP), or for Gopher locations:

Software Archives

Macintosh

Powermac

Windows Demo Software

You wouldn't buy a car without driving it around the block a couple of times, would you? So why invest hundreds of dollars in new software if you're not sure it's what you need? With these Windows program demos, you can try before you buy. Here's where you'll find some scaled-back versions of the real things: morphing software, animation software, viewers, and lots of other stuff on the cutting edge.

How

FTP

Where

garbo.uwasa.fi

Go To

windows/demo/*

Desktop Utilities

Check out some of these fun and practical Windows desktop utilities. You'll find loads of free stuff here, including software to change your Windows startup logo, programs that make your computer load and launch applications faster, file management utilities, and even a Windows trashcan.

How

FTP

Where

garbo.uwasa.fi

Go To

windows/desktop/*

Hey, Got the Time?

This site is strictly for motorheads with an obsession for keeping the correct time. You'll find dozens of displayable clocks and utilities for setting the correct time down to about a jillionth of a second and for adjusting faulty system, real-time, and battery clocks.

How

FTP

Where

oak.oakland.edu

Go To

SimTel/msdos/clock/*

Filename	Description
aclk12.zip	TSR real-time alarm clock (screen upper right)
adclk100.zip	Utility for adjusting inaccurate PC clocks
alarm13.zip	TSR pop-up alarm clock
at-clock.zip	Corrects for AT CMOS clock time slippage
Bclock.zip	Time program with large clock face
clkdev14.zip	Keep DOS time in synch with battery clock chip
clkon240.zip	Resident upper-right corner clock and alarm
fixtim10.zip	Compensates for inaccuracy in on-board clock
gettime.zip	Sets system clock from U.S. Naval Observatory
settm1_6.zip	Sets computer's clock via modem to 'real' time
showdt11.zip	Shows date and time without prompt to change
vidclk.zip	Configurable on-screen clock

A sampling of files in SimTel/msdos/clock

VB Dynamic Link Libraries

If you're a Visual Basic programmer, you'll want to check out this FTP site. Why reinvent the wheel with every new program? Instead, take advantage of the great general-purpose DLLs you can find here. You'll find everything you need to make your programs more efficient in less time.

How

FTP

Where

garbo.uwasa.fi

Go To

windows/dlls/*

Full-Screen Editors for Windows

Are you still using EDLIN? Jeez, say it ain't so! You can even do better than Windows' own anemic Notepad. Check out some of the editing programs available here: MicroEmacs, WinEdit, Win-Emacs, and many other full-screen editors to choose from. Unless you're one of those people who thinks that doing things the hard way builds character, you'll want to download one of these editors and make your online scribbling life just a little easier.

How
FTP

Where
garbo.uwasa.fi

Go To
windows/editor/*

MacLayers

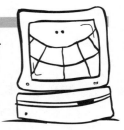

There's multitasking and then there's *multitasking*. If you're a Mac user, you know that your system's multitasking capabilities are pretty limited, thanks to the cooperative multitasking approach used in the underlying system software. But with MacLayers 1.3 for Macintosh users, you can open and work in up to seven windows *simultaneously*. With MacLayers, you can chat with someone across the Internet in one window, Telnet in another window, and download a file while in another window—all at the same time.

How
FTP

Where
rascal.ics.utexas.edu

Go To
mac/communications/MacLayers

Networking from the Internet

This is an excellent site for network administrators, offering dozens of utilities for a variety of LANS and WANS. There are also several programs that allow you to link two PCs via serial or parallel ports. There are even utilities specifically designed to help you use the Internet.

How

FTP

Where

oak.oakland.edu

Go To

SimTel/msdos/lan/*

Filename	Description
archie.zip	Archie DOS client for CUTCP/CUTE/NCSA Telnet
automan.zip	AutoMan: Automatic network management program
bindump1.zip	Lists names of objects in Netware bindery
cmail27c.zip	Free electronic mail program for any LAN
faxbat13.zip	Fax modem networking software for any LAN
ftpnuz10.zip	FTPNuz v1.0: NNTP Usenet Newsreader for PC/TCP
ipxctrl1.zip	LAN node remote control & monitoring with IPX
lanbench.zip	Benchmarks for LANs
lantl124.zip	NETBIOS utility/TSR to send/receive messages
lap101.zip	LapView Pc-to-PC linking, shareware, nagware
lsalv103.zip	List all salvagable files on Netware 3.x drive
lv100b.zip	LanView system analysis tool for LAN's/WAN's
mailcall.zip	LAN: TSR util provides pop-up access to ccMail
nba102.zip	NetBIOS Assist - simple remote console utility
net-co50.zip	Net-Control / Network Monitoring and Recording
netchat.zip	Allows 'live' multi-way conversations on a LAN
spacechk.zip	Tracks network disk usage for users & admins
unet11.zip	Network two PCs together using parallel ports

A sampling of files in SimTel/msdos/lan

Compression/Uncompression Software

So you've found the latest shareware version of Doom, you've down-loaded it, and are ready to start blowing demons back to whatever hell they came from. You start the program and—nothing. Most likely, the problem—and solution—are very simple. Problem: Chances are you haven't uncompressed the file yet. Solution: PKUNZIP

Most files on the Internet, including graphics, programming code, and large text files, are compressed into space-saving binary format before being downloaded. Compressed files not only take up less space on serv-ers, but also require less time to download. But a compressed file is not in a format that your computer can read without a little help. Conse-quently, when a compresed file makes it to your computer, you need to uncompress it. The most popular PC compression/uncompression soft-ware is PKZIP/PKUNZIP, for Macs it's SIT (StuffIt). You can find both all over the Internet, including this site. They're easy to download and come with simple-to-follow instructions.

How

FTP

Where

ftp.cc.utexas.edu

Go To

gifstuff/*

Mission: Impassible

So, you suspect that busybody over in marketing is rifling through your online files, eh? Have we got a surprise for him (or her)—in fact, several surprises. You'll find more than two dozen pass-word protection schemes here, with various levels of password protec-tion for users from the prudently cautious to the totally paranoid. But take these password utilities seriously. We know one user who forgot his password and was forced to reformat his hard disk in order to make his system accessible again. Needlessly to say, he lost many megabytes of invaluable data. Several days later, when he finally remembered his password again, he looked so angry we were afraid even to say "Hello" to him.

How

FTP

Where

oak.oakland.edu

Go To

SimTel/msdos/security/*

Filename	Description
Eeklogin.zip	Restricts certain commands for unwanted users
lkmup251.zip	Password-protects PC from unauthorized users
login.zip	Login password program for PCs
navypass.zip	Password protection system (NARDAC, U.S. Navy)
passwrd6.zip	Installs password on hard disk, w/ASM source
pclock21.zip	Protects hard disk even from floppy boot
pcsntry2.zip	PC-Sentry v2.00b: Security for PCs and networks
pxlgt100.zip	Logs time and displays last time program was run
risk10.zip	RISKIT v1.0: Computer security risk analysis
secure10.zip	Password protected access to subdirectories
slock21.zip	Temporarily locks DOS workstation while user is away
thegate.zip	Limits PC/application access to list of users

A sampling of files in SimTel/msdos/security

For Font Fanatics Only

Are you pushing the envelope of your font usage repetoire when you use italics? If you only knew what you were missing. Here's how to find out: This site includes many useful fonts for business and professional text, as well as some of the most obscure, bizarre, and downright weirdest fonts available.

Font formats here include bitmaps, Adobe Type Manager (ATM), and TrueType. Remember, he who dies with the most fonts wins!

How
FTP

Where
garbo.uwasa.fi

Go To
windows/fonts/*
windows/fonts-atm/*
windows/fonts-tt/*

HP Printer Utilities

Here's a good site for finding DOS-based utilities that enhance the capabilities of your Hewlett-Packard or compatible laser printer. A majority of the files are soft fonts that you can download to your printer, but there are also some great utilities for printing mutliple pages of text per page, creating flowcarts, printing on two sides of a page, and printing on different-size forms.

How
FTP

Where
oak.oakland.edu

Go To
SimTel/msdos/laser/*

Filename	Description
4print41.zip	Print 4 pages/sheet, wide sprdsheet, on HP LJ
adit181.zip	Generates variations of existing HP soft fonts
altrft22.zip	Edit/make/rotate/del/ins+ HPLaserJet soft font
ctable.zip	Determines character widths for HP soft fonts
deartea.zip	'Dear Teacher' (school kid) LaserJet font

A sampling of files in SimTel/msdos/laser

Filename	Description
dingja1.zip	LaserJet Dingbat font
ep2hp.zip	Epson printer emulation on HP LaserJet II
fineprnt.zip	Print small 6 pt font text on HP LaserJet ptr
fontld15.zip	Scale/mirror/invert/rotate LaserJet soft fonts
hp4sign2.zip	Displays messages on HP 4 LaserJet LED display
jetpak11.zip	LaserJet and DeskJet conversion & font utilities
lasrflow.zip	Flowchart maker for HP Laserjet+ compatibles
lb203.zip	Prints MICR encoded blank checks on lasers
lj20.zip	Print 2-sides of page w/LaserJet
lq203.zip	Prints Quicken laser checks on blank stock
lqw203.zip	Prints Quicken 4 Win laser checks on blanks
pcx2font.zip	Converts PCX picture to a LaserJet font
symbol1.zip	Collection of raster pictures for LaserJet
vlj.zip	View LaserJet soft fonts, download to printer
xprt551.zip	Formats text for output to HP LaserJet printer

More files in SimTel/msdos/laser

P.S. I've Found You

Here's a source for some interesting PostScript printing utilities. You'll find numerous ASCII to PostScript conversion utilities, other utilities for converting Epson and IBM print file formats to PostScript, and several Ghostscript fonts (including the Ghostscript program itself).

How

FTP

Where

oak.oakland.edu

Go To

SimTel/msdos/postscrp/*

Filename	Description
2-Up111.zip	Prints two 66 line pages on one A4 page
amaze10.zip	PostScript file creates random maze on printer
ascii-ps.zip	Converts ASCII-to-PostScript, w/QuickBasic source
etsr301.zip	Epson MX80-to-PostScript printer translator

A sampling of files in SimTel/msdos/postscrp

Filename	Description
gs261386.zip	Ghostscript v2.6.1, 386/486 EXE w/extended memory
gs261ini.zip	Ghostscript v2.6.1, required files plus examples
gs261win.zip	Ghostscript v2.6.1, EXE for Windows 3.x
hp2ps18.zip	HPGL to PostScript converter version 1.8
pc2ps11.zip	Converts IBM character-set text files to PostScript
pcps780.zip	Prints ASCII to PostScript 2-up, etc. (DOS/OS2/Unix)

More files in SimTel/msdos/postscrp

I/O, I/O, So Off to Work I Go

You'll find some pretty sophisticated I/O utilities here, including dozens of utilities for managing and monitoring COM, parallel, serial, and other ports. This site is great for computer service technicians, as well as system administrators who are responsible for a company's cadre of PCs.

How
FTP

Where
oak.oakland.edu

Go To
SimTel/msdos/io_util/*

Filename	Description
1pr2a.zip	Swaps LPT1 and LPT2 printer ports
34instal.zip	Adds DOS support for COMM ports 3 and 4
async-ce.zip	COMM port driver
async.zip	Asynchronous communications routines
breakbox.zip	Software-based RS232 breakout box
comchk18.zip	Commchk 1.8: Serial port protocol analyzer
comfix12.zip	Windows COM port 'bug' fix/DOS COM port setup
comprt25.zip	Config COM/LPT ports: Show address, IRQ & UART
comst12.zip	Comset v1.2: Modem/UART/serial port tester
comtrap.zip	TSR to trap unexpected COM port interrupts
dlm140.zip	Data Line Monitor: Turn PC into a datascope
fx16550d.zip	Corrects problem with AMI BIOS and 16550 UART

A sampling of files in SimTel/msdos/io_util

CD-ROMs for (Next to) Nothing

Walnut Creek CD-ROM publishes dozens of different collections of public domain and shareware CD-ROM discs. Some of their CD-ROM discs include:

- Giga Games
- GIFs Galore
- Space and Astronomy
- Project Gutenberg
- Clipart Cornucopia
- Fractal Frenzy
- Internet Info
- C Users' Group Library
- Linux Operating System
- Sprite

Order one of their free catalogs for a complete listing.

How
E-mail

Where
orders@cdrom.com

Ask For
Free catalog

Handy Handicap Utilities

Physical disabilities shouldn't be a barrier to easy computer use. But unlike places of business, the federal government hasn't regulated or even created guidelines for ensuring that computer and software developers provide support for individuals with disabilities. This site can help you or a friend or relative remove many of the barriers that make computers difficult to use for the hearing and visually impaired. There are numerous large-text applications, speech-based programs and utilities for voice synthesizers, and utilities for Braille terminals. In all, there are more than one hundred files here.

How

FTP

Where

rigel.acs.oakland.edu

Go To

SimTel/msdos/handicap

dBASE Yourself

With the advent of Windows, the DOS-based dBASE program, in all of its various incarnations, is starting to give way to Windows-based database management programs. But the changeover has been a long time in coming—millions of copies of dBASE are still in use. The software is especially popular among network administrators and system administrators, thanks to the thousands of applications and utilities that have been written to support this Ashton-Tate mainstay. You'll find some of the better of these utilities at this site.

How

FTP

Where

oak.oakland.edu

Go To

SimTel/msdos/dbase/*

Filename	Description
ags210.zip	Turns dBASE III setups into menu driven system
ashtips.zip	Tips on using Ashton-Tate's dBASE III
c2dbase1.zip	Collection of C utilities for dBASE III+
convdb17.zip	Converts ASCII files to dBASE compatible files

A sampling of files in SimTel/msdos/dbase

Filename	Description
dbfed120.zip	dBASE/Foxbase database editor/viewer/printer
dbfu13.zip	Utility for displaying dBASE file structures
dedit100.zip	dBASE/Clipper programmer's database editor
dscar1.zip	dBASE III+ syntax checker
dxt120.zip	DBASE Exploration Tools: Source code analysis
foxu20.zip	FoxPro/dBASE PD/Shareware ad-ons directory, August 94
foxv20.zip	Directory of FoxPro/dBASE add-on producers, August 94
lib19.zip	dBASE IV procedure/UDF library
printdb4.zip	Ashton-Tate info about dBASE4 LaserJet drivers
swaprv12.zip	Run any program from within dBASE
techs.zip	dBASE technical notes
zipcodes.zip	USA Zip code data in dBASE .DBF format

More files in SimTel/msdos/dbase

Help from an Expert

If you feel like a wounded warrior victimized in the Computer Revolution, take heart! Kim Komando transforms the technical into everyday English through her weekly newspaper computer column and top-rated radio program. Now her expertise is available to Internet subscribers. Great for those who think ROM is some kind of Buddhist chant.

How

E-mail

Where

Komando@aol.com

Ask For

Help with your computing problems

Do-It-Yourself Telnet

Want to use Telnet but don't have access to it through your Internet provider? The files here provide you with everything you need to become your own NCSA Telnet provider, including full documentation for Telnet.

How
FTP

Where
oak.oakland.edu

Go To
SimTel/msdos/ncsatlnt/*

Filename	Description
dev_note.txt	Text file of developer's notes for NCSA Telnet (ASCII file)
info.tel	Description of NCSA Telnet and its utilities (ASCII file)
packets.inf	Guide to installing NCSA Telnet packet drivers (ASCII)
pktdrvr.inf	Pointer to the latest Crynwr packet drivers (ASCII file)
tel2307b.zip	NCSA Telnet 2.3.07 binaries & other utilities
tel2307s.zip	Source code for NCSA Telnet 2.3.07 and utilities
tel23doc.zip	ASCII documentation for NCSA Telnet 2.3

Complete listing of SimTel/msdos/ncsatlnt

Desktop DOS

If you're still a DOS junkie or at least spend a lot of time working in DOS, you'll probably appreciate this collection of desk accessories for DOS. You'll find everything from address and birthday reminder programs to Jewish and Gregorian calendars. There are almost as many calendar programs here than there are weeks in the year, so you'll have to do some browsing and software evaluation to find the program that you like best. Several SideKick look-alikes are here, too. One of our favorites is toadwake.zip, which executes a DOS command at a predetermined time of day.

How
FTP

Where
oak.oakland.edu

Go To
SimTel/msdos/deskaccs/*

Filename	Description
an-101.zip	Advance Notice v1.01 - early warning of events
an300.zip	Ample notice: Powerful appointments/alarm/PIM
app.zip	Use SIDEKICK+ appointment book w/o loading SK+
areacod3.zip	Area Code Finder, C source for MS-DOS, Unix
areafon3.zip	AREAFON 3.02/Areacodes/Foreign Dial/Citynames
callfor.zip	A TSR to keep phone messages
drsc104.zip	Combo desk reference & scientific calculator
jotit2.zip	JotIt: Netbios-compatible phone message taker
pc1420.zip	Clock/calendar/notepad/track reminder/tickler
qdial10.zip	QuickDial: Modem dial voice call in DOS prompt
toadwake.zip	Executes a command at specified time
wuk21.zip	Organizes and prints names, phones, and dates
zodiac61.zip	Hebrew & Moslem calendars moon/sunrise/set/eclipse

A sampling of files in SimTel/msdos/deskaccs

Beating a Better PATH to DOS

PATH is one of the most important commands in DOS because it determines which directories the operating system will look by default to locate programs and files. But PATH is limited both in its size and capability. This site provides several utilities for overcoming some of PATH's limitations, including the ability to use more than 127 characters in the PATH line.

How

FTP

Where

oak.oakland.edu

Go To

SimTel/msdos/pathutil/*

Filename	Description
addpath1.zip	Adds directory to PATH without SET PATH=
apath23.zip	Adds/deletes elements of PATH on the fly
dpath30.zip	Sets a PATH for programs' access to data files
pathfind.zip	Searches for files in DOS's PATH

A sampling of files in SimTel/msdos/pathutil

Alchemical Conversion Magic

Are you determined to be the last Internet jockey on the block to download a GIF viewer? If you're a Windows user, here's another approach. Image Alchemy is a graphics conversion program that will turn your bitmaps into GIF files, your JPEGs into bitmaps, and just about any other coversion combination you can imagine. This shareware version is limited to 640 x 480 display resolution. But if you like the software, become a registered user and get the full-blown professional version.

How
FTP

Where
oak.oakland.edu

Go To
SimTel/msdos/graphics/alch177.zip

Hoosier Shareware Provider?

The Center for Innovative Computer Applications at Indiana University houses the online mother lode of shareware and freeware for Windows— more than 600 megabytes total. Just about every category of software or Windows utility is well represented here, but as you might expect, you'll sometimes have to wait in line to access this site. It's popular and busy during peak hours. Try accessing the site between 7 p.m. and 7 a.m. EST for your best changes. These are the hours that the site administrators request that you use, anyway.

How
FTP or Mosaic

Where
ftp.cica.indiana.edu (FTP) *or* http://www.cica.indiana.edu/cgi-bin/checkftp (WWW)

Go To
pub/pc/win3/*

Get Windows Help-Authoring Help

You don't need to be a programmer to write Windows Help files, although it helps (no pun intended). Windows includes a built-in Help engine that you can use to write custom Help files for applications or just to create online documentation. This *Windows Help Authoring Guide* comes to you free of charge from the "source" itself—Microsoft.

How

FTP

Where

garbo.uwasa.fi

Go To

windows/doc/hag.zip

A Graphical Potpourri

Now there's no excuse for skipping by all those great GIF and JPEG files on the Internet. If you still don't have the appropriate image-viewing software, this site will provide you with all the tools you need. There are image-processing tools, JPEG and GIF viewers, a 3-D landscape modeling program, and more imaging tools. These programs run under Windows.

How

FTP

Where

garbo.uwasa.fi

Ask For

windows/graphics/*

Drive Yourself Nuts

One of the biggest problems with Windows is that every hardware device that Windows controls needs to have its own little management program, or driver. It's a little-known fact, but Microsoft writes very few of the driver programs that are installed with Windows. Most drivers are supplied to Microsoft by hardware manufacturers. And when these hardware companies introduce new devices, Windows usually needs updated drivers to support the hardware. If you've got a device that Windows doesn't seem to know how to support, the problem could be that you have a missing or outdated driver. Check out this source to see if an updated driver is available for your problematic hardware. This site includes printer drivers, video drivers, mouse drivers, and more.

How
FTP

Where
garbo.uwasa.fi

Go To
windows/drivers/*

Teach Your Mouse to Do Tricks

Numerous mouse drivers and mouse utilities can be found here. If you still use one or more DOS programs that don't have mouse support, like dBASE or an older version of Lotus 1-2-3, you'll find several programs here that allow you to use your mouse to emulate arrow keys. There are also programs that let you use the mouse at the DOS command line.

How
FTP

Where
oak.oakland.edu

Go To
SimTel/msdos/mouse/*

Filename	Description
arrmouse.zip	Makes mouse emulate arrow keys for any program
dosmouse.zip	Use Microsoft mouse at DOS command level
drvr624.zip	Logitech Mouse drivers v6.24, from their BBS
gmous102.zip	Genius mouse driver v10.2 (DOS 6.0-compatible)
joymouse.zip	Use joystick as mouse, move cursor, enter keys
k2rod.zip	Simulates series of keyboard strokes with mouse
kme-beta.zip	Emulates a Microsoft mouse with your keyboard
mouse701.zip	Version 7.01 mouse drivers from Mouse Systems
mouseb03.zip	Uses a mouse to cut and paste in DOS' text mode
mswitch.zip	Switches mouse on and off

A sampling of files in SimTel/msdos/mouse

If Icon Do It, So Can You

Tired of using the same old tired icons supplied in the Windows progman.exe and moricons.dll files? You'll find hundreds of unique icons here, so let your imagination run wild. This source even includes some icon editors that you can use to create your own icons or "customize" an existing icon.

How
FTP

Where
garbo.uwasa.fi

Go To
windows/icons/*

Free Stuff That's Fit to Print

This site focuses on printer utilities, but it includes much more. You'll find drag-and-drop print utilities, font management utilities, text searchers, button editors, and lots of other shareware tools for Windows.

How
FTP

Where
garbo.uwasa.fi

Go To
windows/printer/*

DeskJet Utilities

Hewlett-Packard's DeskJet is one of the most popular series of ink-jet printers, noted for their silent operation. However, DeskJets often seem to be limited in their performance capabilities. Try this site for several useful DOS-based utilities, including a utility that provides the ability to print multiple pages of text per page.

How
FTP

Where
oak.oakland.edu

Go To
SimTel/msdos/deskjet/*

Filename	Description
8pdj500c.zip	Prints 8 pages of text per page on HP DJ500
dj-reink.zip	One user's experience with re-inking DJ carts
djdoc8.zip	HP DJ/DJ+/LJ: Print up to 8 pages on one sheet
djfonfmt.zip	How to convet LaserJet soft fonts to DeskJet format
djfont.zip	LaserJet font to DeskJet font converter
djlist.zip	2-up printing on DeskJet
djll.zip	Print landscape on DeskJet
djp4up.zip	Print 4 60-line pages on one page, HP DeskJet
p821_v23.zip	Print up to eight pages to one sheet, HPDJ/LJ4

A complete listing of files in SimTel/msdos/deskjet

Screen Savers Galore!

Windows comes with fewer than a dozen built-in screen savers, and in our opinion, they're all losers. Frankly, we expected a little more graphically interesting screen savers from the company that gave the PC world the most popular graphical user interface. Anyway, you can retire those tired Windows screen savers and replace them with the great selection you'll find here: melting screens, shufflers, slide shows, and many more.

How

FTP

Where

garbo.uwasa.fi

Go To

windows/screen/*

Sounds Like This . . .

Weary of hearing the same old beep every time Windows reports an error? Want to put your musical talent to work online? This source has dozens of .WAV sound files and other samples, guitar scales, MIDI sequencers, and many other sound utilities that you can use with your MIDI device, your SoundBlaster card, or even your PC speaker. Most of these utilities and drivers require Windows.

How

FTP

Where

garbo.uwasa.fi

Go To

windows/sound/*

Sounds Abound for DOS

If you don't have Windows (or if you just don't *want* to use Windows), you can still produce plenty of cool sounds on your PC. This library includes more than 60 sound files and utilities in a variety of formats and for several different sound cards and devices, including that old static-filled standby, the PC speaker. Most of these *do not* require Windows.

How

FTP

Where

oak.oakland.edu

Go To

SimTel/msdos/sound/*

Filename	Description
adl110.zip	Use Adlib/AdlibGold with ModPlay/ScreamTracker
blast13.zip	SoundBlaster driver & direct access routines
bmstr60.zip	Blaster Master: VOC/WAV/SND sound file editor
bunked10.zip	Yamaha-OPL2/FM patch editor v1.0(Adlib/SB/Pro)
c2snd200.zip	Converts DeskMate .SND to/from .WAV and others
cdbox306.zip	VGA/mouse SB sound player/playback shell
cool131.zip	WIN3.x: Professional quality .WAV form editor
fftscop5.zip	Real-time scope display of SoundBlaster input
gldwav21.zip	GoldWave: Digital sound editor for Windows 3.1
mvpshare.zip	Music/Voice/Pictures for Adlib and SoundBlaster
nohiss10.zip	Reduces background noise in voice sound files
nusnd102.zip	Plays .WAV sound files through PC speaker
plany12.zip	Play any file (.AU, .WAV, etc) on SoundBlaster
remac.zip	Plays Macintosh sound files through PC speaker
sbf3.zip	C callable library for SoundBlaster/Pro, with source
sbprog10.zip	SoundBlaster programming routines (C++ src)
voc2snd.zip	Convert SoundBlaster .VOC file to Macintosh .SND
wjmr21.zip	Win3.x MIDI sequencer: Plays MIDI files on SoundBlaster

A sampling of files in SimTel/msdos/sound

Scott Yanoff's Special Internet Connections

This is an especially rich Internet "list of links;" that is, a document listing URLs of interesting and useful resources on the Internet. Scott has been maintaining the list since 1991, which consists of a large HTML page with a table of contents at the top, followed by the links in alphabetical order and a short description of each.

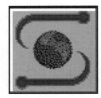

The list is diverse, but also fairly mainstream; this in contrast to lists like Justin Hall's "The Wild, Weird, and Wonderful on the WWW," which emphasizes stuff definitely on the other side of the typical. Topics include art, astronomy, news servers and journals, games, chat, physics, business/financial, law, literature, history, Gopher sites, space, and much much more. This is one of those places you should visit first while setting out on a new research project.

How

Mosaic

Where

http://www.uwm.edu/Mirror/inet.services.html

Power to the PC

In 1991, Apple, IBM, and Motorola formed one of the strangest and most unlikely alliances in the history of technology. The result of their combined efforts has been a new microprocessor technology that threatens the dominance of Intel as the major supplier of CPUs for personal computers. The biggest problem with keeping up with this intriguing new technology is that the PowerPC industry players are continually introducing new chips, new systems, new standards, and new news. You can stay in touch with the PowerPC Revolution by subscribing to this free newsletter.

How

E-mail

Where

news@power.globalnews.com

Ask For

A subscription to the *PowerPC Newsletter*

Dr. Dobbs Journal

Since its inception in 1986, *Dr. Dobbs Journal* has remained one of the most respected and read magazines for programmers. This site contains code listings from all issues of DDJ from January 1986 through March 1994. Filenames indicate the magazine's date of issue. For instance, ddj9303.zip contains code listings from the March 1993 issue.

How

FTP

Where

oak.oakland.edu

Go To

SimTel/msdos/ddjmag/*

PC Magazine Library

Since the advent of personal computers in the late 1970s, literally hundreds of general-computing magazines have started and then quietly died from lack of reader interest. *PC Magazine*, a Ziff-Davis publication, has been one of the survivors and has even thrived through all of the competition. This Internet source is massive, reflecting the wealth of genuinely useful end-user (and some programming) material published throughout the years. There are more than 200 files of magazine articles here, covering more than 300 DOS and Windows utilities (but mostly DOS).

How

FTP

Where

oak.oakland.edu

Go To

SimTel/msdos/pcmag/*

PC Techniques Library

The first issue of *PC Techniques* magazine went to press in March 1990—a latecomer to the programming magazine world. Few in the industry expected the magazine to survive amid the glut of other programming journals. But sometimes quality will win out, and *PC Techniques* is still going strong today, mainly because it manages to mix serious programming content with friendly and highly personable text. Anyway, source code listings from every *PC Techniques* issue from the Vol. 1 No. 1 through June/July 1992 can be found at this site.

How

FTP

Where

oak.oakland.edu

Go To

SimTel/msdos/pctecniq/*

Low-Level Tools for High-Level Tekkies

This site includes dozens of utilities for formatting, diagnosing, repairing, partitioning, and booting disks. Think of the ideal disk drive utility that you'd like to have, then check this directory. It's probably here.

How

FTP

Where

oak.oakland.edu

Go To

SimTel/msdos/diskutil/*

Filename	Description
1seagate.zip	Specs for ALL Seagate drives from Seagate BBS
2format.zip	Formats 2 floppys without hassles
3drvs260.zip	Adds 3 hard drives to AT; mix/match types
4drvu100.zip	IDE hard disk inquiry utility, up to 4 drives
4spd100.zip	Hard drive data transfer rate test
align.zip	Drive alignment program for technicians
amos111.zip	Reads/writes OS/2 files HPFS<=>FAT under MSDOS
ataid010.zip	ATA/IDE diagnostic and identification pgm v1.0
atfmt100.zip	Floppy formatter. Gets 1066K on 720K diskette
bboot.zip	Boots from B: drive instead of A: drive
bios-drv.zip	Award & Phoenix BIOS drive type tables
boot.zip	Create your own custom boot records
chkprt.zip	Determines disk suitability for SMARTDRV.SYS
cleaner1.zip	Cleans floppy diskette drive read/write heads

A sampling of files in SimTel/msdos/diskutil

Where to Find More Goodies

Since this is a computer book by nature, you'll find more software in virtually every other section of the book. Try the *Games* section for a good selection of game programs. The *Kid Stuff* section has lots of programs designed specifically for kids.

FREE $TUFF

When a subject becomes totally obsolete, we make it a required course.

Peter Drucker

Education and Teaching Tools

Financial Help Is a Telnet Away

Each year, the federal government commits over $18 billion to help financially needy students pay for college and trade school. Two government publications are available to guide you through the financial aid maze and help make your dreams of college a reality. The Department of Education's *Student Guide* explains the federal government's financial assistance programs and application procedures for college, technical, and vocational students. The National Commission for Cooperative Education's *Cooperative Education: Experience the Advantage* literature shows you how you can earn money, get practical work experience, and earn college credits.

How

Telnet

Where

fedworld.gov (see page 13 for instructions on how to download files from the Consumer Information Center)

Go To

PREPCOLL.TXT

Videos, Videos, Videos

Allegro Computer Services has over 3,500 special interest and how-to videos on every subject imaginable—everything from Algebra to Zimbabwe! Learn cooking, golf, dancing, and more. Have you ever wanted to learn a foreign language or ballroom dancing? Chinese cooking? Art history? Videos are great teaching tools for children, students, professionals, hobbyists, and teachers, and they make great gifts. Send for a free catalog.

How

E-mail

Where

allegro@mercury.interpath.net

Ask For

Video tape catalog

University Ethics

As universities around the country plug into the Internet, they're faced with potential abuse of their networks. In answer to their concerns, many schools are developing guidelines on responsible behavior and use of their computer systems. Download a copy of your university's policy so you're not caught unaware.

How

FTP

Where

ariel.unm.edu

Go To

ethics/*

Your Kids Can Be Grade-A Students

How well your child does in school may have little to do with I.Q. Research has shown that behavior and attitude are what really affect performance in the classroom.

The Office of Educational Research and Improvement (OERI) publishes *Helping Your Child Do Better in School*, a guide that teaches how to help your child learn the four strategies to becoming a better student:

• Paying attention
• Keeping interested in schoolwork
• Learning and remembering
• Studying

How

Telnet

Where

fedworld.gov (see page 13 for instructions on how to download files from the Consumer Information Center)

Go To

HLPCHILD.TXT

Tall Tales or True Stories?

Certainly there aren't really alligators in the New York City sewers, or are there? Does hot water freeze faster than cold? Did a programming typo really cause a U.S. satellite to self destruct? Hundreds of urban myths and other folklore of all types proven and debunked are found at this Gopher site.

How

Gopher

Where

quartz.rutgers.edu

Go To

Folklore-Urban and Other

Different People, Same Planet

Racism is an ugly word. The irrationality of racism has been used since the beginning of time to tout the inferiority of racial or ethnic groups that are "different." Racial justifications are often accompanied by discrimination, verbal or physical abuse, and even genocide.

Some sociologists suggest that in many people and societies, racism exists at an unconscious level, even when there is no overt discrimination. Stereotypes and preconceived ideas about other groups are damaging to both the victims *and* the offender, as well as the society as a whole.

Here's information that can help. You'll learn about the customs, rituals, and beliefs of other cultures and their ways of life. By understanding and appreciating someone else's way of life, you can learn to tolerate their culture, just as they might learn to tolerate yours. Take a small step to end racism.

How

FTP

Where

ftp.netcom.com

Go To

pub/amcgee/indigenous/my_indigenous_related_lists

Teacher's Aide

The biggest complaint we hear from teachers (aside from their paychecks) is that there aren't enough hours in the day to get their jobs done. Here's a good source of help for busy teachers of all grade levels. Most of the programs here are classroom management and productivity tools. You'll find several grade book packages, test generators, and authoring systems. These are all DOS-based programs.

How

FTP

Where

oak.oakland.edu

Go To

SimTel/msdos/teaching/*

Filename	Description
drill20.zip	Classroom student calling for drills, games
examba20.zip	Exam Bank v2.0: Teacher's test maker
extol30.zip	PC-EXTOL 3.0 computer CAI Language
frames.zip	Programmed textbook CAI, fill in missing words

A sampling of files in SimTel/msdos/teaching

Filename	Description
grade252.zip	Aeius Gradebook: Maintain teacher's grade book
lesson.zip	Maintains school lesson plans for teachers
mathprob.zip	Math problem generator for school teachers
pc-quiz.zip	Teachers aid (test)
pccai205.zip	CAI authoring language; write tutorials, tests
powergrf.zip	Math and Science graphics tool for teachers
quizgen.zip	Quiz generator program
seats20.zip	Classroom seating chart creator: Many features
study.zip	Study helper. Asks questions randomly + score
twrite2.zip	Test Writer 2.0: Tests management and printing program
vargra60.zip	Comprehensive grade entry, analysis, and statistics

More files in SimTel/msdos/teaching

Teacher's Pet

If you're a teacher, you know that you never stop learning. Why not use the Internet to find information to help
you become the best teacher you can be. The Internet
Resource Directory (IRD) is an archive of documents to
help teachers hone their skills and exchange information. This site includes mailing lists and Telnet sites for teachers to exchange ideas and
concerns, as well as information on other teacher-related FTP sites.

How

FTP

Where

tcet.unt.edu

Go To

pub/telecomputing-info/IRD/*

Electronic mail systems have proved their effectiveness in distance
education programs and in other collaborative projects (Upitis, 1990).
Many teachers have effectively used email capabilities to run electronic
pen pal activities with students from other parts of state, nation, or even
the world. This timely and personal involvement with individuals from
other parts of the world can provide many real rewards for students.

Excerpt from the Internet Resource Directory for teachers at tcet.unt.edu

Nevor Mispell Werds Agin

It's late, the library's closed, the paper's due first thing in the morning, and you haven't seen the dictionary Mom bought you since last semester when you used it to prop your dorm window open. Now, how do you spell xenogeneic, and what in heck does it mean, anyway? Search us, or better yet, search Webster's Ninth Collegiate Dictionary online and find out for yourself.

How

Gopher

Where

gopher-gw.micro.umn.edu:4324

Go To

Webster's Dictionary

What's the Word I'm Looking For?

Does your writing suffer from a case of the blahs? Add a little respect and authority to your writing with Roget's Thesaurus online. Here's help for when you need just the right/correct/proper/appropriate word. With Roget's, you'll develop the grace/refinement/ease/polish that you knew you had all along.

How

Gopher

Where

gopher.aecom.yu.edu

Go To

Internet Resources

Library Resources

Reference Works

Roget's Thesaurus

Geography? Fun? Nah!

Guess what? Learning geography can be lots of fun! No, really! Learning geography doesn't have to mean sitting down with a stack of books and memorizing place names and national capitals. For young children, learning geography can mean taking a trip to the beach or livening up a car trip by playing a license plate game.

The Department of Education's new publication, *Helping Your Child Learn Geography*, is designed to help kindle enthusiasm for the relationships between people and places, the geographical and cultural differences that make each place special, and for just knowing where things are. If you have a child under ten years of age, this is a great time for him or her to discover the wonders of geography, and this book can help.

How

Telnet

Where

fedworld.gov (see page 13 for instructions on how to download files from the Consumer Information Center)

Go To

NFCGEO.TXT

When children understand geographical features on maps, they can learn how lakes, oceans, hills, and mountains affect the weather. Maybe the cold wind that causes them to need a coat comes in from across a lake. Helping Your Child Learn Geography has directions for making a simple weather vane so your child can see where the wind blows in your neighborhood.

People of other regions may dress or build their houses differently from you. They may eat different food because their land and weather may be different. They may even speak a different language. You can fill out your child's knowledge of different cultures with pictures and books. Helping Your Child Learn Geography has a terrific resource list to help you get free or inexpensive maps, magazines, books, and even pen pals that can broaden your child's knowledge of the world.

An excerpt from NFCGEO.TXT

Big Fish in a Little Program

We debated whether to list this program here or in the *Games* or *Science and Technology* sections. It *is* a game and it is science, but mostly it's a tricky way to educate folks about the balance of nature. With Wa-Tor for Windows, you create a hypothetical undersea population of foraging fish and predatory sharks. You determine the number of fish in both populations, the breeding age for both populations, and a few other options. The trick is to keep both populations alive as long as possible. Choose too few foraging fish, and the sharks eat them all and then both populations die. Choose too many foraging fish, and they crowd out the sharks. Choose too old a breeding age for one population, and they can't reproduce fast enough to stay in balance with the other population.

Well, you get the idea. The program graphically shows you both populations over time, and provides different ways to graph the rise and decline of populations. It's fun, addicting, and you learn a little science and statistics totally painlessly. The program requires Windows.

How
FTP

Where
garbo.uwasa.fi

Go To
windows/educgames/*

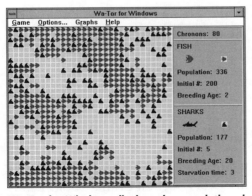

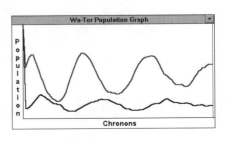

Wa-Tor for Windows displays the populations in action along with graphs showning who's "winning"

Linguistic Lingo

Here's a one-stop shop for the serious linguist, grammarian, or linguistics student. This source includes such specialties as a morphological analyzer, phonological rule simulator, and linguistics data management program. (You practically have to be a linguist just to *pronounce* all this stuff, much less use it.)

How

FTP

Where

oak.oakland.edu

Go To

SimTel/msdos/linguist/*

Filename	Description
babylon3.zip	Worldwide language library linking program
cognate.zip	Identifies related words across languages
englex10.zip	English lexicon (20,000 entries) for PC-KIMMO
fonol421.zip	Fonol 4.2.1 Phonological theory/rule simulator
gramt411.zip	Interpreter for Transformational Grammars
kgen02.zip	Rule compiler for the PC-KIMMO parser
ktext093.zip	Text processing using the PC-KIMMO parser
pckimmo.zip	Two-level processor for Morphological analysis
sh12a.zip	SHOEBOX, linguistic data management program
trans.zip	Translates text to another language
words1.zip	English word list (ASCII), A through D, 1 of 4
words2.zip	English word list (ASCII), E through K, 2 of 4
words3.zip	English word list (ASCII), L through R, 3 of 4
words4.zip	English word list (ASCII), S through Z, 4 of 4
wrdsrv24.zip	Wordsurv: Analyze language survey word lists

A sampling of files in SimTel/msdos/linguist

Where to Find More Goodies

When you really think about it, what information *isn't* educational? You'll find educational material in virtually every section of this book. Especially check out the *Arts and Culture* and *Books and Literature* section for great online information, pictures, and text on liberal arts-related topics.

The *Games* section includes some sites for downloading games that have educational value. For educational software and information on health-related topics, try the *Health and Nutrition* section. For international material, take a look at the *Government and Politics*, *History*, *International Affairs*, *Books and Literature*, and *Travel and Geography* sections. The *Business and Career* section also includes a lot of educational material on doing business domestically and abroad, and on creating a resume and finding the right job.

If you want to learn more about the Internet itself, the *Internet Resources* section is the place to go. If learning about science is important to you, you'll find educational topics and software in the *Nature and the Environment*, *Space and Astronomy*, and *Science and Technology* sections. Of course, if you want to *forget* everything you've ever learned, head for the *Television* section.

FREE $TUFF

We must especially beware of that small group of selfish men who would clip the wings of the American Eagle in order to feather their own nests.

Franklin D. Roosevelt

The Environment and Nature

Fowl Play

If you favor feathered flocks, you'll find a friend in the U.S. Department of the Interior, which has published two free booklets to help you turn your backyard into a bird sanctuary:

- *Homes for Birds* shows you how to select the best birdhouse for your chirpers of choice.
- *Backyard Bird Feeding* describes the styles of feeders available and what to feed your new guests.

How

Telnet

Where

fedworld.gov (see page 13 for instructions on how to download files from the Consumer Information Center)

Go To

BIRDHOME.TXT
BIRDS.TXT

Air Quality

While pollutant levels from individual sources may not pose a significant health risk by themselves, most homes have more than one source that contributes to indoor air pollution. The Environmental Protection Agency and Consumer Product Safety Commission publish a free booklet titled *The Inside Story: A Guide to Indoor Air Quality*. Learn about sources of air pollution in the home that you probably never thought of, and how you can improve the quality of the air you breathe. How dangerous is second-hand smoke? The debate rages on, but you'll find the latest data, along with information on which pesticides are dangerous, household products to watch out for, and other potential contaminants.

How

Telnet

Where

fedworld.gov (see page 13 for instructions on how to download files from the Consumer Information Center)

Go To

AIRQUAL.TXT

U.S.-Japan Environmental Initiative

For a change, allies are truly behaving like allies, and we might all breathe easier for their effort. The U.S.-Japan Environmental Initiative is a joint superpower venture whose goal is to improve the environment in Central and Eastern Europe. Here's the plan in its entirety.

How

Gopher

Where

gopher.gsfc.nasa.gov

Go To

Virtual Reference Shelf

Economic Bulletin Board and Exchange Rates

General Information Files

US-Japan Environmental Initiative

April Showers Bring Big Cleanup Bills

In recent years, nature has been devastating in both the U.S. and elsewhere in the world. Flooding has been an especially serious problem in the Midwest, Georgia, and Florida. If you and your family have been the victims of a flood, the shock and pain of seeing your home and property destroyed can be overwhelming. You shouldn't have to suffer alone. Help is available for flood victims on the Internet with information and aid-related resources.

How
Telnet

Where
idea.ag.uiuc.edu

Login
flood

Environmental Protection Agency

It now seems so long ago, but it's nevertheless true that the Enviornmental Protection Agency was a direct result of the activism of the 1960s. Set up in 1970, the EPA is responsible for regulating water and air quality, commercial waste, pesticides, noise, and radiation in order to minimize the long-term effects of environmental pollution. How successful has this government agency been? You decide. Here's a direct link to the EPA where you can find out more about its regulations, publications, consumer information, and connections to other government Gophers. Now it's easy to remain active about environmental affairs.

How
Gopher

Where
gopher.epa.gov

This is a summary of EPA's Strategic Plan, The New Generation of Environmental Protection. For information on how to order the full plan, please see the last page of this pamphlet.

Introduction

The Environmental Protection Agency (EPA) is at a crossroads in its history. The world is rapidly changing, and the Agency's understanding of the environment is rapidly increasing. The methods EPA has used to protect the environment over the past two decades will not, by themselves, be sufficient in the future.

An excerpt from the EPA's Agency-Wide Strategic Plan Summary

Weather Down Under

For you mates down under: Don't put another shrimp on the barbie till you check out this site and make sure the skies are as blue as a can of Foster's. You'll find the latest weather information for Australia here. Great for travelers.

How

Telnet

Where

vicbeta.vic.bom.gov.au:55555

Login

No Identification of password is necessary

The Latest Dirt

Weekend gardeners and farmers, this site's for you! You'll find all sorts of useful information and tips to help make your hibiscus huge, your lawns lush, and your neighbors green with envy. Get the facts on soil composition, herbicides, and other gardening topics.

How

FTP

Where

sunsite.unc.edu

Go To

pub/academic/agriculture/*

Hot Energy Numbers

What kept the Three Mile Island incident from becoming as disastrous as Chernobyl? On a more local level, how safe and clean is the energy you use in your own home? Here's a directory of Department of Energy toll-free numbers that you can access for information and service about energy matters that matter. This list includes numbers for the Nuclear Safety Hotline, Energy Efficiency and Renewable Energy Clearinghouse, Alternative Fuels Hotline, Clean Cities Hotline, and much more. (See the next topic for still more information on energy alternatives.)

How

Telnet

Where

fedworld.gov (see page 13 for instructions on how to download files from the Consumer Information Center)

Go To

DOE800.TXT

```
        Department Of Energy "800" INFORMATION LINES

The following is a directory of Department of Energy "800 "numbers
offered for information and service:

Nuclear Safety Hotline — accepts complaints or concerns: 800-626-6376.

Building Energy Standards Program Hotline — for questions on DOE
standards and the Energy Policy Act:  800-270-2633.

DOE Occupation, Safety and Health Standards — interpretations and
research service:  800-292-8061.

Energy Efficiency and Renewable Energy Clearinghouse (EREC) — offers
fact sheets, videos, brochures; also handles complex technical inquir-
ies.  EREC is a consolidation of the Conservation and Renewable Energy
Inquiry and Referral Service (CAREIRS) and the National Appropriate
Technology Assistance Service (NATAS).
```

Alternative Energy

Remember the energy crisis of the mid 1970s, complete with hour-long waits in service-station lines? It's a reminder that fossil fuel resources are truly in limited supply. Someday, the use of fossil fuels will be as extinct as the dinosaurs that created them. Read about the research in alternative energy sources that will take their places: hydroelectric, wind, solar, geothermal, and others. This site has lots of books, magazines, and other research information you can download. It's a great source for teachers and parents who are interested in teaching kids more about alternative energy resources. After all, it's their future at stake.

How

FTP

Where

sunsite.unc.edu

Go To

pub/academic/environment/alternative-energy/energy-resources/*

Pesticides

How safe are the pesticides sprayed on your food? Find out if you or your children are at risk and what you can do to minimize any danger. Organic gardening once seemed like a fad; now it's serious business. Learn about the dangers and misconceptions of pesticides, their alternatives, and the use and effectiveness of pesticide-free products.

How

FTP

Where

sunsite.unc.edu

Go To

pub/academic/environment/pesticide-education/general/*

Where to Find More Goodies

The *Arts and Culture* section includes a site for downloading GIFs from the Smithsonian Institution, many of which involve nature and environmental issues.

The *Science and Technology* section includes a "Biologist's Guide to Internet Resources" topic, which provides a wealth of information of interest to naturalists and environmentalists.

The *Health and Nutrition* section includes an important topic on lead-based paints in the home—how to identify and rid your home of all traces of them.

FREE $TUFF

Seeing is deceiving.
It's eating that's believing.

James Thurber

The only thing more exasperating than someone who can cook and won't is someone who can't cook and will.

Robert Frost

Food and Cooking

River View Herbs

Did you know that echinacea can stop your sniffles or that valerian root can help you fall asleep? Maitland Greenhouses, located in Hants County, Nova Scotia, offers a free catalog listing hundreds of varieties of herbs and edible flowers. Gardeners, cooks, and herbalists all will love the freshly cut culinary herbs and scented geraniums, and the plants with medicinal, savory, or aromatic properties. Use the herbs medicinally, as well as to flavor recipes, make teas, scent potpourris and sachets, add color to table arrangements, make dyes and rinses, and to repel insects.

How
E-mail

Where
vmall@hookup.net

Subject
send rvherbs catalog

Robo Cook

Tired of Tuna Helper every night? Why not try this database and download recipes on some creative culinary creations. Search for any ingredient, then choose from the dozens of recipes that appear. Can't decide? Well, there's always the tuna...

1/2 cup milk
4 eggs
2 cups flour
2 tbs. salt

How
Gopher

Where
gopher.aecom.yu.edu

Go To
Internet Resources
Miscellaneous
Search the Food Recipes Database

Rogers' Chocolates

For over 100 years, the historic Rogers' Chocolates has been a Victoria, British Columbia, mecca for chocolate lovers around the world. Today, thousands of mail orders are filled and shipped internationally for these tasty sweets, which are still handmade in the kitchen behind the counter.

Charles Rogers' secret recipes have been jealously guarded and handed down from generation to generation, and the original goodness of his delicious creations remain. These chocolates are quite possibly the best in the world.

There is chocolate almond brittle and many delicious assortments, but we recommend the Victoria Creams. Handmade and covered with dark chocolate, they come in 20 different flavors: cherry, chocolate, coffee, maple, orange, peach, peppermint, and many more.

How

E-mail

Where

vmall@hookup.net

Subject

send rogers catalog

Potent Potables

For your next party, you could do the same old thing—stock up on light beer and wine coolers—or you could get really creative. Download this file to learn how to make hundreds of potent potables your guests will never forget—that is, if they can remember.

How

FTP

Where

ocf.berkeley.edu

Go To

pub/Library/Recreation/big-drink-list

```
----------------------------------------------------------------
General Drink Recipes
----------------------------------------------------------------

Alexander

2 oz. liquor or liqueur
2 oz. white or dark creme de cacao
2 oz. light cream

shake, strain into highball glass


----------------------------------------------------------------

Collins

112 oz. liquor
3 oz. sour mix

shake, strain into collins glass

1 oz. club soda


----------------------------------------------------------------

Cooler

112 oz. liquor
fill with ginger ale

serve in highball glass

lemon wedge


----------------------------------------------------------------
```

An excerpt of drink recipes from the ocf.berkeley.edu "big drink" file

Murchie's Tea and Coffee

In 1894, John Murchie and his sons began selling teas and coffees to discriminating households in and around New Westminister, British Columbia. So began a century-long tradition of selecting, importing, and delicately preparing the finest coffees and teas from around the world. While many things in life have been modernized, Murchies' process of securing and blending the finest quality teas, coffees, and spices has remained virtually the same. Send for a free catalog.

How

E-mail

Where

vmall@hookup.net

Subject

send murchies catalog

Beer Brewing and Wine Making Supplies

Bescaby Lane Vineyards provides winemakers and beer brewers quality supplies and hard-to-find items, including oak barrels, premium corks, and test kits, at prices substantially below retail. Other items they carry include oak chips, fermentation barrels, grommets, bottles, and corkers.

How

E-mail

Where

vmall@hookup.net

Subject

send watson catalog

Coffee Anyone???

How about a steaming cup of coffee to keep you surfing through Cyberspace. "Coffee Anyone??? The Original Computer Coffeehouse," offers a wide assortment of gourmet coffees and teas. Drop a note to Rosemary requesting a free catalog, and get a free sample of one of her fine blends with your first purchase.

How

E-mail

Where

70007.1511@compuserve.com

Ask For

Catalog and free sample—be sure to tell her that you read about it here

Measure Up

When is a pint a pound, an eggplant an aubergine, and a garbanzo bean a chickpea? And just how many pounds is a stone anyway? Measurements and terms for foods vary from country to country, making for a lot of confusion. Here's some information that will help cooks from around the globe communicate with one another.

How

Gopher

Where

quartz.rutgers.edu

Go To

Food, Recipies, and Nutrition
Cooking-FAQ

📁 baseball
📁 books
📁 citadel
📁 computer
📁 cyberculture
📁 disney
📁 economics
📁 etext
📁 folklore
📁 food
📁 gzip
📁 humor
📁 images
📁 internet
📁 jargon
📁 journals

A partial listing of directories (topics) available from the quartz.rutgers.edu site

You Only Need to Supply the Hot Butter

Myers' Gourmet Popcorn offers a variety of delicious popcorns with pizzazz. Whether your interest is in popability or flavor enhancement, you're likely to find what you're tastebuds are searching for in this free catalog.

How

E-mail

Where

mpg@aol.com

Ask For

free catalog

Cookin' Recipe Software

Take your pick from several recipe and meal management software programs available from this site. All of the programs you'll find here are DOS-based.

How

FTP

Where

oak.oakland.edu

Go To

SimTel/msdos/food/

Filename	Description
cchef20.zip	CompuChef v2.0: Full-featured recipe database
dw_cook.zip	Dave Woodall's Recipe/Cookbook Manager v1.10
fdvw233.zip	FoodView: view/print/index recipes (TROFF fmt)
mchef_1a.zip	Recipe, diet & meal management tool. Part 1 of 2
mchef_1b.zip	Recipe, diet & meal management tool. Part 2 of 2
mcook136.zip	Electronic cookbook w/recipes plus add your own

A complete listing of files available in SimTel/msdos/food

Filename	Description
mcook_2.zip	Recipe/nutrition/menu software for Windows
mm-801.zip	MealMaster database program for recipes, v8.01
mm-801ru.zip	Meal-Master Registered User Utilities upgrade
nutri321.zip	Nutritional database helps fine tune your diet
prm.zip	Personal Recipe Manager
qbook096.zip	QuikBook v0.96a: Free-form recipe database program
rec200-1.zip	Recipe database for use with FoodView

A complete listing of files available in SimTel/msdos/food (continued)

It's Meal Time for Windows

Here's a beautifully done Windows-based assortment of recipes—hundreds upon hundreds of them. The author of the USENET cookbook created this as two Windows help files, with full hypertext links so that you can jump between categories and recipes, browsing until your imagination and tastebuds can't take it any longer. This program requires Windows 3.0 or higher. Just click on one of the .HLP files to start the program.

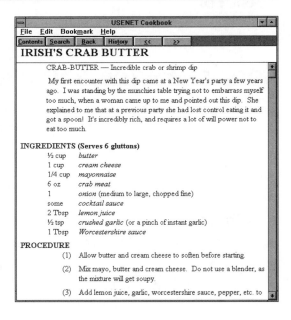

How

FTP

Where

garbo.uwasa.fi

Go To

windows/misc/ucook10.zip

Recipe Organizer

Don't make the same old thing for dinner. It's time to add a little excitement to your menus.This Cardfile-like Windows program allows you to enter and organize all of your recipes online, but takes things one step further. You can enter common measurements, ingredients, and food groups into these three "buckets," and then pick and choose from among them to define recipes. Once you get the hang of this program, recipe creation is a snap.

How
FTP

Where
garbo.uwasa.fi

Go To
windows/util/rcpwin20.zip

What's Cookin'?

Are you looking for great recipes? Then you definitely don't have to look any further. If these recipes don't whet your appetite, then you're not breathing. Are you looking for variety? The folks who maintain this site heard you. We counted seven kinds of chili, three different eggnogs, and over 25 chicken recipes.

No meal is neglected in this database; there's something for everyone, breakfast, lunch, or dinner.

How:
FTP

Where:
gatekeeper.dec.com

Go To:
pub/recipes/*

Make the French Bread dough recipe at least 1 day beforehand if you can. Roll the dough out into the shape of a pizza, put it on a pizza pan,and set it aside. It will keep in the refrigerator overnight.

Preheat the oven to 425.

Prepare the dried mushrooms according to published recipes (soak, wash, cut, resoak, wash, drain).

If the snails are too large (larger than a garlic clove), then cut them in pieces. Drain the snails well.

Melt the butter in a baking dish, add the snails, crushed garlic, (12 tsp" "2.5 ml" salt, and ground black pepper to taste.

Put the bread-dough pan on the top rack of the oven and the snails on the bottom rack of the oven, and cook them both in the preheated oven for 10 minutes. Take them out, and drain the cooking butter from the snails.

Spread the tomato sauce in an even layer on the bread, then sprinkle the Raclette cheese over it. Add the snails, and then the mushrooms. Sprinkle with fresh parmesan cheese, salt, and pepper.

Bake at 425 in the top rack for 12 minutes (bottom rack will burn the crust).

Excerpt from snail-pizza, downloaded from gatekeeper.dec.com.

Where to Find More Goodies

The *Computers and Software* section includes programs for storing and managing recipes.

The *Health and Nutrition* section includes several topics that provide information for eating smart and healthy.

FREE $TUFF

When you're serious about having fun,
it's not much fun at all.

Calvin, from CALVIN AND HOBBES

It was a little all-too-devouring,
just gobble-gobble-gobble.
No social content.

Raph Nader, on Pac-Man

Games

The Leg Bone's Connected to the Hip Bone

Who would ever have thought that learning could be so much fun? It can be when you stop here for the latest in "educational" game software. Tease your brain with these logic puzzles, mazes, word games, and much more. Don't let the word "educational" throw you, either. Most of the games here fit only marginally within that category. These games are fun!

How
FTP

Where
garbo.uwasa.fi

Go To
windows/educgames/*

File	Description
1merlin.zip	Board style game: find treasures and get them to a destination
amaze321.zip	Amazing v3.21 3D, find a way out of the maze
arachnid.zip	Arachnid card game
bcubes.zip	BrainCubes: remember and repeat button sequences
bg4win30.zip	Traditional Backgammon against computer
bog.zip	Bog: Boggle-like word finding game
butmad.zip	Button Madness puzzle
cardws17.zip	Editor/compiler/player for solitary card games
chess321.zoo	GNUChess (v3.21) for Windows (good)
crypto13.zip	Cryptogram puzzle game
cstone1.zip	Cornerstone puzzle
deapsea.zip	Familiar grid game - find ships before yours are found
draw530.zip	Draw 5 v3.0 video poker
mrmind.zip	MasterMind Logic Game
puzzle11.zip	Sliding Tile Puzzle (pictures, BMPs as tiles)
pzl8.zip	Sliding puzzle (numbers as tiles)
stwv150.zip	Story Twister for Windows Version 1.50
watorw.zip	Windows fish & sharks population evolution game
wintris.arc	Tetris for Win3

Files in windows/educgames

Games

Check and Mate

Here's a game that's easy to use but not easy to win. Match your wits against your computer's bits with GNUChess 3.21, a fun and challenging computerized chess program. And with many different levels to choose from, this game will remain challenging, even as your skills improve.

How

FTP

Where

garbo.uwasa.fi

Go To

windows/educgames/chess321.zoo

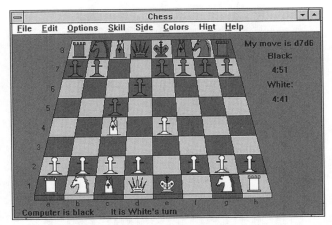

A screen from the Chess program in windows/educgames

Juggling Your Way to Fame and Fortune

Tired of juggling your social life, work, home, money, and family? Try something easier for a change—like chainsaws. Okay, maybe you should work up to that. But you can get started at this FTP site with information on this fun hobby. Download instructions, programs, and publications that will teach you the art of juggling.

How

FTP

Where

moocow.cogsci.indiana.edu

Go To

pub/juggling/*

Whoops! There are lots of fun programs and information on juggling to download from pub/juggling

Bloodthirsty, Back-to-the-Wall Backgammon

And that's just what you see when you log on. Actually, this site offers you a fun and exciting way to kill an evening: backgammon at its finest. Open to all levels, you can match your skills against other players from around the world or just watch (and kibitz) from the sidelines. Rankings and profiles of players are available so you know just who you're playing and what you're getting into.

How

Telnet

Where

fraggel65.mdstud.chalmers.se 4321

Login

guest

Wolfenstein 3D—A Howling Good Time

If you've never played Wolfenstein 3D from Apogee Software, get ready for all the suspense and thrills of a virtual lifetime. And just when you think you've mastered it, you'll find alternate levels, cheat sheets, upgrades, and more for this mega-hit video adventure.

Novices and video junkies alike will find enough additional graphics, sounds, and levels to keep their games from getting boring.

You'll also find some other great video classics here, including Commander Keen, Duke Nukum, Catacombs of the Abyss, and more.

How

FTP

Where

ftp.uml.edu

Go To:

msdos/Games/Apogee/1wolf14.zip

Forever Doomed

Battle cacodemons, spectres, imps, and other nightmarish monsters with Doom, the computer game that's blurring the line of virtual reality. With its awesome 3-D graphics, excellent sound, and nonstop action, Doom has been called "the next step up in PC games." With as many as 5 million players worldwide, it's easy to see why this game is the one used to measure all other shareware games.

Doom can be played solo or against other players across networks. Watch out, this game's addictive and graphically violent. Moms and Dads, parental discretion is advised.

How
FTP

Where
ftp.luth.se

Go To
pub/misc/virtual-worlds/doom/doom1_0.zip

The OTIS/ARCANA Tarot Card Deck

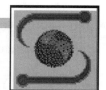

This collaborative effort intends to create an "electronic tarot deck" consisting of images from many artists using digital techniques. Images of the major and minor arcana were gathered until February 1, 1994, and those submitted are now in the process of being judged. The winners in each category will be gathered into the final deck and (finances permitting) eventually printed as physical cards.

The images are beautiful, but some are slightly disturbing; we consider a few of them banal but all are worth a glance. Serious liberties are taken with traditional tarot images here. The Hanged Man, for example, is a "well-hung" man, if you know what we mean (and we're pretty sure that you do)—and most of the rest (aside from the strikingly traditional Tower) are pretty postmodern. There is some nudity on a few of the cards, if this matters to you.

There is a single document containing small thumbnail images of each card. By clicking on a card you find interesting, Mosaic will FTP the full-sized image to your machine and display it using your GIF viewer.

TIP: The thumbnail document alone takes as much as *half an hour* to bring over at 14.4 Kbps. Have Mosaic store it to disk by selecting Load to Disk from the options menu. That way you can read it another day from your hard drive without having to wait another half hour for it to show up. Even if you have read the thumbnail document from local disk, clicking on the thumbnail images will still bring the full-sized images from their respective servers around the world.

The full-sized images are between 75K and 280K in size. Some are black and white; most are in full color. If you don't find the tarot idea itself abominable, you'll certainly find something here worth having.

How
Mosaic

Where
http://oz.sas.upenn.edu/Arcana/cards.html

Fool on a Skateboard card
by Michael Maier, 1994

Tower card
by Les Sattinger, 1994

145

Welcome to Pt. MOOt

Pt. MOOt, a wide spot in the road on the information highway. This virtual town has 350 "residents," and is in no danger of becoming a bustling metropolis anytime soon.

More than just a game, Pt. MOOt is a University of Texas study devoted to "reality modeling." Once you register for citizenship, you're given some pocket money to tide you over until you're gainfully employed (a job bank is provided on Main Street). After that, you're on your own.

How
Telnet

Where
actlab.rtf.utexas.edu

Login
guest

Maur the Dragon

Separated from your friends while exploring a dark and ancient cave, you come across a huge underground cavern. Out of nowhere, a voice fills your head. "Well, a visitor. It has been a long time since anyone has come down this way." You've stumbled upon the lair of Maur, a fierce and ruthless dragon who only wishes a little conversation before he burns you to a crisp.

So begins this interactive computer game at CHAT, the Conversation Hypertext Access Technology site, an experiment in computer-simulated conversation from Communications Canada. Your only weapons against Maur are your words and your wits as you attempt to plead, beg, argue, and con your way to freedom. Will you survive or will you be toast? We're betting on the toast.

How
Telnet

Where

debra.dgbt.doc.ca:3000

Login

chat

Here's MUD in Your Eye

MUDs (Multi-User Dungeons) are Dungeons and Dragons-type role-playing games and are some of the most popular items on the Internet. When playing a MUD, you enter a virtual world in which you become a character in a computer-based fantasy, fighting witches and strange monsters, hunting for treasure, and interacting with other players around the world.

There are hundreds of MUDs of all types on the Internet, and *The Totally Unofficial List of Internet Muds* will help you find the ones that interest you.

How

FTP

Where

rtfm.mit.edu

Go To

pub/usenet/rec.games.mud.announce

Where to Find More Goodies

For more fun and games, take a trip to the *Movies and Videotapes*, *Music*, and *Television* sections.

The *Computers and Software* section includes CD-ROM catalogs that contain plenty of games and lots of Windows utilities that, well, aren't really games, but at least make your computer more fun to use.

The *Kid Stuff* section explains how to find and download lots of games for kids 12 and under, and of course the *Sports, Recreation, and Hobbies* section is pretty gamey. Oh, and one more: Try the *Internet Resources* section for the Internet Hunt.

FREE $TUFF

There's no trick to being a humorist
when you have the whole government
working for you.

Will Rogers

Government
and Politics

Iowa Political Stock Market

Special interest groups have been buying and selling political candidates for decades, so now it's your turn. Following the basic economic principles of supply and demand, you put your money where your mouth is and "buy" shares in politicians when their popularity is low and "sell" when it's high. The Iowa Political Stock Market has proven to be very accurate in reflecting the statistics of opinion polls on many politicians.

How
Telnet

Where
iem.bix.uiowa.edu

Mr. Internet Goes to Washington

The United States House of Representatives Constituent Electronic Mail System is a pilot program being used to test the feasibility of establishing a congressional electronic-mail system. Currently, 30 members of the U.S. House of Representatives have been assigned public electronic mailboxes that you can access, and the number is growing every day.

According to some representatives, E-mail is proving to be an invaluable source of information on constituent opinion. Give it a try and let your congressional representative know what you think.

How
E-mail

Where
congress@hr.house.gov

Ask For
More information

Become a Washington Press Corp Insider

Are you a political junkie? Ever wanted to call in to a talk show to sound off but didn't feel like you were in touch with the latest goings-on inside the Beltway? Well now, you can have White House press releases *automatically* sent to you the instant they're published. This might just be the next best thing to actually being invited to the president's press conferences. (Warning: Press releases are designed to make the White House staff look good. Take 'em with a grain of salt. They're at least entertaining, if not always factual.)

How
E-mail

Where
almanac@esusda.gov

Message
Include the line *subscribe wh-summary* in the body of your message

Say "Cheese," Mr. President

You can use the president's Internet address for more than letting off steam. You can also use it to get some great freebies. Write the White House and request a photo of the president. Won't that look great right next to your autographed photos of Marky Mark and the cast of *Beverly Hills 90210*? Be sure to include your name and postal address.

How
E-mail

Where
president@whitehouse.gov

Message
Photograph of the president (include your name and postal address)

Congressional Listings

Just because your congressperson hasn't hooked up to the Internet yet doesn't mean he or she can hide from you that easily. Here's a listing of phone numbers, fax numbers, and—in some cases—Internet addresses for all U.S. congressional representatives.

How

Gopher

Where

gopher.gsfc.nasa.gov

Go To

US Government

Congress

Congressional Directories

State-By-State Listing of Congressional Directory

Rush Limbaugh on CompuServe

Have you got a gripe on some burning issue that's nagging you? Drop a note to Rush Limbaugh and give him your opinion on the hot issues in the news, or comment on his shows and books. Whether you just want to offer your mega-dittos or you want tell him off, here's where to send your message. Keep in mind that this a CompuServe address. If you're familiar with CompuServe, you probably know that the two parts of a CompuServe address are separated by a comma (for instance, 70277,2502). That won't work when you're sending mail to a CompuServe user. You have to convert the comma to a period, just like we've done below.

How

E-mail

Where

70277.2502@compuserve.com

Legislative Manual

Political science students, as well as anyone interested in the inner workings of the U.S. legislative process, will find this Gopher to be an invaluable source. You'll find information about how committee members are elected, the rules Congress uses to govern itself, and a terrific overview of how our legislative process operates—a great resource for teachers. There's even a list of all the top legislative positions and who holds them.

How

Gopher

Where

gopher.gsfc.nasa.gov

Go To

US Government
Congress
Congressional Directories
Government Manual: Legislative Branch

State of the Union '94

When the Founding Fathers wrote that the President "shall from time to time give to the Congress information of the state of the Union," they couldn't possibly have envisioned the media circus it has become. Thomas Jefferson used to have his report sent over to Congress, not even bothering to read it himself.

From such humble beginnings, the State of the Union address has turned into an annual spectacle of hyped up pomp and PR, sort of a Superbowl of political rhetoric, a Barnum and Bailey side show in which our political leaders cling to the adage, "There's a constituent born every minute."

Here, from Center Ring, is the President's State of the Union address, 1994.

FREE $TUFF from the Internet

How

Gopher

Where

gopher.unc.edu

Go To

What's New on SunSITE

State of the Union Speech 1994

White House Info

Here's where you get the latest information on the President, First Lady, Vice President, and White House staff members. (We don't think Socks the Cat is well represented here, though.) You'll receive daily summaries of White House Press releases through E-mail. Instructions on how to request more information will be sent to you with each summary.

How

E-mail

Where

almanac@esusda.gov

Ask For

send guide

```
Request: 2472
PRESIDENT AND OTHER SPEAKERS AT CRIME BILL EVENT—July 28, 1994—
At the Department of Justice this morning, President Clinton,
Attorney General Reno, Dr. Lee Brown, Secretary Bentsen,
Congressman Brooks, Senator Biden, and Portland, Oregon Police
Chief Charles Moose rallied for passage of the Crime Bill.
The President reminded those present that the Bill is not yet law,
and urged them to "send the message out" that the law enforcement
community and the American people want a 20 percent increase in
police forces, tougher punishment, the capacity for imprisonment,
crime prevention funds, and other provisions contained in the
Crime Bill.
```

An example of a recent White House press summary

House and Senate Committee Memberships

You're the one paying their salaries, so you might as well know what they're doing all day. (Let's hope they're not playing Solitaire on their laptops while congress is in session.) Here's a listing of the House of Representative committees and the members who sit on them. Are you getting your money's worth? You be the judge.

How

Gopher

Where

wiretap.spies.com

Go To

Government Docs (US & World)

Treaties and International Covenants

US Government Today

Review of the Tailhook Investigation

Want to know what really went on behind closed doors at the U.S. Navy's 1991 Tailhook convention? This review of the Navy investigation of Tailhook 91 addresses the actions of senior Navy officials, the Naval Investigative Service, and the Naval Inspector General in their earlier probes into the Tailhook 91 incident.

In part, the findings in this report conclude that the scope of the original investigation should have been expanded beyond the assaults to encompass other violations of law and regulation, and should have addressed individual accountability for the leadership failure that created an atmosphere in which the assaults and other misconduct took place.

How

Gopher

Where

info.umd.edu

Go To

Educational Resources

Academic Resources by Topic

Women's Studies Resources

Gender Issues

Sexual Harassment

Tailhook 91 (part 1, review of the navy investigations)

Major Political Parties Platforms

Find out where the major—and not so major—political parties stand on the important—and not so important—issues. Democratic, Republican, and Libertarian platforms are included, as well as excerpts from the Green Party platform and Paul Tsongas' *A Call to Economic Arms.*

How

Gopher

Where

wiretap.spies.com

Go To

Gov

Political Platforms of the US

Open House at the White House

Wouldn't it be great to get a private tour of the White House? The *White House Photo Tour Booklet* is the next best thing: 40 pages of beautiful color photos, maps, and interesting facts about this historic home to every First Family since 1800. There's also lots of information about the different branches of government, and a fascinating biography of the President and Vice President.

How

E-mail

Where

president@whitehouse.gov

Ask For

White House Photo Tour Booklet
Be sure to include your name and postal address

FedWorld

FedWorld BBS is an Internet surfer's dream wave. Through FedWorld, you can connect to 24 different government bulletin boards, including the Federal Energy Regulatory Commission and Veterans Administration. Each bulletin board offers scores of government resources, connections to other government agencies, and reams of documents you can download. At last, Uncle Sam has entered the Information Age. Now if he would only *dress* a little more contemporary . . . .

How

Telnet

Where

fedworld.gov

Login

new

Go To

Follow the login instructions

Greetings from the President

Make someone's birthday or anniversary extra special with a personalized note from the White House (although we know a few people who, if they received *this* for their birthday, would consider it an act of aggression). Just E-mail the necessary information, including the person's name, the

occassion (birthday, wedding, anniversary, barmitzvah, and so on), the date being celebrated, and the postal address to send the note. This service can get pretty backlogged, so allow a couple of months for delivery.

How

E-mail

Where

president@whitehouse.gov

Ask For

Personalized greeting from the president

Speak to the Vice President

He's just a heartbeat away from the Oval Office, and now you're just a modem away from his heartbeat. E-mail the father of the "Information Superhighway" himself and tell him how he's doing or just ask a question to see if he really knows how to use the fast lane.

How

E-mail

Where

vice.president@whitehouse.gov

Passing the Torch

In addition to being the official bean counter bureau, the Government Accounting Office (GAO) is responsible for preparing detailed reports on all functions, duties, and status reports of an outgoing president's administration. These reports are given to the incoming president and his (or, someday, her) staff to help bring them up to speed as quickly as possible during the transfer of power. This Gopher contains the GAO transition reports for the Bush-Clinton succession.

How
Gopher

Where
wiretap.spies.com

Go To
GAO Transition Reports

Where to Find More Goodies

The *Business and Career* section provides several goverment-sponsored programs for finding jobs and improving your career options.

The *Environment and Nature* section includes several goodies that provide free information from the government on improving the environment or on dealing with environmental regulations.

The *Household and Consumer Finance* section provides government-sponsored material for dealing with consumer issues, especially consumer fraud.

The *History* section includes several topics that explain how the U.S. government got from there to (sigh) here.

The *Law* section includes several topics that explain how to get information on dealing with such legal issues as sexual harassment, child support, copyrights, and privacy issues.

The *Travel and Geography* section explains how to find information posted by the U.S. government regarding warnings, cautions, and notices related to travel in volatile countries.

FREE $TUFF

Let no one suppose that the words "doctor" and "patient" can disguise from the parties the fact that they are "employer" and "employee."

George Bernard Shaw

Health and Nutrition

Growing Up Drug Free

Illegal drug and alcohol use is a major problem, and the threat these substances pose to our children's welfare is all too real. *Growing Up Drug Free: A Parent's Guide to Prevention* published by the Department of Education helps families learn about the drugs children are most likely to try, including alcohol and tobacco. Learn how to prevent and stop drug abuse before it's too late.

How

Telnet

Where

fedworld.gov (see page 13 for instructions on how to download files from the Consumer Information Center)

Go To

DRGFREE.TXT

CancerNet

CancerNet is a government-run bulletin board you can access from the Internet. You'll find all the latest data on cancer research. There's information on research, breakthroughs, prevention, hotlines to call, and a list of support groups to help you if you or your family need it. All information is available in English and Spanish.

How

Gopher

Where

gopher.nih.gov

Go To

Health and Clinical Information
CancerNet Information

Fetal Alcohol Syndrome

How much alcohol is too much when you're pregnant? The damage that alcohol can cause to your unborn baby has only recently been recognized and is still not fully understood. Evidence indicates, however, that even small amounts can disrupt normal fetal development.

The National Institute on Alcohol Abuse and Alcoholism brings you this fascinating and disturbing essay, *Fetal Alcohol Syndrome*, with timely information on alcohol research and treatment.

How
Telnet

Where
fedworld.gov (see page 13 for instructions on how to download files from the Consumer Information Center)

Go To
FETALALC.TXT

No More Stress

Believe it or not, we all need stress to function in our everyday lives. But enough can easily become too much. When stress becomes prolonged or particularly overwhelming, it can be harmful or even lethal. *Plain Talk About Stress* helps you to recognize the early signs of distress and tells you what to do alleviate it. Download these files and then, well, *relax*!

How
Telnet

Where
fedworld.gov (see page 13 for instructions on how to download files from the Consumer Information Center)

Go To
STRESS.TXT

Fighting AIDS

Probably no health topic is surrounded by mystery and misinformation more than AIDS. So educate yourself and your friends and family: Get the latest information on AIDS and HIV research. You'll find helpful advice on preventing the spread of AIDS, the facts and fallacies of AIDS transmission, and what the likelihood is of someone infected with HIV getting AIDS. There's also lots of research data, drug information, and support listings for AIDS victims and their families.

How

Gopher

Where

gopher.nih.gov

Go To

National Library of Medicine (NLM) Gopher
AIDS Information

A Burger and Fries, and Hold the Burger

Health and fitness expert Covert Bailey makes a distinction between the "smart vegetarian" and the "dumb vegetarian." According to Bailey, what you eat is far more important than what you choose not to eat. Whether you're a vegan, a vegetarian, or a lacto-ovo vegetarian, you no doubt have found that the most difficult time to practice what you preach is when you have to dine out. Vegans and vegetarians around the world will love the information provided in this international compilation of vegetarian-friendly restaurants—including fast foods—and organizations. And as for general information: All questions vegetarian are answered here, including tips on proper nutrition, great recipes, and sources for more information.

How

Gopher

Where

quartz.rutgers.edu

Go To

Food, Recipies, and Nutrition

Vegetarian-FAQ

Health Care

You can't pick up a newspaper or turn on a radio without some mention of America's "Health Care Crisis." Cut through the media hype and political scare tactics being waged by Democrats and Republicans alike, as well as the countless lobbyists. Here's the complete text of the president's report on health care. (Warning: If you thought *War and Peace* was long . . . .)

How

Telnet

Where

fedworld.gov (see page 13 for instructions on how to download files from the Consumer Information Center)

Go To

HREPORT.EXE

Americans with Disabilities Act

If you're disabled, it's important that you know your rights. Here are answers to commonly asked questions about the Americans with Disabilities Act of 1990 that everyone should know. There's also information about employment and public accommodations laws and a list of services provided by state and local governments. This is great information for architects, contractors, employers, and others who need to make sure their facilities and services comply with the law.

165

How

Telnet

Where

fedworld.gov (see page 13 for instructions on how to download files from the Consumer Information Center)

Go To

NFCAMDIS.TXT

Eat Right!

Think of all the fad diets you've heard of and all of the people you know who have tried them. Now how many of those people have kept the weight off? The fact is, fad diets don't work! The key to responsible weight loss is learning to eat right and exercise. But reducing your caloric intake without considering the nutritional effects can be harmful—even fatal!

Two publications from the Department of Agriculture's Human Nutrition Information Service are discussed here. *Calories and Weight* includes a calorie table, notes on the different food groups, and a chart to help determine what weight is right for you. *Good Sources of Nutrients* is a set of 17 fact sheets on nutrients from Vitamin A to Zinc, including dietary fiber.

Learn how to monitor your caloric intake and maintain a healthy, balanced diet at the same time.

How

Telnet

Where

fedworld.gov (see page 13 for instructions on how to download files from the Consumer Information Center)

Go To

NFCCAL.TXT

Keep Your Health Care

Your current employer's health insurance has been covering the cost of treating your daughter's ear infections for nine months now, and the doctor says she'll need at least another six months of treatment. Cost is not a problem now, because you're covered by your employer's policy. And with health care costs as high as they are, you know first-hand how important ongoing health insurance is—especially for your family. But since you get your health coverage from an employer-sponsored program, what happens if you lose your job?

The Department of Labor has a free publication that explains how and when the law applies. *Health Benefits Under the Consolidated Omnibus Budget Reconciliation Act (COBRA)* tells about your rights under COBRA. Get this booklet and learn your rights about continuing your health care coverage.

How

Telnet

Where

fedworld.gov (see page 13 for instructions on how to download files from the Consumer Information Center)

Go To

COBRA.TXT

> The law generally covers group health plans maintained by employers of 20 or more people. It applies to plans in the private sector and those sponsored by state and local governments. It also covers spouses and dependent children in the event of divorce or death of the covered employee.
>   While people who continue their health care benefits under COBRA have to pick up the full costs of coverage, it is usually cheaper than buying an individual policy.

An excerpt fron COBRA.TXT

Skin-Deep Safety

Did you know that "hypoallergenic" doesn't necessarily mean that a cosmetic won't cause an allergic reaction, only that it's less likely to do so than other products? Talk about your loopholes. Even those skin-care products labeled "all natural" may be irritating to some people. Here's a way to prevent some of these products from getting under your skin. *Cosmetic Safety: More Complex Than At First Blush*, published by the Food and Drug Administration, will keep you informed about the possible risks from using cosmetics. Here's how to order your copy.

How

Telnet

Where

fedworld.gov (see page 13 for instructions on how to download files from the Consumer Information Center)

Go To

COSMETIC.TXT

Cosmetic Surgery Safety

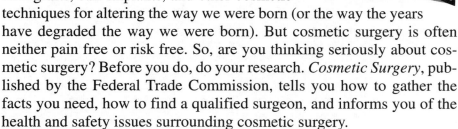

Americans seen to have a romance going with tummy tucks, facial lifts, breast augmentation and reduction, skin grafts, calf implants, and other cosmetic techniques for altering the way we were born (or the way the years have degraded the way we were born). But cosmetic surgery is often neither pain free or risk free. So, are you thinking seriously about cosmetic surgery? Before you do, do your research. *Cosmetic Surgery*, published by the Federal Trade Commission, tells you how to gather the facts you need, how to find a qualified surgeon, and informs you of the health and safety issues surrounding cosmetic surgery.

How

Telnet

Where

fedworld.gov (see page 13 for instructions on how to download files from the Consumer Information Center)

Go To

NFCCOS.TXT

Wife Abuse

Two to four million incidents of domestic violence occur every year. Wife abuse is a leader in this category of violence, and occurs far more often than most people imagine, with many women suffering abuse for years without getting help. *Plain Talk about Wife Abuse* from the National Institute of Mental Health explores what wife abuse is, who experiences it, why it occurs, and why women don't get help. Finally, it looks at what you can do if you're being abused and how to prevent it in the future.

How

Telnet

Where

fedworld.gov (see page 13 for instructions on how to download files from the Consumer Information Center)

Go To

WABUSE.TXT

Caring for Someone with Alzheimer's Disease

Three to four million elderly people have Alzheimer's Disease or a related disorder. But its effects aren't limited to those affllicted. Because Alzheimer's patients require a tremendous amount of emotional, physical, and financial support, spouses, other family members, and friends are also affected. *Useful Information on Alzheimer's Disease,* published by the National Institute of Mental Health, contains important information about Alzheimer's, including the symptoms, treatment, and care of people affected. You'll also learn how the disease is diagnosed, what to expect during its course, what treatment is available, and what research is being done to find a cure. Addresses and phone numbers to get more information are also included.

How

Telnet

Where

fedworld.gov (see page 13 for instructions on how to download files from the Consumer Information Center)

Go To

NFCALZ.TXT

```
The onset of Alzheimer's disease is usually slow and
gradual.  Because none of the symptoms is unique to
Alzheimer's disease, diagnosis is difficult.  In fact,
Alzheimer's disease is the most over-diagnosed and
misdiagnosed disorder of mental functioning in older
adults.  Many other diseases, such as depression, must be
ruled out before a diagnosis of Alzheimer's disease can be
arrived at.  This is called diagnosis by exclusion, and it
has become the most reliable method for determining
whether someone has the disease.  Sadly, this kind of
diagnosis takes a long time.
     Early symptoms of Alzheimer's disease include lapses
in short-term memory and, slightly later, problems with
abstract thinking.  For example, in the early stages a
person might forget to turn off the iron or take
medication.  In time, the person may have increased
difficulty working out the month's bills or engaging in
complex activities they may once have done easily—such as
playing the piano.
```

An excerpt from NFCALZ.TXT

Psychology

Tired of spending hundreds of dollars on self-help books that seem to do nothing for your problems but are doing a great job helping the authors solve their financial problems? Try the freebie approach. Browse this site and check out the tons of valuable psychology-related software for you to download. There are programs to help couples learn to communicate better, tests for attention deficit disorder, I.Q. tests, programs to help you stop smoking, and lots more.

How

Gopher

Where

panda1.uottawa.ca

Go To

Projets de Recherche (Research Projects)
The PSYCGRAD Project
Other Psychology-Related Links
Mental Health Software

Don't Have a Coronary!

Coronary heart disease (CHD) is the number one killer of both men and women in the U.S. Each year, more than 500,000 Americans die of heart attacks caused by CHD. But here's the real tragedy: Many of these deaths could have been prevented, but weren't, through relatively basic changes in lifestyle—such as changes in diet, increased exercise, and quitting smoking. *Facts About Coronary Heart Disease* published by the National Heart, Lung, and Blood Institute shows you how *not* to become a CHD statistic. Share it with a family member who you think might be at risk.

How

Telnet

Where

fedworld.gov (see page 13 for instructions on how to download files from the Consumer Information Center)

Go To

FACTCORO.TXT

Food and Drug Interactions

Most people know that you shouldn't mix alcohol with prescription medicine, but did you know that some foods also interfere with or create side effects with many medications? So, which foods should you avoid when taking certain medications? Knowing the answer may affect whether the medication you're taking does it's job. In fact, some combinations of food and medication can actually be dangerous. The Food and Drug Administration's free fact sheet, *Food and Drug Interactions*, will teach you about the various food and drug combinations you should avoid.

How

Telnet

Where

fedworld.gov (see page 13 for instructions on how to download files from the Consumer Information Center)

Go To

NFCFDINT.TXT

Get Relief from Your Arthritis

More than 37 million Americans suffer from arthritis and its related disorders. And as Baby Boomers get older, arthritis and related disorders are reaching record levels. Hucksters of numerous unproven treatments know that when you're in pain you'll try almost anything in the hope of finding relief. Yet depite the treatments most of these rip-off artists sell won't cure or even alleviate the pain of your arthritis. But two publications from the FDA will help you to understand the disease and teach you how to relieve some of the pain:

- *Hocus-Pocus As Applied to Arthritis* can help you treat the disease and recognize the false claims of quack remedies.
- *Nonsteroidal Anti-Inflammatory Drugs* shows you what you can do to make doctor-prescribed treatments more effective.

How

Telnet

Where

fedworld.gov (see page 13 for instructions on how to download files from the Consumer Information Center)

Go To

NFCARTH.TXT

Oh, My Aching Back!

Next to headaches, lower back pain is the most common ailment in the U.S. Whether it's a slight twinge, a dull ache, or a piercing pain, there's a good chance you'll experience some sort of back trouble sometime in your life. The Food and Drug Administration has two free booklets that explain some common causes of backaches, including how they can be treated and prevented:

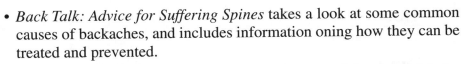

- *Back Talk: Advice for Suffering Spines* takes a look at some common causes of backaches, and includes information oning how they can be treated and prevented.
- *When the Spine Curves* examines scoliosis, a condition in which the spine twists as it grows.

How

Telnet

Where

fedworld.gov (see page 13 for instructions on how to download files from the Consumer Information Center)

Go To

NFCBACK.TXT

> With the exception of headaches, low back pain is the most common ailment in the U.S., and a major contributor to time lost from work. The many causes range from excessive bending and lifting to the shrinkage of disks with age. Inactive lifestyles can also play a role.
> Like other parts of the body, the muscles and ligaments that support your spine, especially the abdominals, need proper care and attention if they're to remain strong. Lack of exercise, poor posture, and poor sleeping habits, including sleeping on your stomach, can weaken these muscles, making them vulnerable to strains and tears.

An excerpt from NFCBACK.TXT

Caffeine Concerns

Did you know that many scientists are actually *less* concerned about caffeine than they once were? The Food and Drug Administration booklet *Caffeine Jitters: Some Safety Questions Remain* gives you the latest information on caffeine and explains how you can order a free, illustrated publication that helps you compare the caffeine contents of many different foods, beverages, and drugs.

How

Telnet

Where

fedworld.gov (see page 13 for instructions on how to download files from the Consumer Information Center)

Go To

NFCCAF.TXT

Get Tested!

Half of all cancers occur in persons age 65 and over, and in the earliest stages most cancers don't show symptoms or cause pain. Make cancer testing a regular part of your checkups. The National Institutes of Health publishes a free booklet called *Cancer Tests You Should Know About: A Guide For People 65 and Over* to help you learn about the different tests used to detect cancer, most of which are performed painlessly, and right in your doctor's office.

How
Telnet

Where
fedworld.gov (see page 13 for instructions on how to download files from the Consumer Information Center)

Go To
NFCCANC2.TXT

Are You at Risk?

Over the past 20 years, colorectal cancer has increased 18 percent among African-American women and 38 percent among African-American men. Learn more about how cancer affects you as an African-American: Get your free copy of *Get A New Attitude About Cancer* from the National Institutes of Health and find out what you can do to cut your risks.

How
Telnet

Where
fedworld.gov (see page 13 for instructions on how to download files from the Consumer Information Center)

Go To
NFCCANCR.TXT

Get the Lead Out

Lead-based paint can create serious health risks, especially for children, pregnant women, and people with high blood pressure. For instance, ingesting lead-based paint chips is a major but preventable cause of retardation in children. An informative fact sheet entitled *What You Should Know About Lead-Based Paint In Your Home* from the Consumer Product Safety Commission will help you learn more about the problems of lead-based paint and what you can do to protect your family. It describes the dangers of lead-based paint, how you can test the paint in your home for lead, and ways you can reduce your exposure.

How

Telnet

Where

fedworld.gov (see page 13 for instructions on how to download files from the Consumer Information Center)

Go To

NFCLEAD.TXT

Obsessive-Compulsive Disorder

Some people spend hours each day washing their hands over and over, convinced they can't get clean enough. Others may constantly rearrange objects in an attempt to have them perfectly placed. Know somebody who fits either of these categories? Surely not *yourself*? Obsessive-compulsive disorder, in which a person deals with unwanted ideas or impulses by engaging in senseless, repetitive tasks, is more prevalent than schizophrenia and other severe mental illnesses. Get more information on this disease, including its causes and treatments.

How

Telnet

Where

fedworld.gov (see page 13 for instructions on how to download files from the Consumer Information Center)

Go To

OBSESS.TXT

Pyramid Scheme

Remember the four basic food groups you learned in school (meat, dairy, fruit, Butterfinger)? But seriously, a healthy diet involves more than just knowing which foods fall into which categories. That's why the FDA, with some prodding from the Center for Science in the Public Interest (CSPI), has revised its basic-food-groups model for the twenty-first century to accomodate what scientists now know about eating habits and nutrition.

Basically, proper nutrition means eating more foods from some groups, and less from others, especially those offering little more than empty calories. This booklet will help you understand the FDA's new pyramid nutritional chart and will help you choose the foods—and quantities—necessary for a healthful diet.

How

Telnet

Where

fedworld.gov (see page 13 for instructions on how to download files from the Consumer Information Center)

Go To

PYRAMIDE.TXT

> The group at the tip of the pyramid, the one that should make up the smallest percentage of your diet, consists of fats, oils, and sweets. These foods are often high in calories, but have little or no nutritional value. Even when you select foods from the lower sections of the pyramid, how you prepare them can increase the presence of those at the top.
>
> For example, a baked potato has about 120 calories and only a trace of fat. The same amount of french fries fried in oil, however, has 11 grams of fat and about 225 calories.

An excerpt from **PYRAMIDE.TXT**

Bringing Up Baby

Is breast milk really better than formula? Or does it matter? New parents will find lots of answers here about nutrition and feeding their babies during the first few months of life.

How

Telnet

Where

fedworld.gov (see page 13 for instructions on how to download files from the Consumer Information Center)

Go To

NFCBABY.TXT

Aerobics the Right Way

Here's an aerobics program created by an M.D. When you use this DOS-based program, you enter your condition along with other workout information. There are entry options for jogging, aerobics, running, stair climbing, and even golf. Based on the information you enter, the program assigns you a number of "points earned" along with your total calorie burn. (Don't expect a lot of points for duffing it on the links.)

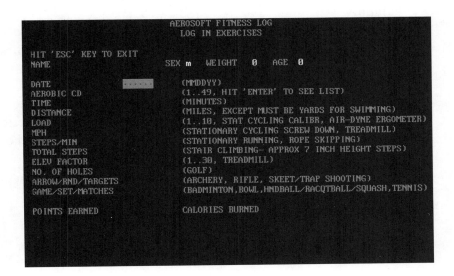

How
FTP

Where
oak.oakland.edu

Go To
SimTel/msdos/database/aerobix.zip

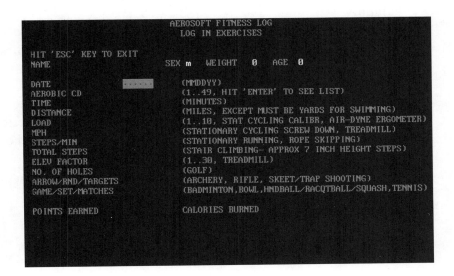

Home Diagnosis

Hypochondriacs will love this. Here's a sophisticated medical diagnostics program that runs under Windows (requires Windows 3.1). Based on information that you enter, the program searches its database and attempts to identify possible diseases and illnesses that might match the symptomotology. The author stresses (as should we) that this software is *not* a substitute for proper medical advice from a professional.

How
FTP

Where
oak.oakland.edu

Go To

SimTel/win3/info/winmed_1.zip, winmed_2.zip, and winmed_3.zip

Where to Find More Goodies

The *Computers and Software* section describes several programs specifically designed to provide health information for you and your family.

The Environment and Nature section describes several topics that either pose or are directly related to health issues that might affect you and your family.

The *Government and Politics* section includes a topic describing how to download the text of the Clinton Health Care Proposal and other health-related information.

FREE $TUFF

History, n. An account mostly false, of events mostly unimportant, which are brought about by rulers, mostly knaves, and soldiers, mostly fools.

Ambrose Bierce
The Devil's Dictionary

History

Climbing the Family Tree

This program will be a big help for anyone tracing his or her family's roots. Created by Everton Publishers, this program includes a listing of unusual record sources, the branch office for the National Archives, and the complete text of the book *Where to Write for Public Records*, published by the Department of Health and Human Services, plus lots more.

How

FTP

Where

ftp.xmission.com

Go To

pub/users/j/jayhall/geninfo.zip

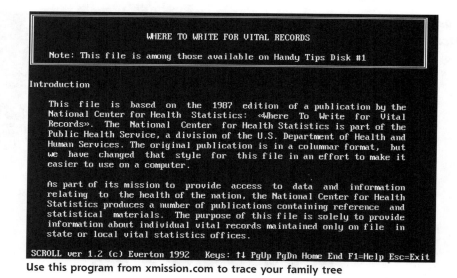

```
            WHERE TO WRITE FOR VITAL RECORDS

  Note: This file is among those available on Handy Tips Disk #1


Introduction

    This file is based on the 1987 edition of a publication by the
  National Center for Health Statistics: «Where To Write for Vital
  Records». The National Center for Health Statistics is part of the
  Public Health Service, a division of the U.S. Department of Health and
  Human Services. The original publication is in a columnar format, but
  we have changed that style for this file in an effort to make it
  easier to use on a computer.

    As part of its mission to provide access to data and information
  relating to the health of the nation, the National Center for Health
  Statistics produces a number of publications containing reference and
  statistical materials. The purpose of this file is solely to provide
  information about individual vital records maintained only on file in
  state or local vital statistics offices.

SCROLL ver 1.2 (c) Everton 1992   Keys: ↑↓ PgUp PgDn Home End F1=Help Esc=Exit
```

Use this program from xmission.com to trace your family tree

It's All in the Genes

Find out more about your family history at this site. Here you'll find numerous genealogical programs, historical research tools, and family-tree chart-making software, so you can choose the software and other tools that you like the most. There's even a database for the first U.S. census, which was tabulated for the period 1880 to 1890. This site also offers useful tools for historical and biographical researchers. Most of the programs here are DOS-based.

How

FTP

Where

rigel.acs.oakland.edu

Go To

SimTel/msdos/genealgy/*

Filename	Description
acc50d1.zip	ACCEPT (v5.0) genealogy research program, part 1 of 3
accnwd4.zip	ACCEPT genealogy research prog. Newsletter #1
artdemo1.zip	Demo: Windows genealogy database program from Everton
bk52ad1.zip	My Brother's Keeper Genealogy SW Mar. 12, 1994, part 1 of 2
census20.zip	Genealogy: EZCensus - 1880/90 census database
chart.zip	Creates 11 generation pedigree charts, Ver. 1.0
crd301.zip	Cemetery Research Database, Ver. 3.01
ctree32.zip	Cumberland Tree 3.2, easy family tree program
fhh130.zip	Family history research tutorial
fhs9105a.zip	FHS (Family History System), May 91, part 1 of 2
fmtrw103.zip	WIN3: Family Tree program with picture support
fru18.zip	Genealogy: Family Records Utils, for PAF files
ft119d.zip	'Family Ties' Genealogy program (Ver. 1.19d)
gbbs9104.zip	Worldwide Genealogical BBS listing - Apr. 1991
gedcht16.zip	Make family tree chart from GED file (LJ3/PS)
genkit15.zip	A toolkit for genealogists
gim_230.zip	Full-featured genealogical information manager
myfmly20.zip	My Family Genealogy program, Ver. 2.0
sdiprt94.zip	Read/print/convert SS Death Index GED Files

A sampling of files in SimTel/msdos/genealgy

Historical Database

Whether you're a student of history or a trivia buff, you'll enjoy browsing this historical database. The Center for Electronic Records offers the

National Archives Gopher to help you research data from such things as the 1970 census, findings on the Challenger Space Shuttle accident, casualty records from the Korean and Vietnam Wars, and much more.

How

Gopher

Where

gopher.nara.gov

Go To

About the National Archives and Records Administration

Civil Rights Act of 1991

In response to Supreme Court decisions that limited the civil rights of individuals, Congress passed the Civil Rights Act of 1991. Its purpose was to restore and strengthen civil rights laws that ban discrimination in employment and to provide a more effective deterrent and adequate compensation for victims of discrimination.

How

Gopher

Where

wiretap.spies.com

Go To

Government Docs (US & World)
US Miscellaneous Documents
Civil Rights Act of 1991

Today in History

Okay, so maybe *your* day wasn't too exciting, but something—*somewhere, sometime*—made big news on this day. Find out what it was with this fun-to-use Gopher, which provides interesting information on the births, deaths, and anniversaries of famous people and events.

How

Gopher

Where

uts.mcc.ac.uk

Go To

Misc Information
Today's Events in History

I Have a Dream

Martin Luther King Jr. may be gone, but his words and actions live on: "I have a dream that one day this nation will rise up, live out the true meaning of its creed: 'We hold these truths to be self-evident, that all men are created equal.'" Here's the complete text of King's moving 1963 Washington speech.

How

FTP

Where

quartz.rutgers.edu

Go To

pub/etext/misc/I_Have_a_Dream.z

African-American History Exhibit

Covering the nearly 500 years of the black experience in the Western hemisphere, the *Library of Congress Resource Guide* for the *Study of Black History and Culture* exhibit represents the start of a new kind of access to the Library's African-American collections. Now the depth, breadth, and richness of the Library of Congress' black history collection is yours to experience.

This exhibit covers four areas:

- Colonization
- Abolition
- Migrations
- WPA

How

FTP

Where

ftp.loc.gov

Go To

pub/exhibit.images/african.american.exhibit/*

One of the numerous JPEG files you can download from the LIBRARY OF CONGRESS AFRICAN AMERICAN HISTORY exhibit

Dead Sea Scrolls Exhibit

The *Scrolls from the Dead Sea: The Ancient Library of Qumran and Modern Scholarship* exhibit brings you over 40 images of the famous artifacts found near Jordan in 1947 and other objects loaned by the Israel Antiquities Authority. The subject of intense public interest and debate over the years, these ancient treasures have raised many questions about their authenticity, the people who hid them, the secrets the scrolls might reveal, and why access to the scrolls has been severely restricted for nearly 50 years.

This Library of Congress exhibit describes the historical context of the scrolls and the Qumran community where they are believed to have originated; it also details the story of their discovery 2,000 years later. In addition, the exhibit encourages a better understanding of the challenges and complexities connected with scroll research.

How
FTP

Where
ftp.loc.gov

Go To
pub/exhibit.images/deadsea.scrolls.exhibit/*

Holocaust Exhibit

Holocaust museums have been established throughout the world so that we might never forget the horror and tragedy of the more than 16 million exterminated during the Hitler regime, including nearly 70 percent of Europe's Jewish population. Now this online exhibit has been created, complete with historical documents, pictures, books, and related works about the Holocaust.

How
FTP

Where

sunsite.unc.edu

Go To

pub/academic/history/holocaust/*

Genealogy Information

Too many of us know nothing about where we came from or who our ancestors were, and most people can only name their closest relatives from a generation or two ago. But tracing your family history can be rewarding, exciting, and even shocking. Begin your search at the National Archives and Records Administration (NARA). The NARA has lots of information to help you learn about your family's roots.

How

Gopher

Where

gopher.nara.gov

Go To

Genealogy
Genealogy holdings

Making History

History buffs will want to check out this site of U.S. historical photographs. Of special interest are the GIFs of the Civil War, World War I, and (sigh) many of the wars after that. Each is documented in this online library of historical photographs. There are also many pictures of old airplanes, old presidents, old military leaders, and many other things preserved on film—in short, history.

How

FTP

Where

grind.isca.uiowa.edu

Go To

image/gif/history/*

Go to image/gif/history to see U.S. Grant taking time out from his busy day of charging through the South to have this picture taken

Where to Find More Goodies

The *Arts and Culture* section includes a site where you can learn more about the history of photography and also explains how to access the Smithsonian collections of online historical documents, photographs, and artwork. For a literary look at history, check out the *Books and Literature* section, which explains where to find online novels and other humanities-related works.

If you want to find historical information on the economy, try the Economic Bulletin Board, which we describe in the *Business and Careers* section.

Since history and education go hand-in-hand, you'll find plenty of historically related educational tools and software in the *Education and Teaching Tools* section. And the *International Affairs* section contains several items relating to world history.

FREE $TUFF

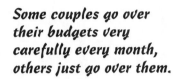

Some couples go over their budgets very carefully every month, others just go over them.

Sally Poplin

Household and Consumer Finance

Give Me Credit or Give Me Debt

Big Brother is alive and well, unfortunately. If you have a charge account, a mortgage on your home, a life insurance policy, or if you've ever filled out a loan or job application, somewhere there is a consumer credit report on you (maybe even *several* reports). These reports show how promptly you pay your bills, whether you've been sued or arrested, filed for bankruptcy, and even more personal information. The Fair Credit Reporting Act protects you against inaccurate or outdated information and helps to ensure that consumer reporting agencies obtain and divulge information about you fairly. Download a copy of it to be sure you know your rights.

How

Telnet

Where

fedworld.gov (see page 13 for instructions on how to download files from the Consumer Information Center)

Go To

FAIR-CRD.TXT

Welcome to the Neighborhood

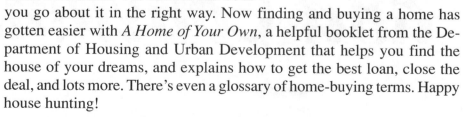

The Great American Dream: owning your own home. Besides the security and comfort it brings, home ownership is also a smart investment—at least it can be if you go about it in the right way. Now finding and buying a home has gotten easier with *A Home of Your Own*, a helpful booklet from the Department of Housing and Urban Development that helps you find the house of your dreams, and explains how to get the best loan, close the deal, and lots more. There's even a glossary of home-buying terms. Happy house hunting!

How

Telnet

Where

fedworld.gov (see page 13 for instructions on how to download files from the Consumer Information Center)

Go To

HOME-OWN.TXT

Know Your Rights

So you bought a service contract for your new car, but have you read the fine print? Does that bumper-to-bumper warranty cover the bumpers? Depending on its conditions, a service contract might be a smart investment or it might be a turkey. Two booklets can help you decide if service contracts are the best deal for you:

- The Electronic Industries Association's *What Consumers Should Know About Service Contracts and Repair Services* explains the differences between appliance warranties and service contracts and helps you select a good repair shop.

- The Federal Trade Commission's *Auto Service Contracts* explains the pros and cons of auto service contracts.

How

Telnet

Where

fedworld.gov (see page 13 for instructions on how to download files from the Consumer Information Center)

Go To

CONSUMER.TXT
SERVCONT.TXT

Credit Card Savvy

So you've got a new, low-interest rate credit card, and you think you're saving money. Maybe you are, but then again . . . .
The differences in credit card rates and features can be substantial—over and above the basic interest rate. Banks have a lot of latitude in the way they can compound interest, in the ability to charge different interest rates for different types of card usage, in the ability to change interest rates periodically (usually by increasing them), and many other tactics designed to help the *bank's* bottom line, not yours. Here's advice to help you learn how much credit you can afford, how to shop for a credit card or loan, the warning signs of debt problems, and more.

How
Telnet

Where
fedworld.gov (see page 13 for instructions on how to download files from the Consumer Information Center)

Go To
CREDCARD.TXT

How you plan to use your credit card determines which card is right for you. It's helpful to classify yourself as one of these three types of credit card users. The "Identification User" generally uses the card for identification when cashing checks, making hotel reservations and renting cars. If you fit this description, you usually don't carry a charge balance from month to month, so the annual percentage rate (APR) charged is not the most important feature to you. More important would be the universal acceptance of the card and the annual fee. Annual fees on credit cards generally range from a low of $12 up to $25, with a few having no annual fee.

The "Non-Revolver" is the person who pays off the balance in full when due. If this definition fits you, the APR, again, isn't the most important feature. Instead, you should give more attention to the allotted "grace" period — usually from 21 to 30 days — between the time a bill is sent out and the time interest is charged on the balance. Be sure to note transaction fees, late charges, or charges if you go over your credit limit.

The "Revolving Credit User" is the person who doesn't pay off the monthly balance and carries a balance over from month to month. If this sounds more like you, the most important factor, then, is the APR. Credit card APRs can vary from 12% to 22%, with an average of about 19%.

An excerpt from CREDCARD.TXT

Building Your Future with Annuities

If you're retired or are planning to retire soon, annuities could play a big part in the quality of life you lead. This booklet gives you the basics of annuities, including how they fit into a retirement savings plan, different types of annuities, and what to consider when buying them.

How

Telnet

Where

fedworld.gov (see page 13 for instructions on how to download files from the Consumer Information Center)

Go To

ANNUIT.TXT

Brighten Those Bad Credit Blues

To many lenders, your lack of a credit record is almost as bad as having a *lousy* credit record. But how do you build a good credit history when no one will help you establish credit in the first place? Get the answers to your frequently asked question about credit cards, credit reports, clearing up bad credit, and establishing good credit.

How

Gopher

Where

quartz.rutgers.edu

Go To

Economics, Business, Finance
Consumer Credit FAQ

Learn the Ups and Downs of Investing

Learning how to invest your money may seem pretty intimidating and as scientific as putting it all on double zero, but armed with a little data and the right plan, you can go a long way. Smart investors know that making money is no accident. Browse this site for information about investment strategies, how to get started, and how to keep from getting burned. Many of your investment questions are answered here.

How
Gopher

Where
quartz.rutgers.edu

Go To
Economics, Business, Finance
Investment-FAQ

Avoiding the Federal Lawnmower

Congress wants to gather a little more green stuff for the federal trough, and your lawn is in their path. You can sit back and do nothing or you can try to beat these lawnmower jockeys using their own rules. Here are some helpful tips on how to avoid being clipped by Washington and the IRS.

How
Gopher

Where
quartz.rutgers.edu

Go To
Economics, Business, Finance
Lawnmower-Strategy

Caution, Merger Up Ahead

Banks across the country are merging with alarming frequency. If your bank gets taken over, you may face changes in account numbers, services, fees and charges, interest rates, federal deposit insurance coverage, and more. While banks try to minimize any disruption, some confusion is unavoidable. Here are some simple tips to help you deal with potential changes and charges.

How

Telnet

Where

fedworld.gov (see page 13 for instructions on how to download files from the Consumer Information Center)

Go To

NFCBANKS.TXT

    The most important thing to check is that the new bank is
covered by the Federal Deposit Insurance Corporation (FDIC) and
that your deposits fall within FDIC rules. The basic insured
amount for a customer is $100,000 at any one bank. Because the
FDIC regulations are full of lots of fine print, covering
everything from joint accounts to mortgage escrow accounts,
people with $100,000 or more in a bank should check with the bank
to make sure it's all covered. If you do have more than $100,000
in any one bank, you may want to move some of the money to
another institution to keep full FDIC coverage.

An excerpt from NFCBANKS.TXT

A Penny Saved . . .

Want to get back a little of what you've paid in to Uncle Sam? Maybe it's time you consider making U.S. Savings Bonds a part of your long-term savings plan. Savings Bonds are safe, offer competitive interest rates, are tax-deferred, and easy to buy. And for most people, bonds redeemed to pay tuition bills are tax free. Download this file for more information about U.S. Savings Bonds.

How

Telnet

Where

fedworld.gov (see page 13 for instructions on how to download files from the Consumer Information Center)

Go To

NFCBONDS.TXT

Don't Just Kick the Tires

Next to your home, a car is likely to be your most expensive purchase. And once you decide to buy a car, you'll probably have to deal with annoying salespeople, choose from a multitude of options, and make decisions about warranties and service contracts. Automobile salespeople often find that their best strategy is to confuse you into signing away your bank account. As David Horowitz would say, "Fight back!" This booklet will give you the information you need to make informed and intelligent car-buying decisions.

How

Telnet

Where

fedworld.gov (see page 13 for instructions on how to download files from the Consumer Information Center)

Go To

NFCCAR.TXT

Cost Is More Than What You Pay

An automobile is something most of us can't do without. Over the life of your car, you can expect to spend more than 10 percent of your disposable income on it—a *lot* more if you're not careful. And that's not just for gas. From car payments to repairs, it all adds up. How you drive, when you drive, how often you maintain your vehicle, what you maintain, and what kind of car you buy (Mercedes parts are a lot more expensive than Chevy parts) all affect the total amount of money you'll spend during the life of a vehicle. Here are some of the hidden costs you should know about before you buy.

How

Telnet

Where

fedworld.gov (see page 13 for instructions on how to download files from the Consumer Information Center)

Go To

NFCCAR2.TXT

```
    When comparison shopping for insurance, remember that you'll
need dependable service, not just low rates.  Check with your state
insurance commission to be sure the company you want is not under
investigation or has serious complaints lodged against it.  To find
the commission, look in the state government telephone listings for
your area or for the state capitol.
    You can also save money by changing your coverage.  Raising
your deductible, the amount of money you pay before making a claim,
could lower your collision cost by as much as a third.  If your car
is older, you may not feel it's worth the expense to pay for
collision coverage.  And you may not need medical coverage in your
auto policy if you have sufficient health insurance.
```

An excerpt from NFCCAR2.TXT

Legal Info You Might Need to Know

This file is actually a DOS-based, menu-driven program that includes a few legal forms in addition to a wealth of consumer-related legal information. The legal forms are marginally useful, but the legal information is invaluable. There's a great glossary of legal terms to help you decipher what your lawyer writes or tells you, a detailed explanation of your mail-order rights under the law, a description of federal child custody laws, premarital agreement stipulations provided under the federal Uniform Premarital Act, and the Taxpayer's Bill of Rights published, ironically enough, by the IRS. Whew! If you can't find something useful here, you gotta be living alone in a cave (tax-free).

How

FTP

Where

oak.oakland.edu

Go To

SimTel/msdos/legal/guide756.zip

Consumer Fraud Quiz

Okay, all you would-be Ralph Naders, just how good are you at spotting consumer fraud. Test your ability by taking this online quiz.

How

Telnet

Where

fedworld.gov (see page 13 for instructions on how to download files from the Consumer Information Center)

Go To

NFCNCW94.TXT

Home Renovation for the Cost Conscious

Costs for major home repairs and renovation can mushroom quickly if you don't track them carefully. Experienced do-it-yourselfers know that hidden costs abound in home repairs. Here's a handy DOS program that will help you get a handle on materials costs. The program is very detailed; it even calculates wasted materials based on asymetrical or uncommon space sizes, such as room openings. After you've entered details about your home repair needs, the program will estimate the total cost of the repairs. Better to get a shock from this total than from the one you'll get at the hardware-store checkout counter.

How

FTP

Where

oak.oakland.edu

Go To

SimTel/msdos/database/handy120.zip

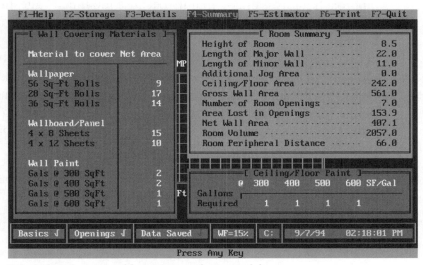

Calculating the costs of home renovation materials

Consumer Contacts

Here's information that will help you resolve complaints about a service or product. The names and addresses of more than 750 corporate headquarters are found here, and in many cases, the name of the person to contact is listed. Most listings also include toll-free "800" numbers.

How:

Telnet

Where:

fedworld.gov (see page 13 for instructions on how to download files from the Consumer Information Center)

Go To:

CRH-II.TXT

Don't Be a Budget Buster

Most families' concepts of a budget is a simple list of income and expense categories, along with estimated monthly values. In reality, this approach rarely works—mainly because too much "guestimation" is involved.

This program takes household budgeting several steps up the ladder. You don't need to be an accountant to use this package, but you will encounter a few bookkeeping terms, such as reconciliation, initialization, and ledger posting. Don't let the language scare you. The program guides you step-by-step through the budget creation process. This program is DOS based.

How

FTP

Where

oak.oakland.edu

Go To

SimTel/msdos/database/hbms430.zip

Software for the Savvy Consumer

This site has an outstanding collection of DOS-based programs for consumers, and even a few Windows programs. Most of the programs here are for personal and household finance, including several loan amortization programs and checkbook programs. There's even a program that your kids can use to start learning smart money-management techniques while they're still young. The files in the following list are just a sampling of the programs that are available here.

How

FTP

Where

oak.oakland.edu

Go To

SimTel/msdos/finance/*

Filename	Description
amortz13.zip	Amortz v1.30: Financial loan calculation
bam361.zip	Bank Account Manager v3.61: Family finance mgr
bondcalc.zip	BondCalc: Bond value and yield calculator
capgains.zip	Calculate capital gains
cfk10t.zip	Cash For Kids: Child's financial plan/track
chekfree.zip	Electronic banking by modem is here!
Cio11.zip	Cheque-It-Out v1.1: Personal money mgmt system
ckmstr31.zip	CheckMaster 3.1, check management program
consol21.zip	Financial mgt: Mutual funds/stocks/bonds/cash
cshfl351.zip	CashFlow: Controls expenses and monthly income
ddmtg.zip	Canadian mortgage amortization month by month
debtfr30.zip	Home mortgage mgr, calculate/record payments
debtmg13.zip	Debt Manager: Finds best way to pay off loans
fads2.zip	Database system for tracking fixed assets
mking102.zip	Mortgage analysis program for Windows 3.1
pcheck22.zip	Prints personal checks & keeps a database v2.2
pfroi39.zip	PFROI v3.9: Portfolio Manager, stocks/bonds
pta47.zip	PTA treasurer's financial database program
sprm24.zip	Stock Portfolio manager,store/manipulate/print

A sampling of files in SimTel/msdos/finance

Taking Stock in Your Home

It's not uncommon for families to learn too late the value of taking careful inventory of all their possessions. Fire and theft can leave you with little in the way of records in order to support your claim to your insurance adjuster. Take inventory of your possessions before it's too late with this very easy-to-use database program. This is little more than a flat-file system in which you enter descriptions of each item along with serial numbers, original cost and replacement value, location, owner, and other fields. After you've taken inventory, make sure you print a report and store it *away* from your home, business, or whatever it is that you're inventorying.

How

FTP

Where

oak.oakland.edu

Go To

SimTel/msdos/database/inv20.zip

Consumer's Resource Handbook

Two out of every three dollars spent in America's marketplace are spent by individual consumers. These dollars help create jobs and contribute to a strong national economy. The ingenuity of American business in meeting the demands of consumers has helped keep our markets growing and made our lives more comfortable. But sometimes problems arise. The *Consumer's Resource Handbook* published by the United States Office of Consumer Affairs explains the resources available to consumers with complaints or problems, including addresses and telephone numbers of sources to contact for help.

How:

Telnet

Where:

fedworld.gov (see page 13 for instructions on how to download files from the Consumer Information Center)

Go To:

CRH-I.ZIP

Where to Find More Goodies

The *Business and Career* section includes topics on economic indicators (including personal income), Wall Street activity, and consumer news.

The *Computers and Software* section includes more than a dozen programs that you can use to manage your financial resources, both at home and at the office.

The *Education and Teaching Tools* section explains where to find financial assistance for college-bound students, and *The Environment and Nature* section includes several comsumer-related topics.

The *Health and Nutrition* section includes a wealth of resources related to consumer issues, including information about drugs, health-care cost issues, and lead-based paints. The *Law* section also includes several topics that relate directly to consumer affairs.

FREE $TUFF

He who laughs, lasts.

Mary Pettibone Poole

Humor

Dilbert Newslettter

Scott Adams, creator of the *Dilbert* comic strip, is now authoring a Dilbert newsletter. Published "whenever I feel like it," or approximately two to three times a year, Adams' newsletter includes information about how to download Dilbert strips off the Internet, FAQs about the strip, and just what the deal is with Dilbert's necktie. Log onto this site and become a Dilbert insider. As the blurb below shows, you'll learn a few things about Dilbert's attire that's off limits to the offline world.

How

E-mail

Where

dilbert-request@internex.net

Ask For

subscribe dilbert_list *<your name>*

Is Dilbert a Virgin?

Sadly, yes. I tried to solve that problem once but my editor decided the funny papers weren't ready. I drew a series of strips where Dilbert had a female co-worker who was a nymphomaniac. She confessed to Dilbert that she had "torrid romances with half of the men in the department in the past year" and asked if Dilbert thought she should seek counseling. Dilbert's reply was "Oh, I'd give it another year." In the strips that followed, it was clear that a happy Dilbert had become her most recent conquest.

I always wished that series had made it through the editorial net. But Dilbert gets another shot at it this summer, when he meets a woman named Liz. Liz will either take Dilbert's innocence or be killed by a meteor. I haven't penned the ending yet. I'm going to monitor my e-mail and see how the sentiment flows after Liz gets introduced. There will be a two month lag while I decide her fate.

Any opinions?

(If Dilbert gets lucky, I'll draw the strip one day this summer with his necktie hanging flat. That's how you'll know.)

Dilbert does Cyberspace

Zippy Should Be Read and Not Seen

This truly minimal Web page presents a bizarre hypertext collection of textual wisdom from Bill Griffith's famous and seminal Zippy the Pinhead cartoon. These are not cartoons! They're...um...right-brain insights into life, the universe, and Velveeta cheese. You can hotlink from one saying into another, seemingly at random—but nothing in Zippy's universe is quite random, is it? Are we having an emotional outburst yet?

How

Mosaic

Where

http://www.cis.ohio-state.edu/htbin/zippy

Wanna See Something Funny?

If you're famous, there's probably a picture of you here in some embarrassing context. The other 99.9 percent of us will get a laugh from the GIFs stored here. George Bush, Dan Quayle, Bill Clinton, Bill Gates, and even Elvis (who, rumor has it will be coming out of retirement to defend himself) can be found here.

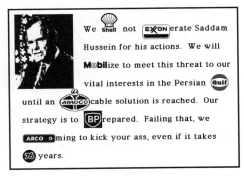

We **shell** not EXON erate Saddam Hussein for his actions. We will **M⊙bil**ize to meet this threat to our vital interests in the Persian **Gulf** until an AMOCO cable solution is reached. Our strategy is to BP repared. Failing that, we ARCO ⊕ ming to kick your ass, even if it takes 76 years.

No one or thing is safe from being picked on, laughed at, or satirized in the humor archives located in image/gif/humor

How

FTP

Where

grind.isca.uiowa.edu

Go To

image/gif/humor/*

Speek Svedeesh Leeke-a Neteef

Here's a program that serves no useful purpose whatsoever. Needless to say, it's one of our favorites. Download it and follow the instructions to get any messages you type on your screen translated into Swedish (sort of).

Inspired by Borg, the Swedish Chef from the Muppets, this program will make you virtually indistinguishable from a true Swiss national. Your friends will be amazed at your grasp of the language, and will no doubt be convinced you had intensive Berlitz training. When they ask how you picked up the language so quickly, smile and say "I gooess I joost hefe-a a geefft fur peecking up fureeegn lungooeges." Won't they be impressed.

How
FTP

Where
ftp.hmc.edu

Go To
pub/chef/ibmchef.exe

pub/chef/ibmchef.doc

Tu be-a, oor nut tu be-a: thet is zee qooesshun:
Vhezeer 'tees nubler in zee meend tu soofffer
Zee sleengs und erroos ooff ooootregeuoos furtoone-a,
Oor tu teke-a erms egeeenst a sea ooff truoobles,
Defuootly tu be-a veesh'd. Tu deee-a, tu sleep;
BORK! BORK! BORK!

Is Shekespeere-a speenning reeght noo? Ooh yeeh, yuoo better beleeefe-a it!

So Sue Me

Q: What's the difference between God and a lawyer?
A: God doesn't think He's a lawyer. . . . And it goes on and on. These two sources of lawyer jokes are absolutely gutclutching, and contribute to the sometimes-

doubted truth that there is in fact justice in the world. We heard some of these jokes years ago, but the majority of them are thoroughly new.

How

Mosaic

Where

http://rever.nmsu.edu/~ras/lawyer.htm and
http://www.ugcs.caltech.edu/~werdna/humor/Lawyer.jokes

Have You Heard the One About . . .

Satisfy your funny bone with this potpourri of humorous jokes, quips, transcripts, and essays. No one or thing is excluded in this equal-opportunity Gopher hole: politics, religion, sex, and, of course, Barney the Dinosaur. There are also transcripts from *Monty Python's Flying Circus Movies*, monologues by George Carlin and Steven Wright, and much more.

How

Gopher

Where

quartz.rutgers.edu

Go To

Humor

The Dinosaur We Love to Hate

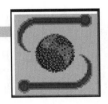

Yep, Barney's on the Web. And hey, he probably drives *you* crazy, but then again Barney would almost certainly forgive you for that. Sickening, isn't it? Anyway, Barney's not intended for mature brains, so stop your griping and point your kids to this Web site. The site itself isn't fully developed yet, but it's working toward providing a total Barney multimedia experience for the little ones—complete with movies, songs, and JPEGs of Barmey and friends.

How

Mosaic

Where

http://www.cam.org/~danvoye/et/barney/barney.html

Everybody's favorite purple dinosaur

A Guy Walks into a Bar Carrying a Chicken . . .

All work and no play makes . . . well, you get the idea. Subscribe to this mailing list for random acts of humor throughout the day (an average of 15 to 20 articles per day). In fact, you ought to have it sent to your computer at the office so you can access it several times a day (when you're not breaking up the monotony with quick games of Solitaire). If your boss wonders why you're laughing out loud, tell her you're filling out your expense account. You'll find all types of humor here for all types of topics and tastes. Enjoy, because if you don't deserve it, who does?

Note: This is not a list for the hyper-sensitive nor persons who are easily offended.

How

E-mail

Where

listserv@uga.cc.uga.edu

Ask For

sub humor <*your name*>

What's So Funny?

Who's on first? Abbot and Costello never did quite get that straightened out. If you're still having trouble with it, download the script and take your best shot. Some of the other great standup comedians you'll find represented here include Emo Philips, Groucho Marx, Rodney Dangerfield, and Steven Wright.

How

FTP

Where

cathouse.org

Go To

pub/cathouse/*

Where the Buffalo Roam

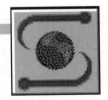

This ragged-edge, black-and-white, hand-drawn cartoon is definitely for the subversive among us. It is far more gonzo than Dr. Fun (see the next entry) and has lots more edge than Doonesbury (though that's not as hard as it used to be . . .). The strip is drawn weekly by Hans Bjordahl for the *Colorado Daily*, where it has appeared since 1987.

If you want, you can view previous cartoons going back several weeks, as well as offer your opinions on the cartoons (or anything else, apparently) over the net.

How

Mosaic

Where

http://xor.com:80/wtbr

Dr. Fun

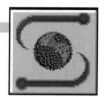

Definitely the electronic *Far Side*, and the first time we've seen a really good cartoon done entirely with electronic means; that is, Dave Farley doesn't draw with a pencil, he draws with his mouse. The cartoon is daily, and "back issues" are available through the Dr. Fun home page reliably for the previous week, and with some hunting for some time beyond that. The images are good size and take some time to download during business hours. Do it early, or do it late—but certainly do it.

How

Mosaic

Where

http://sunsite.unc.edu/Dave/drfun.html

And Now for Something Completely Different

British humor is an acquired taste, no doubt, but once you've acquired it, watch out: it's addicting. If you're a *Monty Python* fan, you'll love this site. There are lots of movie scripts, songs, skits, and more from the *Monty Python* troupe. Lots of pompous British humor ala John Cleese, Eric Idle, et al.

How

FTP

Where

nic.funet.fi

Go To

pub/culture/tv+film/series/MontyPython/*

Where to Find More Goodies

If it's laughs you're after, try the *Government and Politics* section. But seriously, folks, you can find some entertaining goodies in the *Games* section, and the *Television* section includes several sources for information and other trivial pursuits regarding situation comedies and assorted comic geniuses of the tube.

FREE $TUFF

I suggested that she take a trip round the world. "Oh, I know," returned the lady, yawning with ennui, "but there's so many other places I want to see first."

S.J. Perelman, from *Westward Ha!*

International Affairs

World Health Organization

Established in 1946 by the United Nations, the World Health Organization (WHO) is dedicated to the prevention and spread of diseases around the globe. Check out this Gopher site to find out more about this organization and the battles it has waged.

How

Gopher

Where

gopher.gsfc.nasa.gov

Go To

Virtual Reference Shelf
World Health Organization

World Factbook

Put the Central Intelligence Agency's voracious information appetite to work feeding your own brain. Each year, the CIA publishes the *CIA World Factbook*. In it are detailed descriptions of nearly 250 nations, including populations, economic conditions, political information, conflicts and wars, and much more. This book is ideal for political science students or for anyone interested in learning more about the world we live in. Download your free copy.

How

Gopher

Where

gopher.aecom.yu.edu

Go To

Internet Resources

Miscellaneous

Search CIA World Factbook (at the Search prompt, enter the name of the country you want information on, or enter *World* for a table of contents).

```
Cuba, Geography

Location:
  in the northern Caribbean Sea, 145 km south of Key West (Florida)
Map references:
  Central America and the Caribbean, North America, Standard Time Zones of the World
Area:
 total area:
  110,860 km2
 land area:
  110,860 km2
 comparative area:
  slightly smaller than Pennsylvania
Land boundaries:
  total 29 km, US Naval Base at Guantanamo 29 km
 note:
  Guantanamo is leased and as such remains part of Cuba
Coastline:
  3,735 km
Maritime claims:
 exclusive economic zone:
  200 nm
```

An excerpt from the CIA World Factbook file on Cuba

Oh, Canada!

Marshal McLuhan once said, "Canada is the only country in the world that knows how to live without an identity." The more you know about Canada, the more you'll realize how wrong that misconception is. The Province of Quebec alone arguably has more tradition than all of the U.S. And have you ever wondered why language is such a big and divisive issue in Canada? So, how much do *you* know about our neighbor to the north, eh? Here's a site with lots of interesting documents about Canada, including its Constitution, excerpts from the Constitutional Act of 1987, and Shaping Canada's Future. Many of the files are in both English and French.

How
Gopher

Where
wiretap.spies.com Gopher

Go To
Government Docs (US & World)
Canadian Documents

Made in Hong Kong

Hong Kong has become one of the world's leading financial centers, with four stock market exchanges and a booming export trade. It also has a fascinating political history that has seen it controlled by China, Japan, and finally Great Britain. In 1997, control of Hong Kong will revert back to China. What effect will this have in Hong Kong, as well as on the economy of the Pacific Rim?

Now here's an online exhibit tracing the upheavals and economic booms of this tiny territory, including an exceptional collection of GIFs and historical documents.

How

FTP

Where

sunsite.unc.edu

Go To:

pub/multimedia/pictures/asia/hongkong/hkpa/*

A GIF file downloaded from asia.lcs.mit.edu

China Exhibit

View the beautiful artwork, architecture, and history that has shaped the culture of China. You can also download pictures that show examples of China's people and such fascinating landmarks as the Great Wall and the Gezhouba Dam.

How
FTP

Where
sunsite.unc.edu

Go To
pub/multimedia/pictures/asia/china/gif/*

Russian Exhibit

The Soviet Union is no more, but Russia lives on. Once you get past the rhetoric and "Evil Empire" propoganda, what you'll see is a country rich with tradition and culture. This online exhibit examines the culture, politics, and history of Russia and its people. Explore the fascinating history through pictures and documents that are yours to download. Particularly fascinating are the GIFs of priceless artwork and architecture.

How
Gopher

Where
gopher.gsfc.nasa.gov

Go To
Virtual Reference Shelf
Other Online Libraries
Russia
Russian Archive
Images

Constitutions from around the World

Here's a site that you can access to download over two dozen historic documents from around the world, including Australia, Germany, Canada, the Confederate States of America, Italy, the former USSR, and more. Great for history and geography students.

How

Gopher

Where

wiretap.spies.com

Go To

Government Docs (US & World)

World Constitutions

International Treaties

In 1864, the Geneva Convention agreement was signed to regulate the treatment of prisoners of war, the types of weapons used, and the protection of civilians in wartime. Get the full text of this historic international treaty, as well as others, including the Hague Convention, the League of Nations, many Mideast treaties, and more.

How

Gopher

Where

wiretap.spies.com

Go To

Government Docs (US & World)

Treaties and International Covenants

News from Croatia

Millions of Americans have ancestral ties to Croatia, and interest in this region is still strong. Subscribe to this mailing list and you'll get first-hand accounts of what's happening in Croatia, horrifying though it might be. There are also highly informative and highly charged debates about what can be done to stop the fighting. If you're trying to get a better understanding of the confusing issues surrounding this bloody conflict, this mailing list is a must.

How
E-mail

Where
cro-news@well.ox.ac.uk

Message
Subscription to Cro-News

Have You Got the Time—in Rangoon?

As a friend of mine once said, it's always Happy Hour somewhere! Find out exactly where with this handy Gopher that will tell you what time it is anywhere, anytime. Great for broadcast and print journalists or for determining a good time to call a friend or family member abroad.

How
Gopher

Where
gopher.aecom.yu.edu

Go To
Internet Resources
Miscellaneous
Local Times around the World

News from Ireland

Authors Jill and Leon Uris, who have called Ireland the "Terrible Beauty," once wrote: "Ireland, England's first colony, is destined to be her last." It sometimes seems as though the conflict between the Irish and the British is the sole political force at work within Ireland. Not so, although this conflict does significantly shape the political climate there. Are you of Irish descent and interested in learning more about your heritage and contemporary political issues? Here's a forum for the discussion of Irish politics North and South. Topics include Ireland's economy, security, foreign policy, and relations between Northern Ireland and the Republic of Ireland.

How

E-mail

Where

listserv@irlearn.bitnet

Ask For

subscribe irl-pol *<name>*

NAFTA Implementation Resource Guide

Author and business guru Tom Peters has this advice for businesspeople: "Always think global, even if you're running a two-person lemonade stand." And Harvey Mackay advises small businesses to go global, noting that 97 percent of all businesses in the U.S. are categorized by the Bureau of Labor Statistics as "small businesses," but only a tiny fraction of these are doing business in foreign countries. A great way to get an edge on your competition is to expand your business abroad, and thanks to NAFTA, opportunities in Mexico now are better than they've ever been. The Department of Commerce's Office of Mexico has put together a guide to answer questions U.S. exporters may have about implementing NAFTA. This guide is a road map directing exporters to valuable resources, and covers a variety of topics, including how to obtain business visas, information on specific industries, labor issues, and more.

How

Gopher

Where

gopher.gsfc.nasa.gov

Go To

Virtual Reference Shelf

Economic Bulletin Board and exchange rates

General Information Files

NAFTA Implementation Resource Guide

```
                         AGRICULTURE

For information regarding NAFTA agriculture provisions...

     202-720-1340 TEL—  Mexico Desk/Foreign Agriculture Service
     202-690-2079 FAX    U.S. Department of Agriculture
                         14th & Independence Ave., S.W. South
                         Bldg.
                         Washington, D.C.  20250

     202-720-1336 TEL—  Canada Desk/Foreign Agricultural Service
                         (FAX and address, same as above)

For information regarding the export services of USDA, including
commodity fact sheets, state fact sheets, and business guide...

     202-720-6343 TEL—  AGEXPORT Services, U.S. Department of
                         Agriculture
     202-720-4374 FAX    (address same as above)
```

An Excerpt from the NAFTA Implementation Resource Guide

Russian Text

Here's a fascinating library of Soviet documents that puts a Russian slant on the shooting down of Gary Powers' U-2 spy plane in 1960, the Cuban Missile Crisis of 1962, and many other Cold War scraps and scrapes. There's also a lot of interesting literature on Russian history, politics, and cultural life.

How

Gopher

Where

gopher.gsfc.nasa.gov

Go To

Virtual Reference Shelf
Other online Libraries
Russia
Russian archive
Text

The Japan That Can Say No

This book has been a best-seller in Japan, and has gotten a lot of attention in the U.S. Co-authored by Akio Morita, chairman of Sony, and Shintaro Ishihara, a powerful member of Japan's Liberal Democratic Party who placed third in the race to succeed Prime Minister Sosuke, this book is an eye-opener on the business philosophy of Japan. It's a great resource for any businessperson who currently does or plans to do business in Japan. Know your market!

How

Gopher

Where

quartz.rutgers.edu

Go To

Economics, Business, Finance
Japanno

Does America Say Yes to Japan?

Read this book for a fascinating look at how "Japan Inc." functions. We couldn't put it down and we'll bet you won't be able to, either. It will wake you up, it will disturb you, and it will lead you to ask some serious questions about the future of the U.S. as a world leader.

How

Gopher

Where

quartz.rutgers.edu

Go To

Economics, Business, Finance

Japanyes

Where to Find More Goodies

The Internet is truly an international resource, so many topics in this book have some relevance to international affairs. Specifically, see the *Arts and Culture* section for information on museums and galleries in New York City and elsewhere in the U.S. The *Business and Career* section includes information on overseas jobs, careers, and other business opportunities abroad.

The *Nature and the Environment* section includes topics on the U.S.-Japan Environmental Initiative and weather information in Australia. Even the *Food and Cooking* section goes global, with a topic on food measurements used in different parts of the world and how to convert from one measurement system to another.

It probably goes without saying that the *Government and Politics* section includes several topics that are of international interest, but we've said it anyway. The *History* section also is rife with topics of international concern.

The *Languages and Linguistics* section obviously provides a separate slant on international affairs. The *Literature* section also includes several topics relating to international authors and literature. This same fact holds true for the *Movies*, *Film*, and *Music* sections.

The *Travel* section, of course, also provides a wealth of information on other countries and related travel information.

FREE $TUFF

Not only is the Internet a cool place, but all the hot topics keep piling into it, like overheated people into a midsummer swimming pool.

Ted Nelson

Internet
Resources

Hitchhiker's Guide to the Internet

DON'T PANIC! An indispensable companion for anyone trying to make sense of traveling through the complexities of the Internet. It may not always be right, but it does make the claim that "where it is inaccurate, it is at least definitively inaccurate. In cases of major discrepancy it is always reality that's got it wrong." Douglas Adams couldn't have said it better.

How

Gopher

Where

gopher.unc.edu

Go To

Internet Dog-Eared Pages

Guides to the Internet

Hitchhikers Guide to the Internet

The Cello Web Browser

Most people surf the World Wide Web through the University of Illinois' Mosaic browser, but Mosaic is by no means the only way to go. Developed at the same time as Mosaic is Cornell University's Cello browser, a Windows-specific GUI Web utility available for free from Cornell.

Cello does most of what Mosaic does, and isn't nearly so resource-intensive. You can run Cello effectively on a 4 Mb Windows system, whereas the latest version of Mosaic requires Win32s and at least 8 Mb of RAM, more being, of course, better.

Cello also has a reputation for being easier for a beginner to pick up, and there is a very well-written set of FAQs on the server at Cornell, which is required reading for anyone contemplating the use of Cello. Cornell has prepared a package of viewers for use with Cello, available via FTP from the same site where Cello is distributed. The viewers package is applicable to other Web browsers, and may be worth downloading even if you're using Mosaic or something else. Unfortunately, the VIEWERS.ZIP file is not always present in the Cello FTP area. The individual drivers, however, are there. Make sure to grab VIEWERS.ZIP if you see it.

How

FTP

Where

ftp.law.cornell.edu

Go To

pub/LII/Cello/cello.zip
pub/LII/Cello/viewers.zip

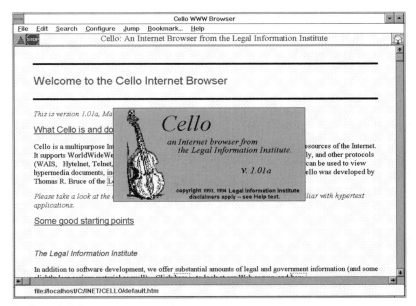

A view of Cello

Internet White Pages

Trying to locate someone on the Internet? This online directory compiles E-mail addresses from around the world to help you find businesses, universities, and people lost in Cyberspace.

How
Telnet

Where
wp.psi.net

Login
Fred

An Electronic Tattletale

As we get ready to send this book to press, so to are the publishers of the *Internet Informer*, an online Internet-based magazine that promises to provide information and perspectives on the effects of the Internet on business, education, and society. We haven't seen this publication yet, because, as we say, it doesn't yet exist. But it'll be available by the time you've bought this book. You did *buy* this book, didn't you?

How
E-mail

Where
informer@cris.com

Ask For
Subscribe to informer

The Thrill of the Chase

Detectives and detectettes will enjoy the thrill of this chase with The Internet Hunt. Each month, you're given a set of 10 questions to answer using only the resources found on the Internet. The questions cover a wide spectrum of available information on the Net, and each question carries a weight of difficulty (1 to 10). Each hunt usually includes an extra-credit question (1 point), and a mystery question.

The Internet Hunt will help you to learn about the different ways people use the Net, how to access different resources, and the types of information available to you. What a great learning tool—and fun, too!

But what about prizes, you ask. There's no money awarded, but you will receive the recognition of thousands of peers around the world that you have achieved Internet Guru status. Now isn't that better than just silly old cash?

How

Gopher

Where

gopher.cic.net

Go To

The Internet Hunt

Zen and the Art of the Internet

Brendan P. Kehoe's *Zen and the Art of the Internet* is a great reference book to help you explore the far reaches of Cyberspace. If you're looking for a good overview of what's waiting for you on the Internet and don't want to be weighed down with mind-numbing details and statistics found in many of the Net books on the market, this online version of the hardcopy classic is for you.

How

FTP

Where

ftp.cs.widener.edu

Go To

pub/zen/*

Incomplete Guide to the Internet

According to the author, "This guide will be finished when the Internet is." In the meantime, download a working copy of it to get some great tips on what's available in Cyberspace and what it takes to get you there.

How

FTP

Where

ftp.ncsa.uiuc.edu

Go To

misc/directory

EFF's Guide to the Internet

Published by the Electronic Frontier Foundation, *EFF's Guide to the Internet* is a great source for all kinds of information about the Internet. Filled with tips on how to use the tools available in Cyberspace, definitions of common terms, and places to visit, this book is a must-have in any electronic library.

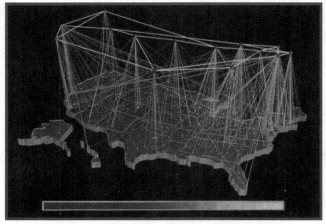

Map illustrating Internet links across the United States

How

FTP

Where

ftp.eff.org

Go To

pub/Net_info/EFF_Net_Guide/netguide.eff

Internet Monthly Report

Merit's Network Information Center publishes this monthly report to the Internet Research Group on the accomplishments, milestones, and problems encountered by the participating organizations around the world. You'll get interesting technical details and statistics on Internet usage, problems, minutes of meetings, and new sites to check out.

How

FTP

Where

nic.merit.edu

Go To

newsletters/internet.monthly.report/*

Information Guide

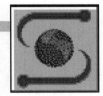

The InterNIC InfoGuide is a comprehensive online information service that brings you information about the Internet and resources that you can access online. Get valuable information about new services such as *The Scout Report* and an online hypertext version of the NSF Network News.

How

Mosaic

Where

http://www.internic.net

Go To

infoguide.html

Cruising the Internet

A Cruise of the Internet, by Merit Network, is a computer-based tutorial to help keep you off the rocks and sailing in smooth waters on the Internet. Your cruise begins with an interactive overview of the tools used on the Internet and then introduces you to resources you can access: space, software, gateways to other systems, and more. No shuffleboard yet, but you will pick up some valuable knowledge about what's waiting for you in Cyberspace. There are Windows and Mac versions.

How

FTP

Where

nic.merit.edu

Go To

internet/resources/cruise.dos/meritcrz.zip

internet/resources/cruise.mac/merit.cruise2.mac.hqx

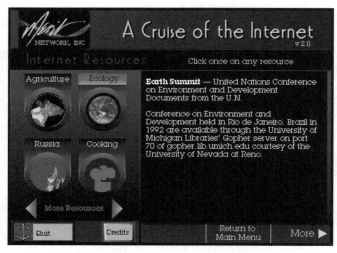

A view of the Windows version of A CRUISE OF THE INTERNET

Scouting Cyberspace

The Internet is growing so fast and is in such a constant state of change, it's nearly impossible to stay abreast of what's new in Cyberspace—at least, it used to be. *The Scout Report*, a weekly summary of Internet highlights, will keep you up to date. Offered by InterNIC Information Services to the Internet community as a fast, convenient way to stay informed on network activities, *The Scout Report* highlights new resource announcements and other news that occurred on the Internet during the previous week.

A wide range of resources is included in the report, with the emphasis being on topics of interest to researchers and educators.

How
Gopher

Where
is.internic.net

Go To
Information Services

Public Dialup Listing

Now there's no excuse for not being wired into the Internet. PDIAL, the Public Dialup Internet Access List, is a listing of Internet service providers offering public access dial-ins and outgoing Internet access (FTP, Telnet, and so on). Most of the providers on the list also provide E-mail and Usenet news, as well as other services.

How
E-mail

Where
info-deli-server@netcom.com

Ask For
Send PDIAL

Chicano/LatinoNet

Chicano/LatinoNet is a joint project of the Chicano Studies Research Center at the University of California at Los Angeles and the Linguistic Minority Research Institute at the University of California at Santa Barbara to provide ready access to networked information of interest to the Latino community.

The Chicano/LatinoNet Gopher brings together Latino research, as well as linguistic minority and educational research efforts being carried out around the U.S. It also serves as a gateway between faculty and students engaged in Latino research and studies.

Some of the highlights of this Gopher include information on:

- Newsletters, research guides, and library resources of interest to the Latino community
- Scholarships and employment opportunities
- Statistical data related to Latino research
- Student organizations and other resources of general interest to students

How
Gopher

Where
latino.sscnet.ucla.edu

Go To
AboutCLNET

Just How Big Is the Internet?

The growth of the Internet is extremely hard to fathom. Words like "astronomical and "exponential" really only scratch the surface of comprehension. A lot of graphs have been sketched on bar napkins in vain efforts to illustrate its explosiveness (yet another descriptor).

Finally, the effort has been made to document and make available online graphs to illustrate where the Internet began, where it is today, and, more important, where it's going. Download copies of these to use in your own presentations or publications.

How

Gopher

Where

gopher.tic.com

Go To

Matrix
Growth
Internet

The Online World Handbook

The Internet is moving so fast that printed books can be obsolete as soon as they're printed (except this one, of course). Not so with *Online World*. A new version appears every second month. *Online World* teaches you how to use the Internet to cross continents, countries, and networks to get the most out of the online information available to you.

In this online resources handbook, author Odd de Presno shows examples ranging from databases, entertainment, and the bizarre to special services for professionals and organizations. In addition, his insights on using major global networks and services that you can access around the world are invaluable.

Version 1.6 has new pointers to:

- Services that can help you learn and use foreign languages
- Sources for information about books in many different languages
- Six different news digests on Africa
- New sources on China
- International political and economic news from the British Broadcasting Corporation

- Current currency exchange rates
- The Information Bank on African Development Studies (a World Bank project)
- Encyclopedia Britannica

For the more technically inclined, there are new pointers on satellites, amateur and packet radio, information about an Internet clipping service, finding the best Gophers in the world, a database of World Wide Web information pages, Internet tools, and more.

How

Gopher

Where

cosn.org

Go To

Networking Information

Reference

The Online World - Odd de Presno

online1.6.txt (compressed)

Where to Find More Goodies

If you're not already a Web browser, it's probably time to head over to *The Tightwad's Guide to Mosaic* section, which explains how to get up and running with Mosaic. If you don't know what Mosaic or the Web are, then you definitely want to read that section ASAP. *The Poor Man's Passport to Cyberville* also provides local-access online services, many of which include access to the Internet.

FREE $TUFF

The quickest way for a parent to get a child's attention is to sit down and look comfortable.

Lane Olinghouse

Kid Stuff

Online Coloring Book

Save this program for a rainy day when the kids are driving you nuts. Coloring Book Version 2.0 is a painting program that includes 10 pictures kids can color online (35 pictures come in the registered version). There are 50 colors to choose from and sound effects, too. Kids use a keyboard, mouse, or joystick to color their pictures; they can even print their artwork when they're through. Coloring Book is so simple to use, it can be learned and played with no adult supervision.

How
FTP

Where
garbo.uwasa.fi

Go To
pc/passtime/cbook20.zip

An easy-to-use coloring book for kids

Blue Dog Can Count!

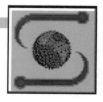

Kids of all ages will love this one, although it requires Mosaic so you might want to supervise or even play along with the little ones. It's totally offbeat—the sort

of thing that makes the Internet and Mosaic so gonzo great. Yes, it is a blue dog that can do arithmetic. Enter a simple formula (such as 5 + 6), and Blue Dog will bark out the answer. Try it—that's all we'll say, other than to point out (as the page does not) that you must have multimedia-capable hardware for it to work.

How

Mosaic (requires forms; use version 2.0)

Where

http://hp8.ini.cmu.edu:5550/bdf.html

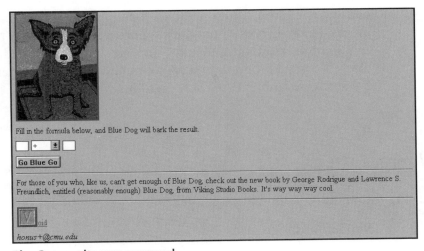

Blue Dog awaits your command

Toons of GIFs

It's a small, small world, and the Internet's making it smaller. Travel to this Cyberspace, Toon Town where you'll find loads of GIFs you can download. There are lots of great pictures of your (or your kids') favorite Disney characters. Sorry, but we can't show any of them here (lawsuits and all that).

How

FTP

Where

garfield.catt.ncsu.edu

Go To

pub/disney/*

Software for Kids

Except for the boolean logic and circuit tutor and a few other higher-level educational and oddball programs (an *air conditioner repair self test*, for cryin' out loud!), the vast majority of the software in this library is for kids. In fact, most of the programs are designed for kids 12 years and younger. You'll find several educational math and math-game programs, coloring books, and drawing programs, as well as spelling, word recognition, reading, and kids' foreign-language-learning programs. There's even a program to help your child learn how to tell time. All of the software here is DOS-based—almost 100 programs.

How

FTP

Where

rigel.acs.oakland.edu

Go To

SimTel/msdos/educatin/*

Filename	Description
123tlk22.zip	Talking Teacher: Child learns numbers/counting
aalpha.zip	Animated Alphabet for pre-school to first grader
abc430.zip	ABC Fun Keys: Teaches children ABCs, v4.30
abctlk25.zip	Teaches children to talk, read/alphabet/spell
aclockmp.zip	Animated Clock: Teaches kids to tell time
addalotm.zip	Educational math game for 6 to 12 year olds
amath1.zip	Animated Math: counting/addition/subtraction
amdcm1a.zip	Animated multiplication/division game, 1 of 2
amdcm1b.zip	Animated multiplication/division game, 2 of 2

A sampling of files in SimTel/msdos/educatin

Filename	Description
amem20.zip	Animated Memory Game: aids kids' memory skills
amy-v22.zip	LARGE char. typing fun for infants/toddlers
amy23.zip	Educational children's games (age 4 to 8)
animals.zip	Number games for children
animshap.zip	Animated Shapes: shape and color identification
awcmp1.zip	Animated Words spelling game for children, 1 of 2
awcmp2.zip	Animated Words spelling game for children, 2 of 2
babydraw.zip	Simple drawing program for children
bertaa40.zip	Bert's African Animals: Kids coloring pgm, 1 of 2

More files in SimTel/msdos/educatin

Disneyland Fun Facts

Here's where to go *before* you go to Disneyland. This site has all the answers a kid (or kid at heart) wants to know about Disneyland and Disney World. Read about upcoming events, new rides, the best times to go, even how to get free stuff when you visit.

How
FTP

Where
rtfm.mit.edu

Go To
pub/usenet/news.answers/disney-faq/disneyland

Teach Your Child the Joy of Reading

Books for Children, published by the Children's Literature Center in the Library of Congress, is for parents, teachers, librarians, publishers, and anyone interested in learning about the best the United States has to offer in current children's literature.

The editor and an advisory committee of children's book specialists examine over 5,000 newly published titles each year to choose the 100 they consider to be the most noteworthy.

Quality of plot, theme, style, pace, characterization, and setting is essential for satisfying stories. In addition, for the picture-story book, the art—and its harmony with the text—is vital. For nonfiction, accuracy, organization, timeliness, clarity of presentation, and quality of writing and illustration are all evaluated.

Selected books include rhymes, picture stories, adventure, fantasy, natural history, biography, science, and more. Books are selected for readers from the toddler stage to the teenage years. Some are to be read aloud; some are for instruction; and some are for fun. All are chosen to stimulate the imagination of children and adults alike.

How

Telnet

Where

fedworld.gov (see page 13 for instructions on how to download files from the Consumer Information Center)

Go To

BOOKSFOR.TXT

THE BIG ALFIE OUT OF DOORS STORYBOOK
|By| Shirley Hughes. New York: Lothrop, Lee & Shepard Books |1992| $17.00   ISBN 0-688-11428-8
Special events in young Alfie's busy life are highlighted in delightfully pictured stories and poems.

CLAP YOUR HANDS
|By| Lorinda Bryan Cauley. New York: G. P. Putnam's Sons |1992| unp. $14.95   ISBN 0-399-22118-2
A variety of simple movements are introduced here in catchy rhyme and vigorous pictures.

COUNT!
|By| Denise Fleming. New York: Henry Holt |1992| unp. $14.95   ISBN 0-8050-1595-7
A well-designed counting book features a menagerie of exuberant animals, among them gnus, toucans, kangaroos, and worms, representing numbers.

DADDIES
|By| Adele Aron Greenspun. New York: Philomel Books $15.95   ISBN 0-399-22259-6
A photographic essay highlights special relationships between fathers and their children.

A partial listing of the best children's books from BOOKSFOR.TXT

Your Source for Seuss

Who *didn't* grow up reading Dr. Seuss? Only the seriously deprived. *Green Eggs and Ham, Horton Hears a Who, How the Grinch Stole Christmas, The Cat in the Hat, Yertle the Turtle* . . . . Ahh, the memories! If your parents already hauled off your Seuss collection to the Salvation Army, you can still carry on the fun and tradition by pointing your kids to this site. They'll enjoy reading these stories online from the original master of kiddie rap.

How
Gopher

Where
quartz.rutgers.edu

Go To
Electronic Texts
Seuss

Dinosaurs Galore

In 1978, Skullduggery began producing fossil replicas for museums around the world. They quickly found out, however, that there was a significant interest among the general public for high-quality fossil replicas as well.

Skullduggery's unique molding process, along with its expert detailed casting procedures, makes owning a Skullduggery replica the next scariest thing to having the real thing roaming your backyard. (*That* would keep those stray cats away.) Send for your free catalog. An educational booklet for each item is also provided at no extra cost.

How
E-mail

Where
vmall@hookup.net

Subject

Send skull catalog

Space Stickers

Kids love space and kids love stickers. Double the fun with these stickers commemorating the Apollo and Space Shuttle missions. (Of course, kids also love destruction, so you might want to restrict their sticking options.) Other memorabilia is also available. Send E-mail requesting the stickers and more information.

How

E-mail

Where

kdurham@smtpgate.osu.hq.nasa.gov

Ask For

Apollo and Space Shuttle stickers, plus information on other NASA memorabilia. Be sure to include your name and postal address.

Songs from the Magic Kingdom

Song lyrics from *The Little Mermaid, Aladdin*, and other Disney hits are transcribed here. There's also information on upcoming movie releases and lots of other fun Disney stuff.

How

Gopher

Where

quartz.rutgers.edu

Go To

Disney—The Wonderful World of Disney

Dear Pen Pal

Kids love learning when learning is made fun. And there's no better way to learn about other countries, cultures, and people than through letters from a pen pal. This service will match your child with kids around the world to share thoughts and experiences through E-mail. Things your kids take for granted will fascinate someone on the other side of the globe and vice versa.

How
E-mail

Where
pen-pals-request@mainstream.com

Ask For
Information on getting a pen pal

Solar System Puzzle Kit

Building your own solar system may seem a bit daunting, but now it's easy—and fun. This puzzle kit from the National Aeronautics and Space Administration Education Publications helps children learn about the solar system they live in and the planets that share it.

How
E-mail

Where
kdurham@smtpgate.osu.hq.nasa.gov

Ask For
Solar System Puzzle Kit. Be sure to include your name and postal address.

Discovery Toys

The employees at Discovery Toys believe that play is a child's work. Children play to learn, to grow, and to experience the world around them. With outstanding developmental toys, books, and games, Discovery Toys offers the finest products of the highest quality for your baby, toddler, or older child. Send for a free catalog of toys that will let your children learn while they play.

How
E-mail

Where
vmall@hookup.net

Subject
Send dtoys cat

KIDLINK

Learning can also be fun, and nowhere is this more true than on the Internet. KIDLINK, a global service for children between 10 and 15 years old, lets kids around the world talk to each other. Operated by a grassroots network of volunteers, KIDLINK grew from an idea in 1990 to over 23,000 participating children in 61 countries by June 1994.

Kids from around the world meet at the the KIDCAFE to discuss everything from pop music to what it's like to live in other countries. Participation is free, and kids can write in any language.

Schools all over the globe integrate KIDLINK with their classes in language, geography, other cultures, history, environment, art, and more. Send a request for more information and find out why KIDLINK is a great place for kids to learn about computers, the Internet, and the world.

How
E-mail

Where

listserv@vm1.nodak.edu

Ask For

Get kidlink general

Where to Find More Goodies

The Internet's certainly not just for adults anymore. The *Education and Teaching Tools* section explains how to get lots of educational information and software for kids, as does the *Computers and Software* section.

Some of the items in the *Games* section will provide great fun for kids, as will some of the software and topics in the *Sports, Recreation, and Hobbies* section.

For more serious kid stuff, head over to the *Space and Astronomy* section, which tells you where you can find observatory programs and other educational astronomy software.

The *Travel and Geography* section also includes software that helps kids learn U.S. and world geography in a fun and painless manner.

FREE $TUFF

I took an estimated two thousand years of high-school French, and when I finally got to France, I discovered that I didn't know one single phrase that was actually useful in a real-life French situation.

Dave Barry

Language and Linguistics

French Tutor

Viva la France! And *viva la* Internet for bringing you these French-language tutors. Before you know it, you'll be speaking like a Parisian *bon vivant* having a *tête à tête* with a *femme fatale à la* Brigitte Bardot. *Oh la la!*

How

FTP

Where

oak.oakland.edu

Go To

SimTel/msdos/langtutr/fren1-23.zip
SimTel/msdos/langtutr/fren2-23.zip

It's All Greek to Me

Tu Parle Francais? Se habla Español? Sprechen sie Deutsch? If not, try the World Wide Web Human-Languages page. It offers foreign language dictionaries (like English-German), tutorials (like *Let's Learn Arabic*, and *Travelers' Japanese Tutorial*), foreign literature, and other references and resources.

How

Mosaic

Go To

http://www.willamette.edu/~tjones/Language-Page.html

Achtung, Cyberpunks!

If you garnered your knowledge of the German languages from reruns of *Hogan's Heroes*, you may want to take this refresher course. You'll learn the fundamentals of German, as well as important phrases to help you blend in with the Berliners. You'll need to supply the glockenspiel and lederhosen.

How

FTP

Where

oak.oakland.edu

Go To

pub/msdos/langtutr/germ1-23.zip

pub/msdos/langtutr/germ2-23.zip

Japanese for Business 101

Sure all the talk is about NAFTA and Mexico's emerging economy, but Japan is still an important money-maker for U.S. markets. This tutorial for American businesspeople wheeling and dealing with the Japanese is sure to help you rise above the competition.

How

FTP

Where

oak.oakland.edu

Go To

pub/msdos/langtutr/japan14.zip

Japanese for the Mac

If you're a Macintosh user, check out this interactive software to help you learn beginning Japanese. You'll get an introduction to the basic verb forms and sentence patterns of the modern Japanese language through grammatical explanations coupled with interactive exercises.

Seventeen lessons in grammatical instruction plus drills for checking your progress will have you talking Japanese better than you ever thought you would. Plus, two of the lessons are devoted specifically to mastery of the Japanese *hiragana* and *katakana* writing systems. (No, we don't know what they are.)

How

Gopher

Where

boombox.micro.umn.edu

Go To

Japanese

When in Rome . . .

Ah, Italy: Naples, Florence, Venice! See it for yourself, but brush up on the language first. This tutorial program can help. You'll learn more than enough to make your trip all the more memorable.

How

FTP

Where

oak.oakland.edu

Go To

pub/msdos/langtutr/ital1-23.zip

Español, Olé!

Here are several programs to get you started in Spanish. You'll learn the basics: how to spell, proper pronunciation, and more. When you're feeling confident, run south to the border (or maybe just go to L.A.) to practice your new tongue.

How

FTP

Where

oak.oakland.edu

Go To

pub/msdos/langtutr/span1-23.zip

pub/msdos/langtutr/span2-23.zip

pub/msdos/langtutr/spanwd15.zip

pub/msdos/langtutr/spnsh102.zip

Language Smorgasbord

Nine languages are included in this vocabulary tutorial. You'll be drilled in Spanish, French, Italian, and more. This progam is designed to give you a working knowledge and solid foundation for each of the languages covered. Won't that look good on your resume?

How

FTP

Where

oak.oakland.edu

Go To

pub/msdos/langtutr/vocab217.zip

Chinese for the West

As China continues to open up to the West, travel and business are increasingly popular between China and the West. Here's a program that will quiz you on your knowledge of Chinese characters and phrases. Each lesson is designed to help you learn at your own pace and to build on previous lessons so you'll be fluent in no time.

How

FTP

Where

oak.oakland.edu

Go To

pub/msdos/langtutr/kong1_1a.zip

pub/msdos/langtutr/kong1_1b.zip

Russian Language Tutor

With the demise of the Soviet Union and an increase in tourism and business opportunities in the Baltic region, learning Russian is possibly more useful for Westerners than it has been in over 100 years. RussianTutor is a shareware program for Windows that teaches the basics of the Russian language. The software guides you through the study of sounds, inflection, and pronunciation differences, rather than just memorization.

Although you need ToolBook V1.53 or above to run RussianTutor, the runtime version of ToolBook is bundled with Russian Tutor, which includes:

- Seven lessons covering the basics of the Russian language, each with digitized recordings of a native Russian speaker
- Use of the Media Control Interface (MCI) for all multimedia functions, which allows for the use of any multimedia hardware that is MCI-compatible
- Recording of students' voices; you can compare your voice with that of the recordings
- An easy-to-use graphical interface

How

FTP

Where

ftp.cica.indiana.edu

Go To

pub/pc/win3/misc/rusntutr.zip

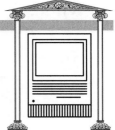

The Mac Looks Greek to Me

Ever wanted to read the New Testament or the Greek philosophers in the original language? No? Ever been told by your prof that you *had* to read the New Testament or the Greek philosophers in the original language? Here's a Macintosh application to help you learn one of the greatest and most difficult of the ancient languages. Specifically, this application provides a hypertext tutorial on Greek verb cases.

How

Gopher

Where

echonyc.com

Go To

Geek Stuff

Software Archives at MERIT (University of Michigal)

Linguistics Archive (Merit Network, USA)

Software

Mac

greekverbhelp1.2.sit.hqx

I'd Like My Esperanto with a Lime Twist

This Hypercard stack is an introduction to Esperanto, a universal language designed by a linguist to be used as a common second language for all cultures. We're not sure how the world can adopt a common language when some of us still can't play well with others. Anyway, the stack contains a lot of information, including a full alphabet and example sentences, and the program speaks. Of course, this program requires Hypercard and a Mac.

How

Gopher

Where

echonyc.com

Go To

Geek Stuff

Software Archives at MERIT (University of Michigal)

Linguistics Archive (Merit Network, USA)

Software

Mac

esperanto.sit.hqx

Linguistic Lingo

Here's a one-stop shop for the serious linguist, grammarian, or linguistics student. This source includes such specialties as a morphological analyzer, a phonological rule simulator, and a linguistics data management program. You practically have to be a linguist just to pronounce all this stuff, much less use it.

How

FTP

Where

oak.oakland.edu

Go To

SimTel/msdos/linguist/*

Filename	Description
babylon3.zip	Worldwide language library linking program
cognate.zip	Identifies related words across languages
englex10.zip	English lexicon (20,000 entries) for PC-KIMMO
fonol421.zip	Fonol 4.2.1 Phonological theory/rule simulator
gramt411.zip	Interpreter for transformational grammars
kgen02.zip	Rule compiler for the PC-KIMMO parser

A partial listing of files in SimTel/msdos/linguist

Filename	Description
ktext093.zip	Text processing using the PC-KIMMO parser
pckimmo.zip	Two-level processor for morphological analysis
sh12a.zip	SHOEBOX, linguistic data management program
trans.zip	Translates text to another language
words1.zip	English word list (ASCII), A through D, 1 of 4
words2.zip	English word list (ASCII), E through K, 2 of 4
words3.zip	English word list (ASCII), L through R, 3 of 4
words4.zip	English word list (ASCII), S through Z, 4 of 4
wrdsrv24.zip	Wordsurv: Analyze language survey word lists

More files in SimTel/msdos/linguist

Where to Find More Goodies

After you've acquired a working knowledge of a foreign tongue, you'll no doubt want to try it out. The *Travel and Geography* section provides plenty of travel information and travel-related goodies to help you on your journey.

If you like foreign languages, you probably also are interested in foreign cultures. Check out the *International Affairs* section for tons of resources and information relating to countries and cultures around the globe.

FREE $TUFF

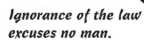

Ignorance of the law excuses no man.

John Selden

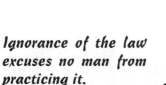

Ignorance of the law excuses no man from practicing it.

Addison Mizner

Law

Child Support Facts

For many parents, receiving the child support they're lawfully entitled to may seem about as likely as winning the lottery. Here's information to help you beat the odds. This file provides answers to common questions, suggestions for improving your chance of receiving the support you've been awarded, and strategies to ensure that you continue to get your support payments.

How

Telnet

Where

fedworld.gov (see page 13 for instructions on how to download files from the Consumer Information Center)

Go To

NFCCHILD.TXT

Supreme Court Bios

Who are they, where did they come from, and just what *do* they wear under those robes? Here are biographies of all current and recent U.S. Supreme Court justices. You'll be surprised at the different backgrounds of each member that makes up the highest judicial tribunal in the land. This is a useful document for teachers and civics students alike.

How

Gopher

Where

info.umd.edu

Go To

Educational Resources
Government

United States
Supreme Court Documents
Justices of the Supreme Court Biographies

Not Just for Lawyers

Is it true that a person who represents him/herself in court has a fool for a lawyer? A traffic-court judge once told us that it's fairly routine for defendants to try to plead their own cases. For minor offenses and citations, this approach can help consumers to save hundreds or even thousands of dollars in attorney's fees. The only problem is that most of the time these individuals haven't even read the statutes that they've allegedly violated! So, it can be cost effective and sensible to act on your own behalf, providing you invest some time in research. The Internet has tons of law-related information—if you know where to look. Here's a great place to start. There are files containing Supreme Court decisions, copyright information, patent and trademark rulings, and much more. This Gopher is also ideal for law students, political science majors, or anyone who has an interest in the law. Also check out *The Legal List* topic in this section.

How

Gopher

Where

tmn.com

Go To

Law

Copyright Info

So you think you've written a sure-fire hit song? Have you checked to make sure that your ideas are truly yours alone? Find out with LOCIS— the Library of Congress Information System. LOCIS contains copyright data and records from 1978 to present. If it's already been written, sung, or performed, you'll find out about it here. You can even register your

work online. One important note, though. Searching LOCIS can be an exercise in frustration if you're a new user. The commands are many and they're complex. Be sure to download and read a copy of the *Guide to Quick Searching LOCIS*.

How

Telnet

Where

locis.loc.gov

Go To

Follow login instructions

```
BROWSE SEARCHING:
    You type:    b clancy, tom      (author search)
        or       b burden of proof  (title search)
        or       b solar energy--   (subject search)
        or       b call na109       (partial LC call # search)

SELECTING:
    Select the line number on the left of the screen that matches your search:
        You type:    s b6
DISPLAYING:
    Your screen will show one or more SETS.  To display a set:
        You type:    d 1      (or the appropriate set number)
    To change display to ascending (earlier items first):
        You type:    set da     Return to descending:  You type:    set dd
    To return to the most recent alphabetical index:
        You type:    b b6--

TIPS:    Capitalization is not necessary.
         Exclude initial articles.
         Advance to the next screen, press  ENTER.   Over --->
```

Instructions on how to quick-search the LOCIS database

The Legal List

There's no shortage of legal information on the Internet. In fact, in doing legal research, your biggest problem might be trying to determine where to start looking for information. So, for all you legal eagles, here's an in-depth list of law-related resources on the Internet and directions on how to find them. You'll find loads of FTP, Telnet, and Gopher sites, as well as BBSs and government resources.

How

FTP

Where

ftp.midnight.com

Go To

pub/Legallist/legallist.txt

```
            Law, Politics and Government

Listname: aba-unix Topic: unix interest group of the ABA Law Office
Management Section Mail address: aba-unix@cayman.com

Listname: ai-ed Topic: Artificial Intelligence in Education Subscription
address: ai-ed-request@sun.com Mail address: ai-ed@sun.com

Listname: aids-stat Topic: distributes AIDS statistics Subscription address:
aids-stat-request@wubios.wustl.edu Mail address: aids-stat@wubios.wustl.edu

Listname: aidsnews Topic: AIDS news Subscription address:
listserv@rutvml.bitnet Subscription Instructions: subscribe aidsnews YOUR
NAME Mail address: aidsnews%rutvml.bitnet@cunyvm.cuny.edu

Listname: ail-1 Topic: artificial intelligence in law Subscription address:
listserv@austin.onu.edu Subscription Instructions: subscribe ail-1 YOUR NAME
Mail address: ail-1@austin.onu.edu

Listname: amnesty Topic: amnesty international Subscription address:
listserv@jhuvm.bitnet Subscription Instructions: subscribe amnesty YOUR
NAME Mail address: amnesty@vms.cis.pitt.edu or amnesty@jhuvm.bitnet

Listname: animal-rights Topic: animal rights Subscription address:
animal-rights-request@xanth.cs.odu.edu Mail address: animal-rights@cs.odu.edu

Listname: apda Topic: American Parlimentary Debate Association Mail address:
apda%pucc.bitnet

Listname: arms-1 Topic: policy issues related to peace, war, national
security,
arms race Subscription address: listserv@buacca.bu.edu Subscription
Instructions: subscribe arms-1 YOUR NAME Mail address:
arms-1@buacca.bu.edu or arms-1@buacca.bitnet

Listname: aviation Topic: information of interest to pilots including laws
Subscription address: aviation-request@mc.lcs.mit.edu Mail address:
aviation@mc.lcs.mit.edu

Listname: biomed-1 Topic: biomedical issues including ethics and the right
to die Subscription address: listserv@ndsuvml.bitnet Subscription
Instructions: subscribe biomed-1 YOUR NAME Mail address:
biomed-1%ndsuvml.bitnet@vml.nodak.edu

Listname: bpwsp-1 Topic: Bureau of Public Water Supply Protection Mail
address: bpwsp-1@albnydh2.bitnet

Listname: cjust-1 Topic: criminal justice Mail address: cjust-1@iubvm.bitnet
or
cjust-1@iubvm.ucs.indiana.edu
```

Partial listing of sources for legal information

Sexual Harassment

There's a fine line between friendliness and sexual harassment. And overt physical acts are not the only forms of harassment. In fact, you might be surprised to learn how easily a casual conversation can be interpreted as harassment. Protect yourself from becoming a victim of sexual harassment or even from inadvertently committing an act that might be viewed as harassmenet by others. The U.S. Equal Employment Opportunity Commission (EEOC) Library has compiled this selective list of books, articles, and videos on the topic of sexual harassment for the convenience of business people, their employees, and the general public who wish to familiarize themselves with this important issue.

How
Gopher

Where
info.umd.edu

Go To
Educational Resources

Academic Resources by Topic

Women's Studies Resources

Gender Issues

Sexual Harassment

Sexual Harassment Resources

Privacy Act of 1974

The purpose of the Privacy Act of 1974 was to prevent government agencies from misusing the data it collects. This means that information gathered on you for one purpose cannot be used for another. But some people feel strongly that government agencies routinely try to circumvent the law in order to acquire information about citizens. Have you had an experience that makes you wonder whether information about you is being shared by different government agencies, possibly illegally? Learn more about the Privacy Act, how it affects you, and your rights by downloading your own copy.

How
Gopher

Where
wiretap.spies.com

Go To
Government Docs (US & World)
Treaties and International Covenants
Privacy Act of 1974

Brady Bill Becomes the Brady Law

Few topics elicit stronger reactions from people than gun control. The Brady Handgun Violence Prevention Act establishes waiting periods for handgun purchases, as well as the establishment of a national instant criminal background check system. But many court challenges to this law have already been filed. In fact, a sheriff in Arizona won his case against the Brady Law by arguing that the government can't require a local agency to enforce an unfunded federal law. Other challenges have been based on Second-Amendment rights issues. Find out for yourself what the Brady Law *really* says in the full text of this controversial law.

How
Gopher

Where
wiretap.spies.com

Go To
Government Docs (US & World)
Brady Handgun Violence Prevention Act

Electronic Frontier Foundation

The Electronic Frontier Foundation (EFF) was founded to "ensure that the principles embodied in the Constitution and the Bill of Rights are protected as new communications technologies emerge."

The EFF works to ensure freedom of electronic speech, including the establishment of communications services accessible and affordable to everyone so that all citizens will have a voice in the Information Age. Read about the efforts being made by the EFF to ensure your First-Amendment rights are protected in Cyberspace.

How
Gopher

Where
gopher.eff.org

Go To
About the Electronic Frontier Foundation

Various State Laws

We are in the *United* States, right? So why do laws vary so widely from state to state? Get up-to-date information on various state statutes, including privacy laws, environmental and nuclear safety, computer systems protection, and computer crime. This is an excellent education resource for demonstrating the rights of states over the mandates of federal law.

How
Gopher

Where
wiretap.spies.com

Go To
Government Docs (US & World)
Various US State Laws

Help Solve a Crime

The spirit of Elliot Ness lives on. The FBI has offered a $1 million reward for help in solving a series of 14 bombing incidents that have occurred across the United States from May 1978 to June 1993. So far, no motive has been found, and no person or group has taken responsibility. The explosions have taken place in seven states across the country, killing one person and injuring 23, some critically. In July 1993, a special task force, dubbed "UNABOM" was created and dedicated exclusively to solving these crimes.

Among the clues in the case is a note possibly written by the bomber as a reminder to make a telephone call: "call Nathan R—Wed 7PM." The UNABOM Task Force believes that "Nathan R" may be associated, perhaps innocently, with the bomber, and that "Nathan R" may have received a telephone call from the bomber on a Wednesday prior to the June 1993 bombings. If you can help, contact:

William L. Tafoya, Ph.D., Special Agent, FBI.
UNABOM Task Force
San Francisco, CA

How
E-mail

Where
btafoya@orion.arc.nasa.gov

Ask for
Information on what you can do to help solve UNABOM

Where to Find More Goodies

The *Business and Careers* section explains how to find rules, regulations, and other legal notices from government agencies. Much of this information can impact you if you are a small-business operator. In this same section, you'll also find out how to get a free consultation with Information Researchers, an organization that provides information-location services, including searches for legal information.

The *Government and Politics* section tells you how to download a copy of the Tailhook '91 investigation, which might be of interest to legal students.

The *Health and Nutrition* section includes a download site for information about the COBRA health benefits law.

The Environment and Nature section explains how to find regulations imposed by the Environmental Protection Agency on businesses, states, and consumers.

The *Household and Consumer Finance* section includes a wealth of legal-related information, including the text of the Fair Credit Reporting Act, and the rights of consumers in dealing with repair shops, service contracts, and product warranties.

The *International Affairs* section points you to the text of NAFTA, which explains the legalities of doing business in Mexico and Canada.

FREE $TUFF

Several tons of dynamite are set off in this picture—none of it under the right people.

James Agee, reviewing
Tycoon, 1947

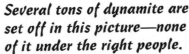

Movies and Videotapes

Imart

Imart is your one-stop shopping mart on the Internet for audio and video entertainment. Through Imart, you can order compact discs, laser discs, VHS music video cassettes, and CD-ROMs, all from the convenience of your home. With its extensive collection of online catalogs containing thousands of selections you can order through E-mail, online shopping has never been easier.

How
E-mail

Where
imart@netcom.com

Subject
info

Videotapes by the Thousands

Here's your one-stop shop for buying videotapes. There are over 60,000 videotapes available for you to order, with topics covering automation, motorcycles, aviation, boating, business skills, child care, cooking, investment, sexuality, sports, and tons more. Get a free *Special Interest Video Collection* catalog by ordering one or more videos, plus a $10 certificate towards your next order of at least $50. Video prices start as low as $9.95.

How
E-mail

Where
slide@mailserv.nbnet.nb.ca

Message
Please send me your catalog of videos

Two Thumbs Up

This site won't tell you who's lead gaffer or best boy of your favorite movie, but it does list the actors, directors, writers, and other celluloid heroes who helped bring your movies to life. There are also plot summaries, bloopers, movie trivia, scripts like *Airplane*, *Terminator*, and *Aliens*, and much more. And just what *is* a "key grip," anyway?

How

Mosaic

Where

http://cathouse.org/cathouse/movies/scripts/

Cardiff's Movie Database Browser

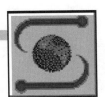

An amazing store of information on all the movies you've ever heard of, and plenty of others. It's completely free to access, can be searched on several different criteria, and allows you to vote for your favorite (or not-so-favorite) movies on a scale of 1 to 10.

You can search by movie title or by name (that is, by the names of people associated with the movie, including directors, producers, and so on). What's in the database is quite accurate, as much as we've checked; however, there are some holes in the more obscure spots, like costume designers for Grade Z horror flicks of the 1950s. The database has been compiled 100 percent by volunteers, and if you know how to fill one of the "holes," you are enthusiastically invited to do so.

Nearly all of the films we looked for were there, including such one-week-wonders as *Kronos*, *Year of the Jellyfish*, and *The Crawling Eye*, but inexplicably omitting the 1959 Three Stooges masterpiece, *Have Rocket, Will Travel*. Can't win 'em all.

Submitting a vote on a film or group of films is awkward, since it can't be done through Mosaic; you must submit E-mail to the server, but apart from this inconvience, the service is a complete delight.

How

Mosaic (requires forms; use version 2.0)

Where (U.S.)

http://www.msstate.edu/Movies/moviequery.html

Where (U.K.)

http://www.cm.cf.ac.uk/Movies/moviequery.html

For Videophiles Only

Is your VCR collection rapidly becoming a video store? Then you need to get organized. Actually, this program is great for film reviewers, film students, retail outlets that rent/sell videos, mail-order outlets that sell videos, and anybody with a whomping collection of tapes. Movie Catalog for Windows is a program that does just that, catalogs information about movies and tapes. (Windows is required, of course.)

For each movie, you can enter the director, star, co-stars, composer, playing time, a category, an MPAA rating, the production studio, a catalog number, the year of the film's release, reviews or review excerpts, a tape number, the tape's cost and quality, and even the date and location of purchase. Talk about your obsessive-compulsives. Hmmm—think we'll watch *The Odd Couple* tonight.

How

FTP

Where

garbo.uwasa.fi

Go To

windows/util/am_mc10.zip

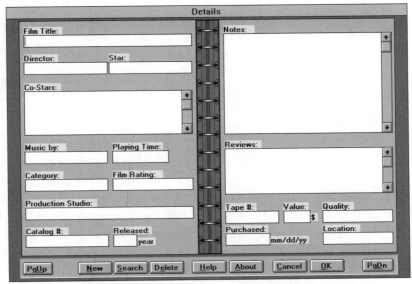

Add detailed information about each video using this screen

In a Galaxy Far, Far Away. . .

"Master Luke, over here! I think I've found something!" If you don't already know every line from the *Star Wars* trilogy, you can download the scripts here. Reading these files is like seeing the movies all over again. Or, give the scripts to your kids and have them and their friends act them out to create their own plays. And by the way, may The Force be with you.

How

Gopher

Where

quartz.rutgers.edu

Go To

Electronic Texts

StarWars

Kid, I'm Gonna Make You a Star!

Interactive Videosystems Inc., a Vancouver-based multimedia company, will make your child a star in his very own personalized animated cartoon. With this amazing Starmaker computer technology, your child's color photograph is digitally scanned into a program that converts it into a cartoon character, which is then placed into a full motion, animated cartoon.

The narration and read-a-long video subtitles are also personalized with your child's name for a completely customized feature cartoon, called *The Festival of the Forgetful King*. The characters were designed by award-winning Al Sens Animation Ltd., and the 12-minute story follows guidelines set by the National Association for the Education of Young Children.

And for children who have access to a personal computer, Interactive Videosystems will soon introduce a computer version of the Starmaker video. Featuring the same personalized story as the video, the computer version will also include a paint program, talking storyteller, music teacher, and editor, as well as arcade-style video games. Children will be able to interact with their personalized stories by repainting the images, changing the narration, re-editing the sound track, solving puzzles and learning other educational video games.

In addition, Interactive Video is currently developing six new titles it plans to introduce in 1994.

How
E-mail

Where
vmall@hookup.net

Subject
send ivideo catalog

Where to Find More Goodies

If you're into films, you might also have an avid interest in Television. If so, the *Television* section provides several Internet sites that are TV-related.

For children, the *Kid Stuff* section explains where to find the lyrics to songs from favorite Disney films.

The *Shopping* section also tells you how to get free catalogs from mail-order video companies.

FREE $TUFF

*I don't know anything about music.
In my line you don't have to.*

Elvis Presley

Music

Internet Unplugged

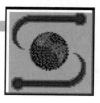

Acoustic guitarists will love the treasures waiting to be dug up at this musical archive site. There are lots of song transcriptions and online magazines devoted to professional acoustic guitarists and fans of their music.

How

Mosaic

Where

http://fedida.ini.cmu.edu:5550/bdf.html

The Official Rolling Stones Web Site

This is one of the best rock fan hangouts yet erected on the Web—and certainly, if you're looking for drawings and photos of tongues, there will never be a better one. Seriously, the page presents promo audio clips from the band's new CD, *Voodoo Lounge*, along with pictures of the band and lots of other things relating to the Stones, their current tour, and recent recordings.

To celebrate the new *Voodoo Lounge* CD, voodoo images of various sorts are available in the picture archive. And we're not kidding about the tongues! (Jagger is well-endowed, in that respect at least.) Obviously, you're going to need multimedia hardware to listen to the audio clips.

How

Mosaic (audio clips require multimedia hardware)

Where

http://www.stones.com/

Is It Live or Is It Dead?

The Grateful Dead have been selling out shows longer than many of us have been alive, and they're "bound to cover just a little more ground." Check this site out for loads of information about the Dead, including song transcriptions, tour dates, bios, and lots more.

How
FTP

Where
gdead.berkeley.edu

Go To
pub/gdead/*

Playing Musical Computers

Here's a great source for making and playing music on your computer. There's more Bach here than you can shake a baton at. You'll find lots of stuff for MIDIs and SoundBlaster cards, but you'll also find plenty of music that's playable directly through the PC's anemic little speaker. This site has lots of Christmas and holiday music, too. The following list is just a sampling. There are dozens more files here.

How
FTP

Where
rigel.acs.oakland.edu

Go To
SimTel/msdos/music/*

Filename	Description
ac37musd.zip	Create music, print it, transpose it, play it
bassv25.zip	Bass/percussion/chord sound generator for MIDI
bgp11.zip	Play Basic-like music in background mode

A sampling of files in SimTel/msdos/music/*

Filename	Description
chrstmas.zip	Christmas songs - menu driven
cwb135.zip	Composer's Work Bench: MIDI notator/seqencer
d10ctl11.zip	Roland D-5/10/20/110 synthesizer MIDI ctl pgm
dousound.zip	Demonstrates how to make two channeled sound
getit30.zip	MIDI data transfer and sequencer program v3.0
midimod2.zip	Makes MIDI files from MODs automatically
moded301.zip	4-track digitized music composer, PC speaker/SoundBlaster
musicbox.zip	Write & play music, for PC-compatibles only
st224.zip	4-channel digitized music composing utility
tmodpl.zip	Turbo MODplayer: Play modules through SB/PRO/LPTx
tmusic.zip	Menu-driven classical music program
winplay.zip	Polyphonic music player for MS Windows 3.x

More files in SimTel/msdos/music/*

MTV (Not!)

Old VJs never die, they just lose their hairspray endorsements. No, actually, they switch mediums. Take Adam Curry (please). He may be gone from MTV, but he's alive and well in Cyberspace. His new home includes all the music news that's fit to download, chart listings, details on upcoming concerts and events, and pictures of today's hottest bands.

How

Gopher

Where

metaverse.com

Guitar Music

Tablature guitar music for all styles. Jackson Browne, Jimmy Buffett, Bruce Springsteen, and more. A must for aspiring and expiring rockers, motorheads, Deadheads, and anyone else who's ever tuned a guitar.

How

FTP

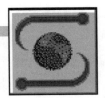

Where

ftp.nevada.edu

Go To

pub/guitar/*

Princeton's Scramble Band

The very first college football marching band in the U.S. in now the first such band to have their own home page and hypertext archives. The Princeton University band (PUB) is one of perhaps a dozen "scramble bands" in the country, meaning that they change from one formation to another by what looks like (but is *not*) a lot of random milling around, all done in strict time to the music. It's truly something to see—along with their trademark blinding-bright orange and black plaid outfits.

Seeing it in motion still requires a trip to Princeton, (at least until the speed of our links improves) but hearing it is a lot easier, and only requires multimedia hardware. Numerous recordings can be downloaded, along with halftime scripts, pregame scripts, photos, and lyrics.

The music is recorded in MULAW format (12 bits compressed to 8) and an online test is available to test whether or not your workstation can understand that format.

How

Mosaic

Where

http://www.princeton.edu:80/~puband

Japanese Pop

Looking for the latest on Yumiko Takahashi? Or perhaps you're wondering what Yamaguchi Momoe is really like? Find out here. This list is for the discussion of Japanese pop music, including its artists, new release

lists, bestseller charts, reviews of albums and singles, and more. Discussion is primarily in English although JIS-encoded Japanese characters may be understood by some subscribers.

How
E-mail

Where
majordomo@tcp.com

Ask For
Subscribe JPOP

Here Comes Jordan Music Productions

Order a free catalog to find out about this catchy, creative series of songs designed to help make learning fun. Conceived, written, and produced by Toronto teacher Sara Jordan, these cassettes can be played in the home, car, or classroom.

3r Rap helps children with arithmetic, and *Funky Phonics* will help them to read. Embracing the traditional and current methods of teaching youngsters, there are songs about vowels, consonants, and the alphabet. More importantly, though, the other songs cover a wide variety of topics children learn about many different things while beginning to read including animals, telling time, days of the week, months, seasons, money, and the environment.

In addition there are many more songs and subjects to choose from in English, French, and Spanish, including:

Songs and Activities for Early Learners
Kids learn about the alphabet, farm animals, counting, family members, parts of the body, days of the week, colors, fruit, opposites, and shapes through these lively, action-packed songs. Available as a packaged kit with a lyrics/activity book, with fun assignments and crossword puzzles!

The Presidents' Rap from Washington to Bush

Here's a great way to learn American history using classical, gospel, light opera, rock, pop, and rap. Eleven catchy songs written in the musical style of each historical period. This kit comes with illustrated lyrics book.

How

E-mail

Where

vmall@hookup.net

Subject

send jordan catalog

Ain't Whistlin' Dixie

Billed as "the Internet's first collection of folk music in album format," this is a suite of 12 Irish and American folk tunes, executed by David Walker on the ocarina and penny whistle. The tunes are available in two forms, AU and AIFF. AIFF is better quality but not as widely supported, and the music in AIFF format will take 2-3 times longer to bring down to your system.

The music itself is sharp and lively and well-recorded, and I suspect that most of you will not ever have heard anything like it. James Galway frequently plays a piece or two on the penny whistle during his concerts, and this is very much the same thing.

There is a little background discussion about the instruments, including a photo of the instruments and the artist's dog, which is as close as it comes for album art. David considers himself a local artist, and this format is an interesting way for such a local artist (and he is a good one indeed) to obtain fame at the national or even international level. One hopes more of this sort of recording will appear on the Web over time.

You'll need Mosaic 2 to support the push buttons that initiate the music download—and of course, sound hardware to reproduce it!

How

Mosaic 2

Where

http://mothra.nts.uci.edu:80/~dhwalker/dixie/

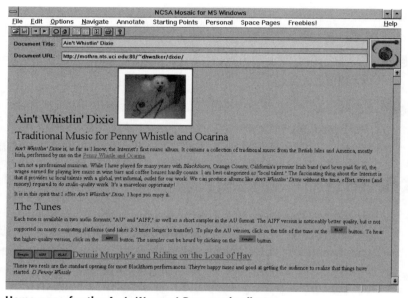

Home page for the AIN'T WHISTLIN' DIXIE music album

A Gentleman and a Sailor

Here's a site just for parrot heads: all the songs and writings of Jimmy Buffett. So crank up the blender, make a few boat drinks, and enjoy a pirate's look at the world.

How

FTP

Where

147.226.57.196

Go To

pub/Buffett/lyrics/chords

Who's the Boss?

For millions of rock fans, Bruce Springsteen is simply "The Boss," with no other rocker coming close to matching his energy, dedication, and popularity. From his reputation for perfection in the studio to his legendary marathon road shows, Springsteen has managed to surprise and inspire his followers for over 20 years.

This mailing list is devoted to serious Boss fans only. There are some great discussions about Springsteen's albums and concerts, as well as the latest information on bootlegs, concert info, film projects, and more.

How
E-mail

Where
backstreets-request@uvaarpa.virginia.edu

Ask For
Subscription to Backstreets

Compact Disc Connection

Regardless of your tastes in music, you'll find what you're looking for at the Compact Disc Connection. Their online catalog of over 80,000 titles is the ultimate in CD selections. Come see how easy and convenient it is to find and order your favorite CDs.

How
Telnet

Where
cdconnection.com

Login
No ID or password is necessary

Go To

Follow the login instructions

Beatlemania

In 1964, they sparked a pop explosion that still influences musicians today. With the loss of John Lennon, it's now impossible for the Beatles to provide the reunion that many millions of fans having been begging for since the group's breakup. But in Cyberspace, Beatlemania is still alive and kicking. Check out this site for loads of news, trivia, pictures, and more of the Fab Four that you can download for free.

How

FTP

Where

bobcat.bbn.com

Go To

pub/beatles/*

Music Bonanza

Crank up the volume! This is the best place to go to get hundreds of song lyrics, tablature music, artist bios, pictures, and more from your favorite rockers, rappers, and toe tappers.

How

FTP

Where

ftp.nevada.edu

Go To

pub/*

Where to Find More Goodies

The *Computers and Software* section explains where to find lots of sound clips in SoundBlaster, MIDI, and other formats, along with programs and utilities for composing and playing music on your computer.

The *Kid Stuff* section explains where to find the lyrics to songs from your favorite Disney films.

FREE $TUFF

When we talk to God, we're praying. When God talks to us, we're schizophrenic.

Lily Tomlin

Religion and New Age

Bible Bootup

Prayerware on the Internet! Put this program in your AUTOEXEC.BAT file and get a random quote from the King James Bible every time you turn on your computer. (Maybe this will help prevent crashes.)

How
FTP

Where
oak.oakland.edu

Go To
pub/msdos/bible/biblepop.zip

If the Spirits Move You

Spirit-WWW is a Web-based collection of resources for the paranormal/New Age/metaphysical subculture. There are a number of articles on the channeling of higher entities, out-of-body experiences (OBEs), yoga, UFOs, Theosophy, Eastern philosophies, Light studies, healing and alternative medicine, New Age music and music reviews, spirit-related art, and even movies.

There is a search engine attached to the page that lets you look things up in the material presented. For this you'll need Mosaic 2, which supports forms and command buttons.

As good as the page is, connections to the host machine seem to be very slow, and regardless of how fast your own link is into the Internet, accessing Spirit-WWW will take some time. Consider it a meditation.

How
Mosaic 2 (needs forms and command buttons)

Where
http://err.ethz.ch/~kiwi/Spirit.html

Paranormal resources on the Web

Electric Mystic's Guide to the Internet

This site contains a directory of over 200 major religious documents, archives, and services available on the Internet, including reviews, books, dissertations, major sacred texts, software programs, electronic mail addresses, electronic journals, newsletters, online discussion groups, and more.

How

FTP

Where

panda1.uottawa.ca

Go To

pub/religion/electric-mystics-guide-v1.txt

Bar Mitzvah Planner

A bar mitzvah is an important time in a boy's life and can be a huge undertaking. How they were planned for thousands of years before computers we'll never know. But planning one now is a little simpler thanks to Bar Mitzvah Planner 1.0. This program helps you to keep track of expenses, guests, gifts, dates, times, whether your Aunt Alice will be able to attend, and whether she still refuses to sit next to your cousin Marvin after what he tried last time. You can even print mailing labels, expense reports, and guest lists by table.

How

Telnet

Where

fedworld.gov (see page 13 for instructions on how to download files from the Consumer Information Center)

Go To

BARMITZ1.ZIP

Vatican Online Art Exhibit

In addition to being a separate nation with all the rights and provisions accorded to a nation under the U.N. Charter, the spiritual focal point for millions of Catholics worldwide, and home to a priceless historical collection of Christian manuscripts, artwork, and other religious documents, the Vatican is now wired to the Internet. No, you can't E-mail in your confessions, but you can view and download an invaluable collection of rare documents and art. *Rome Reborn: The Vatican Library and Renaissance Culture* is an online religious art exhibit containing over 200 GIF files of the Vatican Library's priceless manuscripts, books, maps, and other historic documents.

How

FTP

Where

ftp.loc.gov

Go To

pub/exhibit.images/vatican.exhibit/*

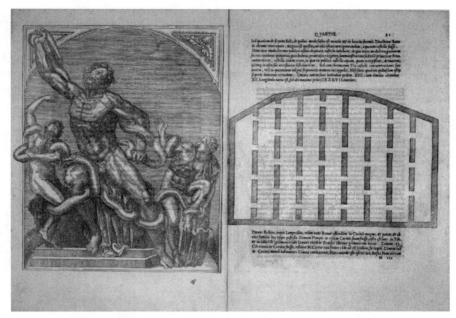

A sampling of GIFs available in the Vatican online exhibit

American Jewish Information Network

The American Jewish Information Network was formed to promote the use of electronic communication by the American Jewish community with other Jewish organizations worldwide. It is part of an international networking project that includes the Global Jewish Information Network in Israel and the British Jewish Information Network in Great Britain.

How

E-mail

Where

ajin@israel.nysernet.org

Ask For

Information on joining the Jewish Information Network

Buddhism

Originating in India around 500 B.C., Buddhism is the world's major religion, a fact that many Westerners find surprising. Find out more about the fascinating teachings of Buddha that have attracted more than 250 million followers worldwide—many are newcomers from the West. With this question and answer format, you'll discover the history of Buddhism, learn about karma, enlightenment, and many of the other beliefs and principles central to the Buddhist philosophy.

How

Gopher

Where

etext.archive.umich.edu

Go To

Religious.Texts
DharmaNet
Buddhism
q-and-a.zip

Koran

Made up of 114 chapters, the Koran (or *Quran*) is the primary holy book of Islam. Believers say it was given to Muhammad by God about 616 A.D. Maybe so, but it fell down this Gopher hole and is now yours for the reading.

How

Gopher

Where

etext.archive.umich.edu

Go To

Religious.Texts
Quran

King James Bible

Here's your very own copy of the Old and New Testaments from the King James Bible. This electronic copy makes searching for words and phrases a snap, so you can quickly find the scripture you're looking for.

How
FTP

Where
etext.archive.umich.edu

Go To
Pub

Religious.Texts

King James Bible

Bible Studies

Here's a site where you can get many different translations of the King James Bible. Download a copy in Latin, French, German, Swahili, and many more.

How
FTP

Where
nic.funet.fi

Go To
pub/doc/bible/*

---

4 Yohane Mbatizaji alitokea jangwani, akahubiri kwamba ni lazima watu watubu na kubatizwa ili Mungu awasamehe dhambi zao.

5 Watu kutoka sehemu zote za Yudea na wenyeji wote wa Yerusalemu walimwendea, wakaziungama dhambi zao, naye akawabatiza katika mto Yordani.

6 Yohane alikuwa amevaa vazi lililofumwa kwa manyoya ya ngamia, na mkanda wa ngozi kiunoni mwake. Chakula chake kilikuwa nzige na asali ya mwituni.

7 Naye alihubiri akisema, "Baada yangu anakuja mwenye uwezo zaidi kuliko mimi, ambaye mimi sistahili hata kuinama na kufungua kamba za viatu vyake.

The New Testament's Book of Mark in Swahili (in case you didn't recognize it)

Directory of Religious Texts

Here's a listing of religious texts you'll find scattered around the Internet. Download a copy to help you along your electronic pilgrimage as you search for religious documents stored throughout Cyberspace.

How
FTP

Where
coombs.anu.edu.au

Go To
coombspapers/otherarchives/soc-science-directories/religious-e-texts-93dirctry.txt

Online Bible Quiz

Now we'll find out who paid attention in Sunday school and who slept through it. Here's a file that will test your knowledge of the Old and New Testaments.

How
FTP

Where
oak.oakland.edu

Go To
pub/bible/bibleq.arc

Online Hebrew Quiz

Not another quiz! Afraid so. This one tests your knowledge of the Torah, other historical and prophetic books, and psalms that make up the Hebrew Bible.

How

FTP

Where

oak.oakland.edu

Go To

pub/msdos/hebrew/hebquiz.zip

Christian Denominations

These fascinating essays discuss the beliefs, rituals, and customs of many different Christian denominations. You'll learn about the common roots that the many branches of Christianity share and what makes each of them different.

How

Gopher

Where

wiretap.spies.com

Go To

Wiretap Online Library
Religion

LDS Scriptures

Compared to many age-old religions, The Church of Jesus Christ, Latter-Day Saints (LDS) is still a swaddling babe. However, it's currently one of the world's fastest growing religions. This site contains some of the most important LDS scriptures online:

- Book of Mormon (file bom.zip)
- Doctrine and Covenants (in file d-and-c.zip)
- Pearl of Great Price (in file pofgp.zip)

How

FTP

Where

oak.oakland.edu

Go To

SimTel/msdos/mormon/*

Where to Find More Goodies

The *Books and Literature* section includes a few sites that include online copies of religious texts and religious writings.

The *History* section tells you where to access an online version of the Scrolls from the Dead Sea exhibit as well as documents, pictures, books, and related works about the Holocaust.

And the *Travel and Geography* section explains how to view the Vatican's online art collection.

FREE $TUFF

We owe a lot to Thomas Edison. If it wasn't for him, we'd be watching television by candlelight.

Milton Berle

Science and Technology

Online Periodic Table

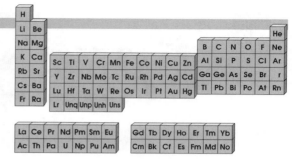

This utility displays the Periodic Table of Elements as classified by atomic weight. What better way to learn the elements than online. Plus, since the table is only a mouse click away, it's always handy when you need it.

How

FTP

Where

garbo.uwasa.fi

Go To

pc/science/peri20.zip

Better Living through Chemistry

Here's a sparse but useful directory of programs for chemists and serious high school and college chemistry students. The table of elements database (elements.zip) is a great study aid for students, and the atomic-structures display program (mv130.zip) is a good tool for students and professionals alike.

How

FTP

Where

oak.oakland.edu

Go To

SimTel/msdos/chemstry/*

Filename	Description
ccal9116.zip	Chem Calculator for MW, %composition, equations
chemical.zip	Molecular modeling program CGA or EGA
chemref.zip	Chemistry database/reference
elements.zip	Study aide: data on the 106 chemical elements
jmr1_20.zip	Raytrace renderer for organic molecules
jmr_bs.zip	Molecule ball and stick demo
molwin20.zip	WIN3: Read atomic coordinates display molecule
mv130.zip	Displays and prints pictures of atomic structures
periodic.zip	Displays the periodic table of elements, (EGA)
teddemo2.zip	Thermodynamics: Kinetic gas model simulator
torg320.zip	Simulates qualitative organic analysis
vsdem101.zip	3D molecular modeling set for Windows (DEMO)

A sampling of files from SimTel/msdos/chemstry/*

Dissect a Virtual Frog!

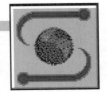

No muss! No fuss! No formaldehyde! Learn all you ever wanted to know about frog innards without ever having to croak one of the poor critters. You have your choice of two separate virtual frog dissections, one (from Lawrence Berkeley Laboratory) using computer-generated images of a frog, and the other (from the University of Virginia) using actual photographs and even movies of a dissection of a real frog.

Both simulations are free—with the caution that like all good simulations, these are very resource-intensive. You'll need plenty of RAM, and plenty of patience on any link slower than ISDN speed. Even at 28.8 Kbps, you'll wait several minutes for some of the bitmaps to move down the line, especially at times of the day when net traffic is intense.

At this writing, the Lawrence Berkeley dissection will not work with the Windows version of Mosaic due to a bug in the current Alpha 6 release of Mosaic. This bug may be corrected by the time you read this; Mosaic is a project in motion and it's certainly worth a try. The Mac and X Windows versions work fine.

These simulations are excellent prototypes of the sorts of cutting edge (no pun intended) educational software that will be widely used over our eventual Information Superhighway.

How

Mosaic (requires the 2.0 release; the Windows version of Mosaic might not work with the Lawrence Berkeley dissection!)

Where

http://curry.edschool.Virginia.EDU:80/~insttech/frog/ (University of Virginia)

http://george.lbl.gov/ITG.hm.pg.docs/dissect/info.html (Lawrence Berkeley Laboratory)

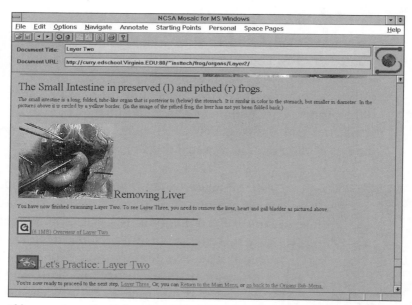

This page from the University of Virginia's dissection provides a detailed view of the frog, along with excruciatingly detailed descriptions of the steps to take to probe its innards

Earth Sciences Resources

Originally, the Internet's sole basis for existence was to allow scientists of all fields to communicate with one another, and in spite of its exponential growth, the Internet has never lost site of its original charter. Today, more scientists are linked into Cyberspace than ever before, and much of their data is yours to review and download. And it's not just limited to computer science or physics; the Earth sciences are equally well represented.

Whether you're a geologist, meteorologist, oceanographer, paleontologist, or work in any of the other Earth sciences fields, you'll find dozens of resources on the Internet. This list of Internet resources is useful to anyone interested in the Earth sciences. Use it to point you in the right direction.

How

Gopher

Where

gopher.unc.edu

Go To

Internet Dog-Eared Pages

Guides to the Internet

Internet Resources for Earth Sciences

Software for Biologists

Most of the software here is for professional biologists, although some of the programs are great for college students, and the longevity analysis program (hrap.zip) is a valuable aid for just about anybody who wants to live long and die beautiful.

How

FTP

Where

oak.oakland.edu

Go To

SimTel/msdos/biology/*

Filename	Description
bbhlp087.zip	Windows 3.x Help file for molecular biologists
bbseqf12.zip	Converts sequence file formats in Windows 3.1
bed100.zip	Molecular Biology input feedback echo w/speaker
biomrf.zip	Demos cumulative small chg, Darwin evolution
bldfsh21.zip	Identify and graphically display fish
cura22.zip	Autocidal pest control simulation for Windows 3
esee109e.zip	DNA/protein multiple sequence editor Ver 1.09e
gep208a.zip	WIN31: Simulation of biochemical pathways
gsrc208a.zip	Source code of GEP208A.ZIP simulation package
hrap.zip	Diet+Lifestyle=Longevity: compared w/average
pedhlp13.zip	Pop-up hypertext help for PEDRAW13
pedraw13.zip	Scientific pedigree-drawing program
stages14.zip	Research tool predicts spermatogenesis cells/t
tierra40.zip	Create virtual worlds and virtual life
toxins.zip	Snake and toad toxins, diagnosis, and treatment

Complete listing of files in SimTel/msdos/biology

The Electronic Zoo

This archive was originally created by Ken Boschert, DVM, to provide information and resources for all-things animal, especially for biologists, zoologists, and veterinarians. But it's grown to become more all-encompassing. Here you'll find online issues of *Discover* magazine, *Environmental Magazine, Issues in Science and Technology, Journal of Neuroscience*, subscription sites for professional organizations and newsletters, and a variety of other scientific and medical information.

How

FTP or Mosaic

Where

wuarchive.wustl.edu (FTP) or http://netvet.wustl.edu/On:\e-zoo.html (Mosaic)

Go To

doc/techreports/wustl.edu/compmed/elec_zoo.x_x (the x's indicate the current version)

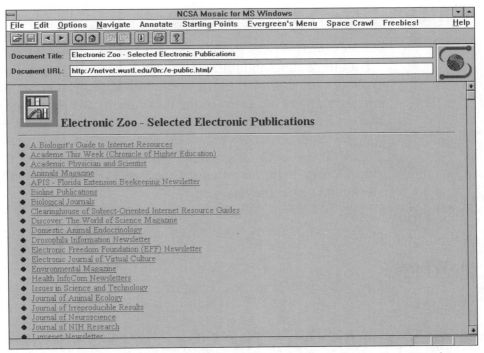

A partial listing of electronic publications available at the Electronic Zoo (from Mosaic)

Shake, Rattle, and Roll

In the twentieth century, earthquakes worldwide have accounted for the deaths of millions of people and caused inestimable billions of dollars in damages. While most likely you only hear about the big ones, the fact is dozens, often hundreds, of earthquakes occur every day, most of which can only be detected by sensitive instruments.

Now on the Internet you can get up-to-the-minute reports on tremors around the world, including locations, times, magnitudes, and more.

How

Finger

Where

quake@gldfs.cr.usgs.gov

Batten Down the Hatches

A quick quiz: What's the difference between a hurricane and a typhoon? About three thousand miles. Hurricanes occur in tropical regions while typhoons are confined to the northern Pacific. But no matter what you call them, these are some of the most destructive forces of nature, with violent winds and torrential rains that can level coastal cities.

This FTP site at Colorado State University provides the latest tropical storm forecasts for the Atlantic Ocean and surrounding land, along with storm updates as they happen.

How

Finger

Where

forecast@typhoon.atmos.colostate.edu

Are You Missing THE LINK?

The Link, a newsletter devoted to academic computing, is published five times a year. It features articles about networking, new trends in computing, and innovative uses of computing, as well as highlights of new technology or features in the areas of microcomputing, training, and mainframes.

How

E-mail

Where

zdeb@umd2.umd.edu

Ask For

Subscription to The Link

Climb Aboard NETTRAIN

When you read reviews of computer books, make sure you consider the source. Not much validity can be put into the words of someone reviewing a UNIX programmer's guide who the day before was reviewing cookbooks.

If you want in-depth analysis and critiques of the latest computer books hitting the shelves, NETTRAIN is definitely for you. Subject-matter experts working in the computer industry pull no punches in these informative analyses of technical books.

How

E-mail

Where

listserv@ubvm.cc.buffalo.edu

Ask For

sub nettrain *<your name>*

New Book Bulletin

Get your free subscription to the *New Book Bulletin*, an informative catalog jammed with the latest and greatest computer books. Published by Computer Literacy Bookshops, with the world's largest selection of computer books, each quarterly issue reviews more than 100 new computer titles, including books on:

- Software engineering
- Power PC topics and PowerMacs
- Internet guides and directories
- LANs

How

E-mail

Where

info@clbooks.com

Ask For

Free subscription to the New Book Bulletin (be sure to include your postal address)

Note: You can also get an online copy of the *New Book Bulletin* by FTP from ftp.netcom.com in pub/clbooks/*

Simulation Digest

Computer simulation is used to represent the real world by a mathematical model solved by a computer. For instance, population growth for a specific area can be predicted through a mathematical model run on a computer.

Global warming, community disasters, even forest fires can all be simulated on computer. *Simulation Digest* covers the field of computer simulation.

How

E-mail

Where

simulation-request@cis.ufl.edu

Ask For

Subscription to Simulation Digest

Here's a Shocking Site

Plug in here for more than a dozen software packages for electrical and electronics engineers. There's a program to perform common electric calculations, Windows and DOS-based circuit simulation packages, and quite a bit more.

How

FTP

Where

oak.oakland.edu

Go To

SimTel/msdos/electric/*

Filename	Description
daubwave.zip	Wavelet analysis program, w/C source
demand20.zip	Calculate/report residential electrical demand
dlanet.zip	Polynomial/circuit analysis, w/built-in editor
dspice0b.zip	128Mb Spice 2g6 circuit simulator. Req. 386/387
dspice0s.zip	C Sources for Spice 2g6. Req. DJGPP and F2C_LIB0
dwelcalc.zip	Residential NEC electrical code calculations
ee11.zip	Electrical engineering design and analysis program
Electrc3.zip	Performs most common electrical calculations
faisyn20.zip	Electronic filter synthesis program
filtry10.zip	Aids in design of active and passive filters
logisy30.zip	Logisym v3.0 Digital Logic Simulator, VGA req.
Pspic54a.zip	PSpice analog/digital circuit sim for Win 3.1, 1 of 3
pspic54b.zip	PSpice analog/digital circuit sim for Win 3.1, 2 of 3
pspic54c.zip	PSpice analog/digital circuit sim for Win 3.1, 3 of 3
rascal10.zip	Antenna design and analysis using GUI
sim120bn.zip	SIMIC logic and fault simulator,1 of 2
sim120dc.zip	SIMIC logic and fault simulator, 2 of 2
simic104.zip	SIMIC logic simulator, student version 1.0.4
spctr3e2.zip	386/486 vers. of SPICE 3e2 ckt simulation pgm.
Sspice10.zip	Symbolic SPICE: Circuit analyzer and approximator
timecrft.zip	WIN3: Electronic circuit timing diagram generator

The complete listing of files in SimTel/msdos/electric

STIS Information System

The Science and Technology Information System allows you to access information on upcoming workshops, minority study programs, research information on biology, anthropology, and lets you perform sophisticated text searches on National Science Foundation publications and its database of award abstracts.

How

Telnet

Where

stis.nsf.gov

Login

public

Life Sciences

Whether you're a scientist or are just interested in scientific research, you'll find a huge assortment of resources here you can browse and download. There are dozens of resources for biologists, anthropologists, or anyone interested in the life sciences. You'll find pointers to AIDS information, shareware, grants and research information, links to the World Health Organization, and much more.

How

Gopher

Where

una.hh.lib.umich.edu

Go To

Science
Life Sciences

Anatomy 101

If your idea of studying anatomy back in college consisted of hanging out on sorority row, then this site is *not* for you. But if you're interested in viewing some excellent photographs and illustrations on human anatomy, you won't be disappointed.

How

FTP

Where

grind.isca.uiowa.edu

Go To

image/gif/anatomy/*

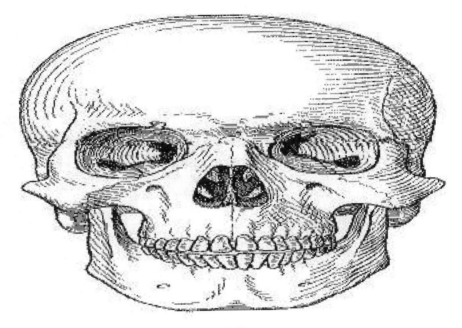

An illustration downloaded from image/gif/anatomy

Math That's Definitely Not for Dummies

Stay away from this site if you're math-phobic or even arithmetically challenged. This directory is for serious number lovers. You'll find several curve fitting programs, FORTRAN routines, calculation packages, and logic programs for truth tables and syllogisms.

How

FTP

Where

oak.oakland.edu

Go To

SimTel/msdos/math/*

Filename	Description
cf427.zip	Curvefits: Science/engineering curve fitting
cla20.zip	Displays info on a matrix (incl. Jordan form)
csa.zip	Analyzes categorical syllogisms for validity
delp.zip	Fast non-iterative multi-exponential fitting
delpx03.zip	Time-series data analysis, exponential fitting
femis.zip	Finite-Element Matrix Interpretive System
fit2-117.zip	Linear/non-linear modeling, analysis/transform
fsultra1.zip	High quality, fast, versatile random numbers
grad.zip	Automatic Differentiation of FORTRAN programs
lgsolv1.zip	FORTRAN routines: Solving Large Linear Systems
lie43.zip	Lie analysis of differential equations, exact solutions
linsys10.zip	Solves linear systems (including homogenous)
lp100210.zip	Linear programming, solve optimizing problems
mafia2b.zip	Complex math calculation utilities package
poly.zip	Fits polynomial equations to data points
polyrt1.zip	Finds polynomial roots, w/interactive graphics
sgnls313.zip	Illustrates signal processing concepts w/plots
spectr20.zip	Spectral analysis of random time series
tsfima12.zip	Programs of financial mathematics, T.Salmi
ttm120.zip	Make/print truth tables from keyboard input

A partial listing of files in SimTel/msdos/math

Let's Get Physical

Physicists, chemists, astronomers, and other physical scientists are sure to find this Gopher an invaluable source for research. There's information on oceanic and atmospheric research, publications from the National Science Foundation, a database for compiling extragalactic research, and *The Scientist*, a newspaper for research scientists.

How

Telnet

Where

hepburn.ipac.caltech.edu

Login

ned

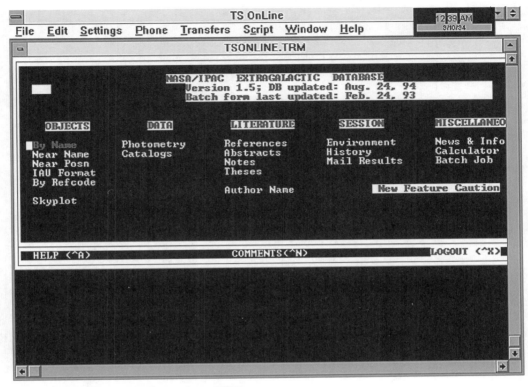

The NASA/IPAC Extragalactic Database (NED)

For FORTRAN Fans

Ten years ago, we thought the FORTRAN language was showing signs of age, but it refuses to die. For many mathematics and science professionals, FORTRAN is still the programming language of choice. Here's a site with more than two dozen FORTRAN libraries, code checkers, and programs.

How
FTP

Where
oak.oakland.edu

Go To
SimTel/msdos/fortran/*

317

Filename	Description
bcf7713b.zip	Fortran-77 compiler/linker/debugger ver 1.3b
elmop10.zip	Library of MS FORTRAN callable DOS functions
extenpr.zip	FORTRAN pgm - Extend the precision of decimals
f2c-exe.zip	Binaries & Libs for f2c Fortran to C converter
f2c-src.zip	Source for f2c, Fortran 77-to-C converter
fatdos.zip	Library to access DOS from within FORTRAN
fckdemo1.zip B	Forcheck: Fortran code verifier DEMO (Win3.1)
fort-fmt.zip	Text to FORTRAN FORMAT statement generator
ftnchk26.zip	Robert Moniot's Fortran source code checker
ftnchk27.zip	Robert Moniot's Fortran source code checker
fv121s.zip	FORTRAN library for video-regs/pop-down-menus
fxt120.zip	FORTRAN Exploration Tools: Source analysis
libry51.zip	FORTRAN library - mathematics and thermodynamics
linpkdrv.zip	Complex math equations for Fortran - 1 of 2
linpklib.zip	Complex math equations for Fortran - 2 of 2
pcrng.zip	Random number generator for use with Fortran
random.zip	Random number generator - one of the best
tidy642.zip	Clean up Fortran-77 programs, w/Fortran source
token.for	Tokenize a string (C 'StrTok') for Fortran 77 (ASCII file)
weekday.for	Calc weekday of date, Zeller Congruence algorithm (ASCII file)

Caption: Complete listing of files in SimTel/msdos/fortran

Biologist's Guide to Internet Resources

From anatomy to zoology, there are hundreds of Internet sources that biologists can tap into for current research data and other news. Here's a list from Yale University that includes information on newsletters, mailing lists, newsgroups, software archives, and lots more.

How

E-mail

Where

smith-una@yale.edu

Go To

nfcunemp.txt

Hurricane Tracking Software

The Atlantic Hurricane Tracking System (version 5.0) provides detailed information on recent Atlantic-region hurricanes and displays the information in several graphical map formats and tables. The shareware version available here is a good educational tool, but it provides data only for the years 1982 through 1992. For more current and more historical hurricane information, you'll need to register the software.

Two registered versions are available. Both registered versions include a 107-year database that can be used to examine hurricane history for a particular region and to make forecasts for anticipated hurricane activity.

The professional version includes several features that aren't available with either the shareware or registered hobbyist versions. Some of these features include:

• 27 detailed tracking charts covering the entire East Coast of the U.S.
• Optional county boundaries on maps
• Optional highway and road depiction on maps
• Ability to enter and display National Hurricane Center information

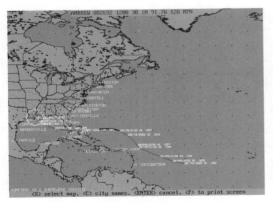
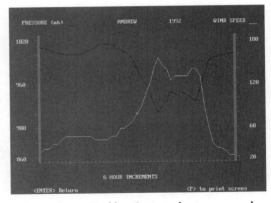

These two screens from the shareware version of the Atlantic Hurricane Tracking System show maps and statistics of 1992's Hurricane Andrew

How

FTP

Where

rigel.acs.oakland.edu

Go To

SimTel/msdos/weather/hurrtr50.zip

Medical Practice Guidelines

The National Library of Medicine, sponspored by the National Institutes of Health, has recently put its clinical practice guidelines and other consumer guidelines on the Web for you to download. This resource is for physicians and consumers alike and includes documents to help physicians, patients, and familes make difficult decisions about patient diagnosis and care, avoid malpractice situations, and determine how well physicians are serving the needs of their patients.

The online site is actually called HSTAT (for Health Services/Technology Assessment Text) and includes quick-reference guides for physicians and several brochures for consumers.

How

Gopher or Mosaic

Where

gopher.nlm.nih.gov (Gopher) or
http://www.nlm.nih.gov/hstat (Mosaic)

Go To

NLM Online Information Services
HSTAT

USMetric Will Make You a Convert

Advocates of the metric system have been predicting for years—make that decades—that the United States would be fully converted to the metric system by . . . 1985. Hmmm, that's one date we're not likely to make.

While our archaic system of measurement is no longer state of the art, few are willing to change. But computers have simplified so many other parts of our lives, maybe it's time someone made learning the metric system a little easier for us dinosaurs of the old school.

Well whaddaya know, someone has! Before you know it, USMetric will have you wearing 37.854-liter hats, giving pinches to grow 2.54 centimeters, and walking 1609.344 meters for a Camel.

How

FTP

Where

oak.oakland.edu

Go To

SimTel/msdos/science/usmetr11.zip

Where to Find More Goodies

For more science, see the *Education and Teaching Tools* and *Games* sections, which point you to educational software and games that deal with science themes. The *Environment and Nature* section also includes some great topics for ecologists, naturalists, biologists, and environmentalists. The *Space and Astronomy* section explains how to get lots of great astronomy and simulation software. *Travel and Geography* points you to still other programs that provide education and information about U.S. and world geography.

If "technology" translates into "computers" for you, be sure to browse through the *Computers and Software* section for access to hundreds of programs and computer utilities.

FREE $TUFF

You know why women are better car buyers than men? Because they're not ashamed to admit that they don't know diddly about cars.

Tom and Ray Magliozzi (Click and Clack)

Shopping

Electronic Car Showroom

Toyota Motor Sales of America has joined Ford Motor Co.'s Lincoln-Mercury Division on the Internet to develop a business information center in Cyberspace. Located at the Electronic Newsstand's Electronic Car Showroom, this information center is for anyone interested in learning more about Ford and Toyota's products and services. You can even download pictures of automobiles and send E-mail requesting more information.

How
Gopher

Where
gopher.internet.com

Go To
The Electronic Newsstand
The Electronic Car Showroom

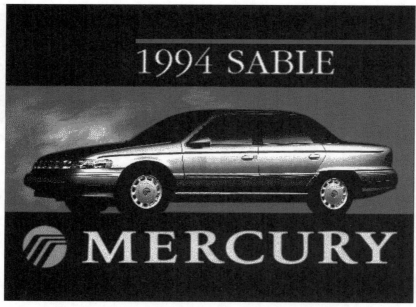

The Mercury Sable, downloaded from the Electronic Car Showroom

Consumer's Resource Handbook

Here's information that will help you resolve complaints about a service or product. The names and addresses of more than 750 corporate headquarters are found in the *Consumer's Resource Handbook*, and in many cases, the name of the person to contact is listed. Most listings also include toll-free "800" numbers. Be sure to download parts 1 and 2.

How

Telnet

Where

fedworld.gov (see page 13 for instructions on how to download files from the Consumer Information Center)

Go To

CRH-I.TXT

CRH-II.TXT

Let Me Talk to the Manager

Two out of every three dollars spent in America's marketplace are spent by individual consumers. These dollars help create jobs and contribute to a strong national economy. The ingenuity of American business in meeting the demands of consumers has helped keep our markets growing and made our lives more comfortable. But sometimes problems arise. *How to Be a Smart Consumer,* published by the United States Office of Consumer Affairs, explains the resources available to consumers with complaints or problems, including addresses and telephone numbers of sources to contact for help.

How

Telnet

Where

fedworld.gov (see page 13 for instructions on how to download files from the Consumer Information Center)

Go To

CRH-I.ZIP

Perfume D'Europe

Parfums D'Europe has, for the last seven years, been a distributor of designer miniature fragrances to stores across Canada. Five years ago they started to sell by mail order, with thousands of Canadians purchasing their products. Now their fragrances are available to you through the Internet.

These fragrances are from the leading French, Italian, Canadian, and American designers, and they come in convenient travel sizes so they can be easily placed in your purse or suitcase. Some of their most popular fragrances include: Creation, Creature, Armani, and Perry Ellis. Send for your free catalog.

How

E-mail

Where

vmall@hookup.net

Subject

Send eperfume catalog

Children and Games Go Hand in Hand

Kids will have hours of fun playing with the great products from Hand in Hand. These high-quality toys, games, puzzles, books, videos, and nearly 400 other items are yours to order from this terrific selection of children's products. All items are selected by childcare experts for their durability, quality, safety, and, of course, fun. Order your free catalog.

How

E-mail

Where

fsd@world.std.com

Ask For

Free catalog (be sure to include your postal address)

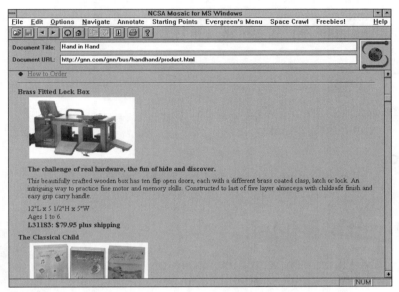

This brass-fitted lock box is great for one- to six-year-olds to practice their fine motor skills

Image Is Everything

Images International provides corporate identification and promotional advertising products to businesses throughout North America. Make sure your clients know how to reach you by putting your name and phone number at their fingertips. Some of the promotional products Image International carries are pens, caps, mugs, keychains, mailing labels, and much more. Send for your free catalog.

How

E-mail

Where

vmall@hookup.net

Subject

Send IMAGES catalog

Purchase Tickets Online

Plan your next vacation online. You can purchase your tickets, reserve hotels and rental cars, and get information about your destination all through your computer—all with *no* service charges.

How

E-mail

Where

travel@msen.com

Ask For

Information on buying airline tickets online

Say It with E-Mail

Merlin Olsen would be proud of this service: Sending flowers anywhere in the world is easy on the Internet. This unique service lets you order flowers and other gifts from the convenience of your computer. Concerned about how a bouquet will look? You can even download pictures of the arrangement you're sending so you're sure it's perfect. Now there are no excuses for not sending flowers.

Pictures of arrangements can be downloaded so you can see what you're buying

How

Gopher

Where

florist.com

Go To

Grant's FTD Flowers on the Internet

Branch Information Services - Ordering Flowers

Home Inventory Manager

If your home is damaged or robbed, the first thing the insurance company wants—and the last thing you want to deal with—is a list of valuables. With all the other headaches you're dealing with, the last thing you want to do is try to remember everything you own(ed). You're bound to have some items slip through the cracks in your memory.

To avoid this situation, use Inventory Manager 1.0. This home inventory program is a great tool for organizing and keeping track of your valuables around the house. You can list your inventory by item and location, add and delete items whenever necessary, include each item's value and serial number, and more.

One note of caution: Make sure you save your file to disk, then store the disk at your office or safety deposit box in case anything happens to your computer. Better safe than sorry!

How

Telnet

Where

fedworld.gov (see page 13 for instructions on how to download files from the Consumer Information Center)

Go To

HOME1.ZIP

Handcrafted Gifts

Remember when you'd visit Grandma on the farm? As soon as you arrived, you smiled and marveled at how the house always smelled inviting, like fresh-baked oatmeal cookies or raisin bread, and how she always seemed busy with some stitchery, weaving, or other arts-and-crafts project. What, you *can't relate?* Okay, so maybe we're a few decades out of synch. Grandma really lives in a condo that always smells like Chinese take-out, and her idea of crafts is sticking decals on her rollerblading helmet.

But you can still experience the good ol' days at McCrerey Farm of Pennsylvania, where you'll find lots of handcrafted dolls, arts and crafts supplies, and traditional gifts to order. With this catalog, you can fill your house with beautiful country collectibles—no thanks to your too-contemporary, "with-it" Grandma.

How
Gopher

Where
telerama.lm.com

Go To
Shopping Plaza

Gifts from the Great White North

You don't have to battle the elements to bring a little of the beauty and history of Canada into your home. Check out some of the fun and eclectic gifts available from this virtual trading post. You'll find a wide assortment of Canadian crafts and gifts available from Red Eagle, including Indian blankets, handcrafted decoys, hats, hand-knit sweaters, and more. No, the goods aren't free, but you *can* send for your free catalog.

How
E-mail

Where
vmall@hookup.net

Subject
Send redeagle catalog

Get Me to the Church On Time

Weddings and headaches: The words are almost synonymous. As the Big Day nears, thoughts of elopement become more and more appealing. Wouldn't it be

wonderful if you could turn some of the 1,001 things you're trying to keep track of over to a professional wedding planner and let her manage them for awhile? Here's a program that can help.

Wedding Planner 3.1 will keep track of who's invited, who's RSVPed, and who will manage your wedding expenses, maintain appointments, and organize many of the other details that can get lost in the shuffle of this once (maybe twice) in a lifetime event. It will help to ensure your wedding is as special as it can be. It will even help get you away on your honeymoon. After that, you're on you own.

How

Telnet

Where

fedworld.gov (see page 13 for instructions on how to download files from the Consumer Information Center)

Go To

WEDDING3.ZIP

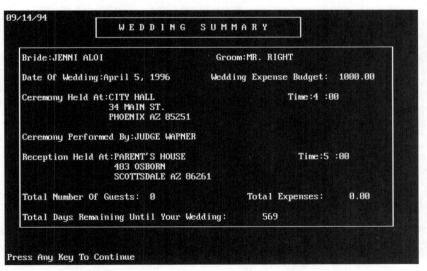

A view of Wedding Planner 3.1

U.S. Marshals Property List

The United States Marshals Service offers a variety of forfeited property for sale to the public. For more information, including a National Sellers List of federally contracted service providers, download this file.

How

Telnet

Where

fedworld.gov (see page 13 for instructions on how to download files from the Consumer Information Center)

Go To

SELLERS.TXT

Where to Find More Goodies

The Internet is essentially one big shopping mall, so every section in this book offers you the opportunity to go shopping without spending a penny (except for your online connect charges, of course. Especially try the *Computers and Software* section to find out where to find hundreds, even thousands, of free software packages, and the *Kid Stuff* section for software written especially for kids as well as catalogs and actual free products for kids.

For free catalogs, try the *Education and Teaching Tools* section for a video catalog from Allegro Computer Services, *Food and Cooking* section for available catalogs on foods and beverages, and the *Music* section for a kids-music catalog from Jordan Music Productions and the online Compact Disc Connection.

Also, the *Household and Consumer Finance* section includes lots of sites that provide information on how to avoid getting ripped off when you shop for everything from homes to automobiles.

FREE $TUFF

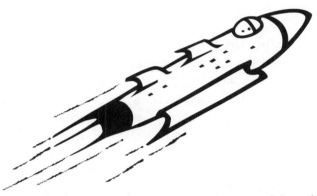

You just won't believe how vastly, hugely, mind-boggling big [space] really is. I mean, you may think it's a long way down the road to the chemist, but that's just peanuts to space.

Douglas Adams, from THE HITCHHIKER'S GUIDE TO THE GALAXY

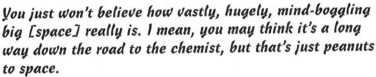

Space and Astronomy

333

Dance of the Planets

This program has a somewhat archaic user interface, which makes it a bit difficult to learn. But once you do, you'll realize how much you can do with the program. It's quite a sophisticated planetarium viewer for serious and experienced astronomy buffs. You can view the orbits of heavenly bodies within our solar systems and display detailed astronomical information about the planets.

The program graphically displays the solar system in a way that looks much like what you woud see with a low-powered telescope. You can scroll to different portions of the solar system, just as if you were scanning the skies from your backyard observatory. You can also accelerate and decelerate the speed of orbits within the solar system, from real-time to many times faster so that you can actually watch the orbits of various heavenly bodies in space. You can even zoom in on different portions of the universe for a closer look at objects there and their rotations and other movements. This program is a demo only, although it's a good one. If you want the full package, you can send the requested donation to the author.

How
FTP

Where
oak.oakland.edu

Go To
SimTel/msdos/astronmy/dance13.zip

Look, up in the Sky!

SkyMap 2.1 is the latest version of the popular Windows 3.1 planetarium program. With SkyMap, you can view the stars as seen from anywhere on Earth and from any date between 6000 BC and 8000 AD. Besides stars, you can display planets, asteroids, comets, deep space objects, and more. Plus, click on any object you're viewing to instantly display information about it. You can even print high-quality charts.

How

FTP

Where

garbo.uwasa.fi

Go To

windows/astronomy/skymp21a.zip

Fun with Binary Stars

This program is limited in its scope, but for what it does, it does well. The program graphically illustrates the diffraction rings for a specific binary star. You enter the name of the star for which you want graphical output, along with data about the star. This tool is for serious astronomers and astronomy students. Frankly, most kids won't have the slightest idea what to do with this program, but for the curious student, it's a great way to stimulate further interest in astronomy.

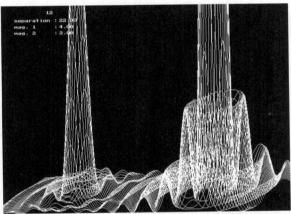

A graphic portrayal of diffraction rings for a binary star

How

FTP

Where

oak.oakland.edu

Go To

SimTel/msdos/astronmy/diff_dra.zip

The Comet Shoemaker-Levy Home Page

The week of July 16, 1994, a comet got into a fight with Jupiter—and lost. The show, however, was spectacular, and was an event that has never before been observed by human eyes. The comet was torn into about 20 chunks by the tidal forces of Jupiter's massive gravitational field, and one by one the fragments blasted into the planet,  leaving scars in its cloud belts that could be seen on Earth with telescopes as small as three or four inches of clear aperature.

The best views were not by human eyes at all, but with the highly sophisticated electronic imaging systems of the world's great observatories and the repaired Hubble Space Telescope in Earth orbit. Tens of thousands of beautifully detailed images are being circulated among astronomers, and the very best of these are available, for free, on the Internet.

NASA has set up a home page for the Shoemaker-Levy event, and through it, you can read about the collision and (most important for the bulk of us non-astronomers) gape at the awe-inspiring electronic images of the giant planet and its brand-new blemishes. The visible light images show distinct violet disruptions in the cloud tops, but the infrared images show searing vortices of heat energy created as the comet fragments were vaporized in Jupiter's upper atmosphere.

Those of us here today may or may not live to see anything quite this peculiar in our solar system again. Certainly we don't want to get a *whole* lot closer to an event like this—but for now, it is something you should *not* miss!

How

Mosaic

Where

http://navigator.jpl.nasa.gov/sl9/sl9.html

A chain of Comet Shoemaker-Levy 9 impact sites on Jupiter
Infrared image in the 1.7 micron methane band taken using MAGIC
on the 3.5-m telescope, Calar Alto Observatory, Spain, 19/07/94   MPIA

The description provided with the photo says it all

Orbits and Bytes

This program simulates the views when orbiting various planets and other
heavenly bodies, and provides a fairly sophisticated set of customizing
options. The more you know about astronomy, the more fun and benefit
you'll get from this program.

How
FTP

Where

oak.oakland.edu

Go To

SimTel/msdos/astronmy/sfs101.zip

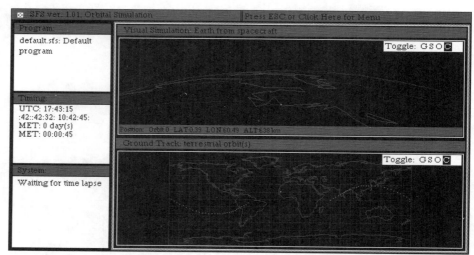

A view of the Earth from an orbiting craft

NASA SpaceLink

Maybe Cyberspace isn't the final frontier, but you can use it to boldly go along on NASA's Shuttle missions. Telnet here to get the latest information about current and planned missions, satellite tracking, and more. It's like having a front row seat at Mission Control.

There's lots of information on NASA educational services, instructional materials for the classroom, news and ongoing reports on NASA projects, answers to frequently asked question, and hot topics about space.

How

Telnet

Where

spacelink.msfc.nasa.gov (you can also Gopher and FTP to this site with the same address)

Login

guest

A Windows Planetarium

Here's a neat little program that displays a grid along with astronomical bodies for different coordinates, based on a view from the Earth's equator, the celestial equator, or the galactic equator. The program provides lots of viewing options, including the ability to speed up celestial movement so that you can actually observe the movement of planets, stars, comets, and other heavenly bodies. This program requires Windows 3.1 running in enhanced mode.

How

FTP

Where

oak.oakland.edu

Go To

SimTel/msdos/astronmy/skyvw30.zip

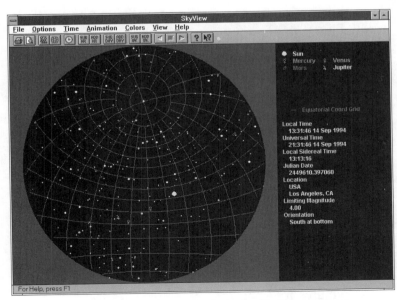

An equatorial view of the solar system from the SkyView program

Astronomy for Couch Potatoes

Maybe you'd like to look at the stars, but the idea of standing outside in the middle of the night getting a crick in your neck doesn't appeal to you. Ah, modern technology comes once again to your rescue. The sky's the limit at this archive of all things astronomy. You'll find shots of Earth rises, moon sets, deep space, eclipses, and other galactic objects. There are also programs, documents, and other files on amateur astronomy. Download a few, turn the lights off in your home office, and ooh and aah over these GIFs. Who needs a telescope?

How

FTP

Where

nic.funet.fi

Go To

pub/pics/space/*

Next Stop, the Moon

Get lost in space at this virtual museum depicting a visual history of U.S. space flight. There are lots of great shots of the Apollo and Space Shuttle missions, the Hubble Space Telescope, and more.

How

FTP

Where

ftp.cis.ksu.edu

Go To

pub/pictures/jpg/space/*

An Apollo lunar expedition module begins its descent to the moon, downloaded from pub/pictures/jpg/space

EnviroNet

Run by NASA/GSFC and the University Research Foundation, the EnviroNET Space Environment Information Service provides information about spacecraft interactions with the space environment for you to download.

How
Telnet

Where
envnet.gsfc.nasa.gov

Login
envnet

Password
henniker

Teach Your Kids to Rotate

Solar Pix is actually a neat little program that teaches kids about the relative rotation of the planets around the sun. The graphics are CGA quality, so the animation is a bit primitive, but it does the job. You (or your kids) can elect to view the rotation of 1 to 5 planets, and you can use the up and down arrow keys to speed up or slow down the rotation.

How

FTP

Where

oak.oakland.edu

Go To

SimTel/msdos/astronmy/solar.zip

Where to Find More Goodies

More photos and information on space and astronomy are available in the Smithsonian Institution's art collection, which is explained in the *Arts and Culture* section. The *Kid Stuff* section tells you how to obtain free space stickers and a space puzzle from NASA. If you've got Mosaic and really want to get spaced out, try the ASTROGOF Project at Rennes' University of France, as mentioned in *The Tightwad's Guide to Mosaic*.

FREE $TUFF

*If people don't want to come
out to the ballpark, nobody's
going to stop them.*

Yogi Berra

*The only reason I would take up
jogging is so that I could hear
heavy breathing again.*

Erma Bombeck

Sports, Recreation, and Hobbies

Start Your Jogging Program

JOG is an exercise program to help you keep track of your running miles, times, progress, and other calculations. Now if someone would only write a program to run the miles for you.

How
FTP

Where
garbo.uwasa.fi

Go To
pc/ts/tsjog15.zip

Go Fly One!

"Jason's Web Kite Site" is an Australian nexus for things that fly on strings. Most people don't realize it, but kites are following technology into the 21st century, and are no longer a couple of willow switches with newspaper glued on. Today's kites use exotic materials like carbon fiber rods (or for teeny-weeny little kites, solid boron rods no thicker than needles!) and ripstop nylon. They can be big, too—sometimes eighty or a hundred feet long. Jason's kite photo collection gives a pretty good feel for the diversity of modern kites. It's presented as a list of thumbnails that you can click on to download the full-sized images. The page also provides pointers to some kite newsletters, newsgroup rec.kites, and other kite sites elsewhere in the world.

Our favorite aspect of this page is the section on kite buggying, which involves sitting in a low-slung motorless go-kart sort of thing, pulled by one or two relatively big kites. The buggies can move as fast as fifty miles per hour, with the pilot's hindquarters only three inches off the ground.

They know how to have a wild good time in Australia, that's for sure.

How

Mosaic

Where

http://www.latrobe.edu.au/Glenn/KiteSite/Kites.html

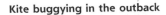
Kite buggying in the outback

Party On, Cyber-Style!

Any excuse for a party! Now there's no excuse for not being organized for one. If you're going to have a party, you've got to learn to party responsibly. And that means making sure there are plenty of Cheetos and onion dip. Party Planner 1.1 helps you organize the big event, keep track of your number of guests, how much the bash is going to cost, what got broken, what to tell your neighbors about what happened to their cat, and lots more. Definitely worth the money (it's free).

How

Telnet

Where

fedworld.gov (see page 13 for instructions on how to download files from the Consumer Information Center)

Go To

PARTY-11.ZIP

Grand Central Station for Electronic Rail Fans

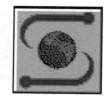

This home page is a sort of "virtual magazine" for rail fans, including to some extent model railroaders. It is an eclectic compendium of links to many places storing information pertaining to rail travel, rail hardware, and rail modeling.

Among many other things, the page has links to a database of all known surviving steam locomotives in the U.S. and Canada, rosters of diesel locomotives in use at American railroads, pointers to non-Internet rail-related BBSs, lists of rail-related newsgroups, and a database of folk songs, many of which are about trains and rail travel. There is a selection of railroad maps available for downloading, and although there's no charge, a few of the maps are disappointingly available only to educational institutions. One of the most unique items here is a discussion of how to use stepper motor technology in model railroads.

When we read the page, there was a wonderful (if large: 214K) image of the Reid Brothers Cumberland Valley N-scale layout that looks as much like a photo of a real rail scene as any layout shot we've ever seen. An absolutely gorgeous piece of work, and in N-scale yet—realism is tough when you get that small.

This is *the* resource for online researchers interested in rail topics.

How

Mosaic

Where

http://www-cse.ucsd.edu/users/bowdidge/railroad/rail-home.html

The Reid Brothers N-scale layout

Flight Planner Makes for Smooth Flying

If man were meant to fly, airlines would have cheaper drinks and better in-flight movies. In any event, here's a program that will at least make piloting your own plane a little easier.

Load your location, destination, type of aircraft, and other detailed flight data in this easy to use flight planner, then let your computer do the rest. It calculates your estimated fuel consumption, route, whether you're overloaded, and lots of other important information for getting you safely back to Mother Earth. Great for pilots of all levels.

How
FTP

Where
oak.oakland.edu

Go To
pub/msdos/database/pcpp121d.zip

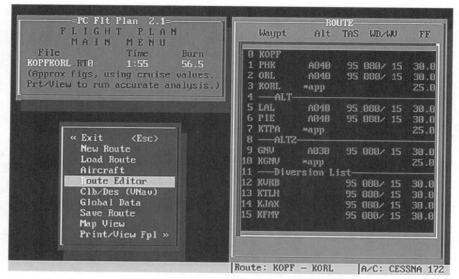

This flight planner will help small-plane pilots map out routes and destinations, and make their flights as safe and worry-free as can be

Football Facts and Stats

Monday-morning quarterbacks will find plenty of ammo to arm themselves for those all-important football debates at the water cooler. Here's a great place to find up-to-date football scores, schedules, and rankings for all your favorite NFL teams.

How

Finger

Where

nfl@spam.wicat.com

Look Out Belooooow!

If freefalling from an airplane at 12,000 feet, performing aerobatics, and opening a parachute a mere 2,000 feet from ground zero (which is 2,001 feet from looking like so many bug parts splattered across someone's windshield) appeals to you, you should try to get psychological help *immediately*. If that doesn't cure you, buy a *large* insurance policy, send it to our attention, then check out the FAQs, GIFs, and thrilling stories at this site devoted to those who have had their common sense surgically removed.

How

FTP

Where

ftp.eng.ufl.edu

Go To

skydive/*

The first step's a doozy, but after that it's all downhill, downloaded from skydive

Take Me Out to the Ballgame

As we write this, the boys of summer are on strike—*again,* and the season's been cancelled. So what to do, sports fans? How about opening a box of Cracker Jacks and downloading the latest about your favorite major league baseball team? There are stats, records, info on trades, and more—and you won't have to cross a picket line to get there.

How

E-mail

349

Where

jtchern@ocf.berkeley.edu

Subject

MLB

It's in the Cards

Sport Card Catalog for Windows 1.0 helps you keep track of your sport card collection in as much detail as you need, including the year of issue, brand, card number, team, type, description, date and price of purchase, and more. The number of entries is virtually limitless. Other program features include the ability to search by any field, print, and much more. A similar format to a physical catalog book makes the program very easy to use. Online help messages are only a mouse click away. This program can be used by both beginners and advanced users.

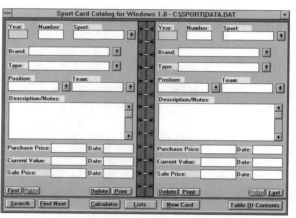

Use this screen to enter detailed info about each sport card in your ridiculously massive collection (the one Mom tried to throw out when you went away to college)

How

FTP

Where

garbo.uwasa.fi

Go To

windows/util/am_spc10.zip

Sports GIFs

If you're looking for great shots of your favorite athletes, look no further than this site. You'll find millions of bytes worth of sports GIFs, including basketball and biking, football and figure-skating, Jordan and judo, and the occasional swimsuit model thrown in for good measure.

How

FTP

Where

nic.funet.fi

Go To

pub/sports/PICTURES/gif/*

Brian Ivie, spiking for the 1984 and 1988 U.S. Olympic Volleyball Team, downloaded from pub/ sports/PICTURES/gif

Take a Powder

It's always snowing somewhere and here's where to go to find out how hard and how much. Downhillers, boogie boarders, snowmobilers, and snow bunnies alike will all want to Telnet to this site and get the latest ski conditions from around the world.

How

Telnet

Where

wind.atmos.uah.edu 3000

Login

No login ID or password is necessary

Minor League Baseball Schedules

It ain't *The Show*, but at least it's *a* show. If the major league strike of '94 prattles on into '95, the second- and third-tier players will be offering the only game in town. If you're a fan of the Albany-Colonie Yankees or the Binghamton Mets (and who isn't), you'll want to check out this freebie. You'll get schedules for A, AA, and AAA baseball teams.

How

Gopher

Where

etext.archive.umich.edu

Go To

Sports

Baseball

Majors or Minors

Schedule

NBA Action

Want the latest info on hot NBA prospects? Find out which players are hot and which will be warming the benches by checking out these NBA scouting and draft reports. Get the jump-shot advantage on your friends in figuring out which college player will be the next Shaq Attack.

How

FTP

Where

sunsite.unc.edu

Go To

pub/academic/athletics/basketball/pro/*

College Basketball

Sports fans are stat crazy, and nowhere is this more true than basketball. Broadcasting hoopsters even have analysts analyzing the analyzers. And if it's college stats you're after, look no further. Here's where to go for ratings, rankings, recruiting picks, and every other stat you can think of for the NCAA. This site is guaranteed to keep you amazing and annoying your buddies with little-known factoids, right through the Final Four.

How

FTP

Where

sunsite.unc.edu

Go To

pub/academic/athletics/basketball/college/*

Ice Hockey Comes to the Internet

The origins of hockey in Canada can be traced back to Ottawa, so it's fitting that the Ottawa Senators hockey club, "hockey's first dynasty," be one of the first NHL team wired to the Internet. Hockey fans will love the souveniers and memorabilia included in the Ottawa Senators Fan Pack available for the asking. This package includes a color photo of the team, logo stickers, information on the history of NHL hockey in Ottawa (a long and proud tradition), team schedules, and more. To receive this package, be sure you include your "snail-mail" address.

How

E-mail

Where

74507.1161@compuserve.com

Ask For

Send your request for an Ottawa Senators Fan Pack to Chris Whiting, Manager Information Systems. Include your name and postal address.

University of Hawaii's NHL Home Page

Perhaps it was serious ice envy that led the U of H to put together their dazzling collection of NHL photos, movies, statistics, and other information about the NHL. Tune in here and you'll find an answer to virtually any hockey question you can think of. You'll find the latest NHL scores, present league standings, 1994 Stanley Cup Playoffs matchups, and a link to individual home pages belonging to several NHL teams, and more.

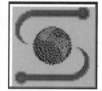

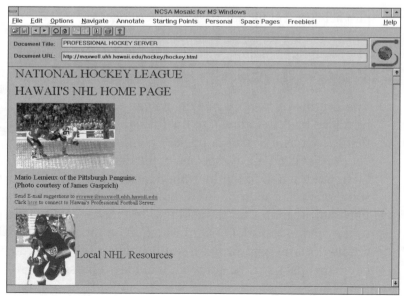

The NHL home page

The scores and standings are maintained automatically by a FORTRAN program that accepts game statistics and re-creates the html pages that present the data over the Web, so you can have pretty fair confidence that the page is up-to-date and accurate.

How
Mosaic

Where
http://maxwell.uhh.hawaii.edu/hockey/hockey.html

Sports Schedules

Sports fans will love this site about as much as sports widows will hate it. Here, you'll find the playing schedules for every major sport, including the NBA, NFL, NHL, and MLB. You don't ever have to miss another game!

How
Gopher

Where
gopher.bsu.edu

Go To
x-Professional Sports Schedules

Puttin' on the FINS

FINS: It sounds like an acronym out of a James Bond flick or even *Get Smart*—maybe a super-secret evil underground spy organization. Actually, this is an under-*sea* organization. FINS stands for Fish INformation Services—a resource for sophisticated aquarium hobbyists and pros. The emphasis here is on saltwater fish and aquariums, but the full spectrum is represented. You'll find pictures, movies, disease diagnoses and treatments, product vendors, catalogs, and much more.

How
Mosaic

Where
http://www.actwin.com/fish/index.html

A Kole Tang from the Reef Aquarium collection

Philatelic Facts

Catalog your stamp collection in as much detail as you need with Stamp Catalog for Windows. Catalog your stamps by

- Country of issue
- Description
- Catalog number
- Value
- Date
- Price of purchase

and more. An unlimited number of entries can be added. The program supports searching by any field, printing, and many others. A similar format to a physical catalog book makes the program very easy to use, intuitive, and straightforward. Online help messages are readily available. This program can be used by both beginners and advanced users.

How

FTP

Where

garbo.uwasa.fi

Go To

windows/util/am_stc10.zip

Go Speed Racer

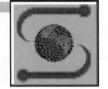

Here's a great site for automotive racing enthusiasts. The r.a.s. Racer Archive, from the University of Hawaii of all places, provides news and information on Forumla One, Indy car, and NASCAR racing. This is a very graphically oriented site, with lots of photos and drawings of cars and drivers.

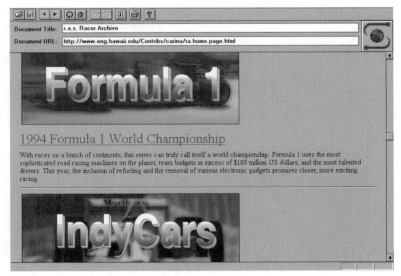

From the r.a.s. Racer Archive home page

How

Mosaic

Where

http://www.eng.hawaii.edu/Contribs/carina/ra.home.page.html

Where to Find More Goodies

If cooking is a hobby of yours, check out the *Food and Cooking* section for great recipe ideas and recipe planning software. The *Games* section also includes several items that might fit in with your recreational or hobby interests. And the *Health and Nutrition* section points you to software for health management, including running and other sports-related activities.

If you're a parent, be sure to check out *Kid Stuff* for recreational ideas for kids. If you're a musician, you'll find plenty to interest you in the *Music* section.

FREE $TUFF

It's amazing how many people see you on TV. I did my first
television show a month ago, and the next day five million
television sets were sold. The people who couldn't sell theirs
threw them away.

Bob Hope, 1950

Television

Dave's Top Ten

Is it *Late Night with David Letterman* or *The Late Show with David Letterman*? We forget. But we do know that this site is the place to go for all of Dave's Top Ten lists. We're still waiting for his Top Ten reasons to buy our book, but we're sure he'll have them any day.

How

Gopher

Where

quartz.rutgers.edu

Go To

Television and Movies
Letterman
Top-ten

Star Trek News and Reviews

"Dammit Jim—I'm a doctor not a net surfer!" If Star Trek is *your* thing, boldly go and send a request to this mailing list for reviews, commentaries, and ratings of all things Trekkie. Definitely for hard-core Star Trek aficionados.

How

E-mail

Where

listserv@cornell.edu

Ask For

subscribe trek-review-l *<your name>*

Beam Me Up, Scotty

If after two television series, at least five movies, countless conventions, and a number of ripoffs from wannabe's, you *still* haven't had enough of Star Trek, maybe these GIFs will finally do you in. You'll get plenty of pictures of all you favorite crew members, Klingons, and Romulons from both series and all the movies.

How

FTP

Where

ftp.cis.ksu.edu

Go To

pub/pictures/jpg/Startrek/*

Everyone's favorite green-blooded, pointy-eared, wild-and-crazy guy, downloaded from pub/pictures/jpg/Startrek

All Things Simpsons

No, this site isn't about O.J.—this one's about the *other* Simpsons. It contains plot summaries for different episodes, lists of guest stars, bios on the people behind the voices, and lots of trivia. So, do *you* know which character on the show calls Bart "little dude"?

How

FTP

Where

quartz.rutgers.edu

Go To

pub/tv+movies/simpsons

Couch Potato Heaven

Why wait for the reruns? Catch up on some of your most loved—and hated—television shows here in couch potato heaven. Get plot summaries for *Seinfeld*, *Twin Peaks*, *Quantum Leap*, and more.

How

Gopher

Where

wiretap.spies.com

Go To

Wiretap Online Library

Mass Media

Television

The Satellite TV Page

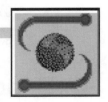

If you think that plates are for eating on but dishes are for watching, don't miss this beautifully executed nexus of satellite TV and radio information. You'll find schedules for most of the popular services, reviews of recent satellite events and equipment, a KU-band FAQ, and much more, including some technical

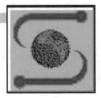
stuff so arcane that we weren't quite sure what it was for, like an Inclined Orbit Satellite Visual Prediction Appendix. If you know what it's for, well, here it is, entirely free and bigger than life.

Well worth reading on the less arcane side are Gary Borgois's articles on Satellite TV for the scrounger and alternative satellite programming.

How

Mosaic

Where

http://itre.uncecs.edu/misc/sat.html

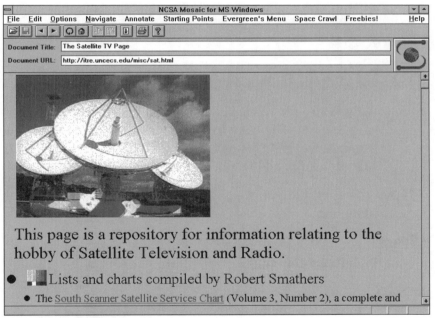

The Satellite TV home page

Home Base for Tube Addicts

The television pointers page gathers together links to a great many TV-related Web sites, with pointers to show-related material as diverse as *Mystery Science Theater 3000*, *Melrose Place*, *The Prisoner*, *The Late Show with*

David Letterman, Fawlty Towers, Max Headroom, Monty Python's Flying Circus, Babylon 5, Red Dwarf, The Simpsons, Seinfeld, and more. Science fiction seems to predominate, but hey, is this Cyberspace or what? Does anyone really want a *Roseanne* page?

In addition to show-related pages, there are pointers to reference pages like a satellite TV page, and a guide to broadcast programming sources. Web surf before you channel surf!

How

Mosaic

Where

http://www.cs.cmu.edu:8001/afs/cs.cmu.edu/user/clamen/misc/tv/README.html

Boob Tube Heaven

If you're a recovering couch potato, stay clear of this site; the temptation is too great. There are tons of television-related trivia, quotes, plot summaries, and FAQ listings for your favorite shows: *Seinfeld, The Simpsons, Cheers, ALF,* and lots more.

How

Gopher

Where

quartz.rutgers.edu

Go To

Television and Movies

The Complete TV Guide

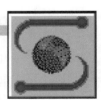

Billing itself as "The Ultimate TV List," this page is a well-organized collection of links to Web-formatted TV material. Most useful are schedules for *The Discovery Channel, The Learning Channel,* and other cable services.

The most fun pointer is to an interactive poll that asks a question and invites any and all Web surfers to respond. The question at this writing is "The best way to have gotten off Gilligan's Island," and the top answer is "Kill Gilligan and wait for the next episode. Now why didn't *we* think of that?

How

Mosaic (TV poll requires Version 2)

Where

http://www.galcit.caltech.edu/~ta/tv

Where to Find More Goodies

TV shows are often spun off into movies, and vice versa. Take *Star Trek* for example. So be sure to visit the *Movies* section for more information about your favorite stars, films, and just all-around video information. The shopping section also explains how to get free catalogs for popular and hard-to-find videos—including TV shows.

FREE $TUFF

Mankind has always had a yen to travel. Millions of years ago, Mankind would be sitting around the cave, eating raw mastodon parts, and he'd say, "Marge, I have a yen to travel." And Marge would agree instantly, because she had frankly reached the point where if she saw one more mastodon part, she was going to scream.

Dave Barry

Travel and Geography

Moon Travel Newsletter

Since 1973, Moon Publications has produced travel handbooks that are both cultural essays and consumer reports. Moon handbooks are packed with more information on historical background, outdoor recreation, restaurants, and hotels than any other series of travel guidebooks. *Travel Matters* is Moon Publications' quarterly newsletter, providing travelers with timely, informative travel news and articles. Regular features include travel trends, transportation, health, book reviews, and much more. Order your free subscription.

How

E-mail

Where

travel@moon.com

Ask For

Free subscription to Travel Matters newsletter. Be sure to include your name and postal address.

Put a Travel Agent in Your Computer

Travel Search, a database of hotels, resorts, and inns in the United States can help you make your travel plans, or at least make planning your travels a little easier. Enter when you'll be on the road and the city or region you'll be staying in, and let Travel Search provide information from its database on hundreds of places weary travelers can rest for the night. There's also lots of information about happenings in the area to check out after you're rested.

How

FTP

Where

oak.oakland.edu

Go To

SimTel/msdos/travel/travma33.zip

Travel Warnings and Consular Information

Up until October 1992, the State Department posted information called "Travel Advisories" (such as warnings, cautions, and notices) to various electronic mailing lists. Since then, the State Department's Bureau of Consular Affairs has revised the Consular Information Program, replacing "Travel Advisories" with "Travel Warnings" and "Consular Information Sheets."

- Travel Warnings are issued when the State Department recommends that Americans avoid travel to a certain country.
- Consular Information Sheets are available on every country in the world and include the location of the U.S. embassy or consulate, unusual immigration practices, health conditions, minor political disturbances, unusual currency and entry regulations, crime and security information, and drug penalties.

STATE DEPARTMENT TRAVEL INFORMATION - Haiti
===

Haiti - Travel Warning
August 3, 1994

The Department of State warns U.S. citizens against all travel to Haiti. On July 31, 1994, all commercial passenger air service to and from Haiti was suspended. The land border between Haiti and the Dominican Republic is closed. The U.S. Embassy in Port-Au-Prince is operating with a limited staff. All U.S. citizens who remain in Haiti are urged to register with the U.S. Embassy. The political situation in Haiti remains unstable with potential throughout the country for random violence, sporadic disturbances and criminal acts. The police and judiciary are unable to provide adequate levels of security and due process. This replaces the Travel Warning dated June 28, 1994 to reflect the suspension of all commercial passenger air travel to and from Haiti.

Excerpt from the State Department's travel warning for Haiti

How
Gopher

Where
info.umd.edu

Go To

Educational Resources

Academic Resources by Topic

United States and World Politics, Culture and History

World

Information for Those Planning to Travel Abroad

Travel Advisories (from the U.S. State Department)

Happy Trails to You

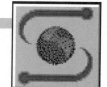

You can use your Web Crawler to search for hot mountain biking sites on the Web, or go straight to this site featuring information for bikers around Northern California. There are mailing lists for you to subscribe to, information about joining ROMP (Responsible Organized Mountain Pedalers), IMBA rules of the trail, and much more.

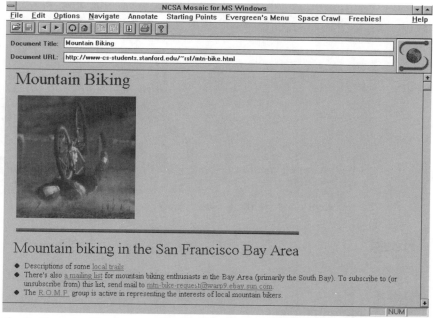

The thrills and spills of mountain biking are yours to check out on the Web

How

Mosaic

Where

http://www-cs-students.stanford.edu/~rsf/mtn-bike.html

Where In the World Is Kankakee, Illinois?

Can you get there from here? You bet! And with this handy utility to show you how, you'll never have to stop and ask directions to Aunt Ethel's again. It's like having your very own service station attendant in the back seat pointing the way to those hard-to-find, out-of-the-way, hole-in-the-wall places.

How

Telnet

Where

martini.eecs.umich.edu 3000

Login

<city, state>

You Can Get There from Here

Over the river and through the woods may be great directions to Grandmother's house, but what if it's over the river, down I-17, then hook into U.S. 89? Things start to get a bit complicated. And how much is this little jaunt going to cost you? Not to worry. With Roadways PC, you'll never take a wrong exit again. Simply select your starting point and your destination, then let Roadways do the rest. In seconds, you'll get detailed directions, including roads to take, cities you'll pass through, distance between cities, total mileage, and more. It will even calculate your costs based on gasoline prices or a cost per mile that you enter. Now if they could just do something about the food at those roadside diners . . . .

How
FTP

Where
oak.oakland.edu

Go To
SimTel/msdos/database/roadw254.zip

Be Sure to Slather on the Tanning Lotion

For those a little less modest and a lot less inhibited than the rest of us, here's a list of nude beaches for you to check out this summer. If you think it hurts *now* when you get sunburned . . . .

How
FTP

Where
rtfm.mit.edu

Go To
pub/usenet/rec.answers/nude-faq/beaches/*

GARDEN OF EDEN is a good change of pace or an alternative when the coast is fogged in. It is in Henry Cowell Redwoods State Park at a spot where the San Lorenzo River makes an "S" bend and has deposited sandy spots on both sides of this small stream ("river" is somewhat of an exaggeration!). This spot is not as nude as it used to be. It may sometimes be occupied by textiles, but you will sometimes find it deserted or nude or mixed. If it appears to be textile, try going upstream a hundred yards or so.

The park is about six miles north of Santa Cruz on Hwy. 9. To get there from San Jose, go south on Highway 17 towards Santa Cruz, but at Scotts Valley take the exit for "Mount Hermon Road/Felton". Take that through Scotts Valley and to the west. When you get to a T intersection (with a park ahead of you) turn right, then left at another traffic signal onto Highway 9 into Felton. Just as the town is fading out, you can turn left into the main parking lot for the park.

The bare facts on nude beaches around the world

372

Welcome to Europe

Europe! by Torpedo Software is a fun way to learn about Western European geography. Kids and parents will have fun learning about different countries, capitals, exports, and landmarks of Western Europe in this easy-to-use program. Race against the clock as you try to match names of countries with their locations on the map, or try to identify major landmarks. Did you fail? (We did.) That's okay, just try again. You can also order maps of all the continents in the world to help you become a virtual world traveler. Great warm-up before a trip to Europe.

How

FTP

Where

oak.oakland.edu

Go To

SimTel/msdos/geogrphy/eurv15.zip

What's Goin' Down—Under, That Is

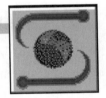

Ever wonder what a laughing kookaburra looks like? Would you like to know what you'll find when you walk the Aboriginal Trail at the Australian National Botanic Gardens? Did you even *know* there was an Aboriginal Trail at the Australian National Botanic Gardens? Did you even know there *was* an Australian National Botanic Gardens?

Well, there is, and if you're planning a trip to Australia, the Gardens are a must-see. But before you go, browse around at this site, which provides a wealth of information for visitors and potential visitors. Many of the brochures that you would receive when you arrive are also available here, online.

How

Mosiac

Where

http://155.187.10.12:80/anbg/birds.html

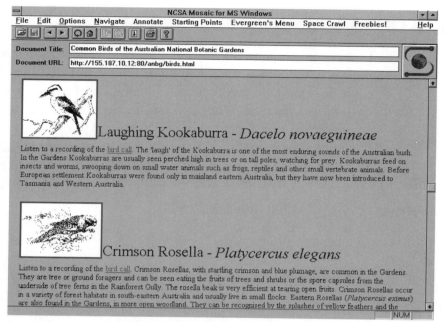

A page from the Australian National Botanic Gardens

An Online Atlas

Atlus is a geography program that gives you information about cities and states in the U.S. Maybe you know your name and address (telephone number, too), but how well do you know the state capitals? Take this quiz and find out. You may be surprised (or embarrassed).

How

FTP

Where

garbo.uwasa.fi

Go To

windows/util/atlus.zip

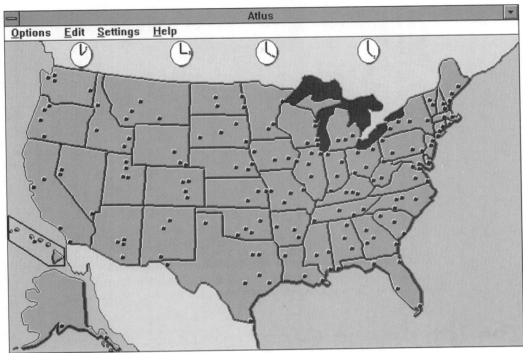

This map from Atlas identifies major cities in all 50 states (there ARE 50 of them, right?)

How I Spent My Summer Vacation

Forgot your camera? No problem. Just tell everybody you took *these* pictures on your last vacation. There are spectacular shots of Monument Valley, the Grand Canyon, London, beautiful deserts, lush forests, and much more.

How
FTP

Where
ftp.cis.ksu.edu

Go To
pub/pictures/jpg/scenery/*

375

A guest appearance of The Golden Gate Bridge, often shrouded in fog, downloaded from pub/pictures/jpg/scenery

The Ultimate in Geography

Want to make learning geography fun? Then Ultimate Geography from Ultimate Software is the program for you. With colorful maps and lots of trivia, you can make learning about the U.S. as fun as playing video games. With Ultimate Geography, you get:

- Quizzes on states and capitals
- Information about the U.S. as a whole, or by state (broken down by population, crime, growth, and more)
- Trivia about each state, such as the state flowers, mottos, birds, and other official info
- Addresses of state tourism offices so you can get even more information

The quizzes let you keep track of high scores so you can play against your friends or try to beat your own best score. Now, if they would just come out with a game for learning geometry . . . .

How
FTP

Where

oak.oakland.edu

Go To

SimTel/msdos/geogrphy/usgeo110.zip

Where to Find More Goodies

The *International Affairs* section is probably the best section to check out before you visit to another country, and it provides a wealth of sites and information to just plain help you learn more about other cultures.

And *The Environment and Nature* section explains how to find the latest weather information for Australia.

Also, the *Business and Careers* section explains where to acces an online database of telephone area codes from around the world as well as ZIP codes for any part of the U.S. If you're traveling in the U.S., check out *The Poor Man's Passport to Cyberville*, which explains how to access regional bulletin boards and even the Internet from local sites that don't require any connect-time charges.

The *Arts and Culture*, *Books and Literature*, *History*, and *Government and Politics* sections all include topics that are global in nature. And if you're planning to travel to a foreign country soon, check out the *Language and Linguistics* section for language-tutorial software.

FREE $TUFF

*If you save your money,
someday it will save you.*

Anonymous

The Tightwad's Guide To Mosaic

Hey, listen up: If this is the first time you've seen this icon, trust us—it won't be the last. It's the symbol of something that is nothing short of a revolution, and while it's only been out there for a little more than a year, it's already become the symbol of Internet's ascent to its role as the whole world's information superhighway.

We're talking about Mosaic, an Internet utility that we consider the most fun you can have for free.

(Well, maybe the second most. But that's a book you won't see us writing . . . .)

Here and there throughout this book, you'll see the icon near the right margin. It indicates a special type of Internet freebie, one that you have to grab using Mosaic. Recent statistics tell us that whereas up to 25 million people may be connected to the Internet as a whole, less than half a million are using Mosaic. So we're going to take a few pages here to shake up those of you who simply haven't caught on.

Nearly everything accessible so far with Mosaic is free.

Learning how to use Mosaic takes so little time that figuring it out (unless you're a New York lawyer billing $500 an hour) is essentially free.

For that matter, Mosaic itself is free. *Completely* free.

It's a tightwad's dream.

What Is Mosaic?

If you use Microsoft Windows, you should be familiar with Windows Help—the lifesaving window that pops up when you press F1. Mosaic is a lot like that help window. It's a software tool that opens up a window onto the Internet, and treats tens of thousands of items scattered around the Internet as one titanic, world-spanning online help file.

You may have been told that Windows Help presents you with a *hypertext document*, a new kind of electronic document file that has little connections from one place to another, and from one document to another. A hypertext document has words and pictures just like a book or a magazine or any other document you might read on paper. But hypertext has more: Here and there in a hypertext document are words or pictures that are colored or bordered a little differently from the others. Click on these special *hot links* with your mouse pointer, and your view will move to a different part of the document, or else to another document that provides you with an aside or a little more depth relating to the discussion at hand.

In a hypertext document, you can read it straight through without following any of the hot links. Or you can click on a hot link for more information, or to follow a thread of discussion more in line with your own interests and needs. You've probably done this time and time again, usually while you're on a tight deadline and are desperate to find out where it says how to format mailing labels out of information imported from a database. Maybe you considered Windows Help a drag—searching the online help file of your word processor is probably not your idea of engrossing leisure-time reading.

But think: What if you had an online help file that discussed virtually any subject you could think of, from the morals of ancient Greece to the development of aspirin to the lyrics of Jimmy Buffet? That would be a *lot* more fun.

Well, you've got it. It's Mosaic.

The World-Wide Web

Mosaic is a program, no different structurally from your word processor or spreadsheet. Like a word processor, you can use it to read a document. (*Unlike* a word processor, you can't use Mosaic to write anything—yet.) Think of Mosaic as a viewer. The things that it views are part of that world-spanning hypertext document mentioned above.

In 1989, the CERN nuclear accelerator laboratory in Switzerland came up with an idea: To tie scattered documents existing all across the Internet into a single, distributed hypertext document. This project and the resulting distributed document are called the *World Wide Web*.

Documents have always been available for downloading from the Internet. The difference is that the World Wide Web project defined a standard way of connecting documents that exist in different places on different computers around the world. The hot links you'll see in a Web document are actually addresses of documents stored somewhere else on the Internet. (Some of the hot links refer to other places within the same document as well.)

Each document on the World Wide Web is informally called a *page*. We say "Web pages" a whole lot more than "Web documents." (Why waste syllables?) A Web page may be connected to other Web pages, but nothing requires it to be. Some Web pages stand alone or are connected to only a handful of other pages.

It doesn't matter whether a page is connected to another. You can "hot link" to a page, or you can simply present Mosaic with its address. The address of a page is called its *URL (Uniform Resource Locator)*. The URL of all web pages begins with the prefix "http://". Other sorts of things available on the Internet have their own URLs, with a slightly different prefix.

What Web Pages May Contain

Most of us think of documents as being containers for ordinary text. There's a *whole* lot more to Web pages than text. A Web page may contain bitmapped images like photographs and drawn diagrams. More remarkably, Web pages may contain multimedia data—that is, sound data and even motion pictures. There are some limitations to multimedia content in a Web page, and we'll return to discuss those limitations shortly. But it's there—and if you have a machine set up to respond correctly to multimedia data, Mosaic will present you with quite a show.

A Web page may also contain fill-out forms and controls like buttons, allowing you to send information to a page's owners and to control the way a page presents information to you. Some interesting tools like the Web Crawler (more on this later) depend on your being able to enter data into a Web page through Mosaic.

Web pages are created using a document spec called the *HyperText Markup Language (HTML)*. HTML is an interesting subject in and of itself, but you don't really have to know a thing about HTML to use Mosaic effectively. Creating your own pages is another matter, but we don't have the time or the space to go into that in this particular book. Very shortly after this book is published, Coriolis Group Books will publish *Mosaic Explorer* and *Mosaic Explorer Pocket Companion*, which will go into a great deal more detail on Mosaic than we have room for here, and will explain how you can create your own Web pages in HTML.

Mosaic as a General-Purpose Internet Front End

Viewing Web pages is certainly Mosaic's primary mission. Its designers had something else in mind as well: creating a single, integrated, easy-to-use front end for all popular Internet services. They wanted Mosaic to be a typical Internet user's "place to stand" on the Internet, from which all popular services such as Gopher, WAIS, FTP, Finger, Telnet and (eventually) E-mail could be easily used, by selecting menu items and filling in dialogs.

People who come from technical backgrounds and have used the Internet for years sometimes forget how complex and cryptic the command structure for all of the various Unix-based Internet utilities can be. Ordinary people with no special interest in computing (much less in Unix, which seems to delight in its needless and completely pointless difficulty) tear their hair trying to get even the smallest thing accomplished. Just as Windows tamed the DOS command line, Mosaic's second but perhaps more important job is to tame the Internet and drive the Unix monster back into its cave forever.

The Line Speed Problem

This is probably a good time to confront the difficulty that most people have with Mosaic: The speed of the connection to the Internet. To use Mosaic effectively, you must have an Internet connection operating at a speed of at *least* 14.4 Kbps (14.4 thousand bits per second) and no less. The richness of Web pages demands a *lot* of data, and that data has to move completely over the net to your machine to be useful, much of it before Mosaic can even begin displaying it.

Even a small bitmapped image (often called a *thumbnail* in Web jargon) can take as many as 20,000 bytes, which can require fifteen seconds or more to transfer on a 14.4 Kbps line. That's time you must simply wait out. Larger images, of course, take even longer to transfer. We routinely wait three or four minutes for a moderately-sized image to come down the line, and have waited as long as fifteen. As you might expect, downloading takes longer during business hours when the Internet is being heavily used and you're competing for bandwidth with millions of other people. We try to bring images home after 8 P.M., when it's high noon over the mid-Pacific, and most of the Western world is fast asleep.

Things have gotten much better over the past year-and-change that Mosaic has been available. Fast modems (14.4 Kbps) are now routinely available for under $100. You can get an even faster modem that runs at 28.8 Kbps (optimally) over ordinary phone lines for about $400, and the prices have been going nowhere but down. These are informally called "Vfast" modems. At 28.8 Kbps, Mosaic starts to become truly compelling.

And of course, if you have a workstation connected to the Internet with a T1 or ISDN connection, well, you're in fat city. Ask at your employer or university if such connections are available, and how you might obtain one. In parts of the country you can even get ISDN connections brought to your home at a reasonable cost. (San Diego and other parts of California are among them.) At T1 speeds (basically 1.5 *million* bits per second) using Mosaic is nothing short of magical.

But even at 14.4 Kbps, Mosaic is an amazing and truly useful thing.

How to Get Mosaic for Free

Mosaic was originally developed at the National Center for Supercomputing Applications (NCSA) at the University of Illinois, and the university makes it available free of charge over the Internet. There are three versions: For X-Windows (Unix), Windows 3.1, and Macintosh. They can be obtained through Gopher or FTP, and reside at the following addresses:

X-Windows :

> ftp://ftp.ncsa.uiuc.edu/Mosaic/Unix/binaries/2.4/

Windows 3.1:

> ftp://ftp.ncsa.uiuc.edu/Mosaic/Windows/wmos20a7.zip

Mac 68K:

> ftp://ftp.ncsa.uiuc.edu/Mosaic/Mac/NCSAMosaicA6.68k.hqx

Power Mac:

> ftp://ftp.ncsa.uiuc.edu/Mosaic/Mac/NCSAMosaicA6.PPC.hqx

The newer releases of Mosaic for Windows 3.1 are 32-bit in nature, and require that Win32s be running. You can get the Win32s ZIP archive from NCSA at the same FTP site as Mosaic itself:

ftp://ftp.ncsa.uiuc.edu/Mosaic/Windows/win32s.zip

It's important for Windows people to keep in mind that these path names are case-sensitive! Don't play fast and loose with caps or you'll never find anything!

If for some reason you can't or don't want to run Win32s, you'll have to go back to Mosaic 1.0, which lacks some features but works well as a 16-bit Windows app. You can get Mosaic 1.0 through FTP at this address:

ftp://ftp.ncsa.uiuc.edu/Mosaic/Windows/old/wmos1_0.zip

All versions of Mosaic—even 1.0—are relatively resource-hungry; you must have at least 8 MB of RAM to run Mosaic, and the more the better, since Web pages are cached in memory as much as possible. A little later we'll explain how to set up Mosaic for Windows.

Mosaic's documentation is online, and once you make Mosaic work on your system you should spend a little time perusing it. Unfortunately, it isn't currently possible to download the Mosaic documentation to local hard disk (on your own machine) and run it locally from your hard disk. (We've tried this, and it doesn't work because some URLs specifying files on NCSA's own servers are "hard-coded" into the HTML document that contains the help information.) You'll have to read it as any other Web page, over the Internet. Furthermore, the current version of Mosaic for Windows does not implement Windows Help. This is one reason we're providing this information here, since Mosaic is a serious work-in-progress without the finish and polish of most commercial applications. In a year or two—who knows? But for now, the whole Mosaic field has a sort of Wild, Wild, Web feel to it.

Other Mosaic-Like Utilities

Mosaic was the first of its kind, and is still almost certainly the best. However, there are other browsers for the World-Wide Web that may also be used to do most of the same things that Mosaic can do.

As with Mosaic, most of these utilities are still freeware or shareware, and can be obtained from somewhere on the Internet without charge. One of the significant trends of late 1994 is that commercial software vendors are creating Mosaic-descendent products that do all of what Mosaic does, and then some. A few providers are creating their own non-freeware Mosaic clones for distribution to their subscribers. These Mosaic look-alikes are not exactly free: You pay for them out of your monthly or annual subscription fee. Some of them are very polished and mostly bug-free, as commercial software must be to compete. I advise you to use them if you can—but there's little advantage so far in buying a commercial Mosaic clone on the open market, when so many good Web browsers are available for free.

The oldest of the freeware Mosaic clones is called Cello, and it is available from the Legal Information Institute at Cornell. Cello was written by Thomas R. Bruce. It isn't entirely fair to say that Cello is a Mosaic clone, since it was created at about the same time as Mosaic, and has a very distinct look and feel of its own. Cello is a little easier to use than Mosaic, since it is entirely menu-driven, but on the flip side it has not been updated as aggressively and is thus not quite as powerful.

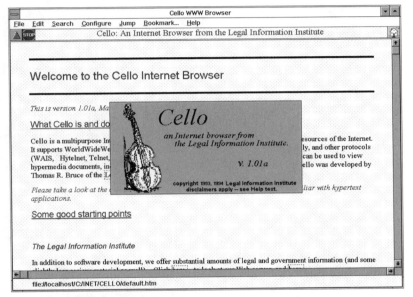

The Cello default home page

To obtain a copy of Cello, FTP from:

ftp://ftp.law.cornell.edu/pub/LII/Cello

One of the newest of the freeware Mosaic clones is WinWeb, which was designed specifically for Windows (Mosaic was ported to Windows from Unix) and created to be used on relatively modest machines, with as little as 4 MB of RAM. WinWeb, like Cello, is a relatively simple program written in the "plain style." It is fast, it does much of what Mosaic does (at least in terms of Web access) and it is free.

You can download your own free copy of WinWeb from EINET's Internet server:

ftp://einet/pc/winweb/winweb.zip

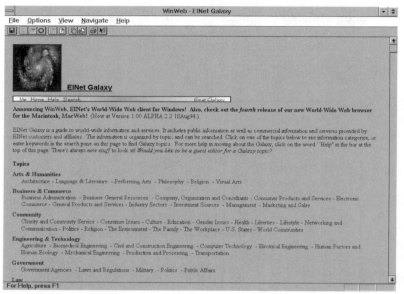

A view of the EINet Galaxy

Viewers and Where to Get Them

Mosaic is capable of handling a wide variety of different types of data. One way it does this is by allowing you to install independent viewers for different kinds of data files. These viewers are separate utilities that are not connected with Mosaic in any way, nor developed by NCSA.

The viewer system works like this: Mosaic associates a file type with a viewer utility. When a file of a given type is transferred down from the Internet, Mosaic launches the appropriate viewer with the name of the file so that the viewer will accept the file and "view" it. This system allows Mosaic to handle file types that didn't exist when Mosaic was designed. As long as a standalone viewer utility exists that can be launched as a child process to handle a data type, Mosaic will accept and handle that data type.

Viewing has become a more general term than applying solely to visual data. A "viewer" may also accept sound files and play them through appropriate sound hardware. It sounds odd, but get used to it: Mosaic can make use of a sound viewer.

NCSA has defined a very handy Web page that describes various viewers known to work with Mosaic. You can read about these viewers and then download them to your disk, in the form of ZIP files. The URL for this viewers page is:

http://www.ncsa.uiuc.edu/SDG/Software/WinMosaic/HomePage.html

To download the viewers from this page, set the **Options|Load to Disk** item on the menu. (Throughout this section we've combined multiple menu selections for ease of description. When you see two commands separated by a vertical bar, these are actually two commands that you select in sequence.) This forces Mosaic to write incoming data to a disk file rather than attempting to display it in some way. Then click on the hot link to the viewer of your choice. Mosaic will ask you for a file name through the standard Windows file name dialog, and then transfer the viewer ZIP file from NCSA to your disk.

Some of these driver ZIP files are very large; the MPEG viewer, for example, is 920K. Download big files after business hours, when net traffic has subsided.

Viewers are installed wherever you want them to be—but you must tell Mosaic where they are or Mosaic won't be able to use them. This is done through the MOSAIC.INI file that Mosaic maintains in your main Windows subdirectory. There is a section of MOSAIC.INI called **[viewers]** that contains path names to viewers for all the various types of files:

```
[Viewers]
TYPE0="audio/wav"
```

```
TYPE1="application/postscript"
TYPE2="image/gif"
TYPE3="image/jpeg"
TYPE4="video/mpeg"
TYPE5="video/quicktime"
TYPE6="video/msvideo"
TYPE7="application/x-rtf"
TYPE8="audio/x-midi"
TYPE9="audio/basic"
rem There can be any number of TYPEs
rem - just use TYPE10, TYPE11, . . . .
telnet="C:\INTERNET\bin\trmptel.exe"
tn3270="C:\INTERNET\bin\tn3270.exe"
application/postscript="c:\internet\ghost\ghostview %ls"
image/gif="C:\INTERNET\bin\lview31 %ls"
image/jpeg="C:\INTERNET\bin\lview31 %ls"
video/mpeg="c:\internet\wmpeg\mpegplay %ls"
video/quicktime="c:\internet\qktime\viewer %ls"
video/msvideo="mplayer %ls"
audio/wav="mplayer %ls"
audio/x-midi="mplayer %ls"
application/x-rtf="write %ls"
audio/basic="C:\INTERNET\bin\wplany %ls"
```

The paths shown here, of course, are those on one of our machines—
you'll have to edit MOSAIC.INI to make the paths reflect where on your
hard disk your viewers are actually installed. Note that the invocation
syntax is already there for you. The only part that you have to modify is
the actual path name showing where the viewers are installed on your
own hard disk.

Obtaining a SLIP or PPP Account

Unless you're tied directly into a digital cable of some sort (ISDN, T1,
etc.) through your school or employer, using Mosaic requires that you
have what is called a SLIP connection to an Internet provider. SLIP stands
for Serial Line Internet Protocol. It's simply a way of handling Internet-
style data transfers across a serial connection (that is, an ordinary phone

line). There is a very similar type of account called a PPP (Point to Point Protocol) which is newer and not as common. Either type of connection will do nicely for running Mosaic. An even more recent sort of connection is called CSLIP, for Compressed SLIP. CSLIP performs some real-time data compression that makes your serial line appear to operate more quickly than it does. Any time you can speed up a Mosaic connection, do it. Get CSLIP if you can.

Your Internet provider will be able to tell you what sort of connection it offers, how much it costs, and often exactly what you'll need to configure the connection. Many providers will hand you a preconfigured install diskette containing all the software you'll need for a SLIP or PPP Internet connection, often including Mosaic itself.

Your TCP/IP Stack

But in order to run Mosaic, you must have a piece of software called a *TCP/IP stack*. TCP/IP is a packet switching protocol that governs how packets of data are sent from your machine out onto the Internet, and from the Internet back down to your machine. Without it, Mosaic simply has nowhere to send its commands, and nowhere to go for incoming data. If you're connecting to Internet through a common serial modem, your TCP/IP stack is your "modem program," and handles things like interrupts for incoming and outgoing data.

A TCP/IP stack is usually a standalone utility. Apple provides one with the newest version of the Macintosh operating system (System 7.5), but Microsoft Windows 3.1 has none. (The upcoming Windows 95—what Microsoft is calling "Chicago"—will have TCP/IP built in, so a separate stack will not be necessary.) Fortunately, there are shareware TCP/IP stacks generally available for Windows 3.1. Before you can even begin configuring Mosaic, locate a TCP/IP stack for yourself. Most of the time, your Internet provider has one that they've had good success with, and since most of these items are freeware or shareware, there's rarely an extra charge for the software. Ask your Internet provider for a TCP/IP stack before you run yourself ragged looking for one!

One of the most popular is called Trumpet Winsock. This shareware product can be obtained without charge from the Internet via anonymous ftp from:

ftp://ftp.utas.edu.au/pc/trumpet/winsock/twsk10a.zip

In addition, from the same site there is an archive of cool Internet mini-apps for Windows:

ftp://ftp.utas.edu.au/pc/trumpet/winsock/winapps.zip

Configuring a TCP/IP stack is not trivial, as you'll see once you install one and start looking at its configuration screens. Most TCP/IP stacks, as with most modem programs like ProComm, require a script file that allows it to automatically dial up and log into your Internet provider's host machine. The first place to go for help is your Internet provider. Most of them can provide you with a script that handles login and logoff to their system, preconfigured with all the correct options.

If your employer or school provides you with a workstation to work at, ask if that workstation already has a configured Internet connection. Some people we know have spent their own money and struggled to set up an Internet connection from their home PCs, not knowing that their machines at work could access the Internet—for free—at the touch of an icon.

Riches are often where you find them. But as we like to point out in this book, if you don't look, you won't find them.

Setting Up Mosaic for Windows

If your provider hands you an install diskette set for their Internet services, you're home free. Just install it, and the install program will create a program group with icons for all the various Internet utilities that they provide—including, presumably, Mosaic. You won't have to fool with creating directories or program groups or anything else. Most providers are moving in this direction, but some of the smaller ones (including our own) have not quite gotten there.

If your provider doesn't give you Mosaic, or if you're setting up all your software on your own, your Internet configuration bears a little thought. Here's how we do it, and it works very well: Each of us has a subdirectory on our hard disk called INET. Beneath the INET directory is a separate directory for the TCP/IP stack, and also for each of the major Internet utilities we use, like Windows Eudora. Mosaic gets its own subdirectory, which we call MOSAIC2, because we're using the 2.0 version of Mosaic.

When you retrieve Mosaic from NCSA, it will be in the form of a ZIP file. Copy that ZIP file into the MOSAIC2 directory, and use a PKZIP compatible utility to extract all of the files into that directory. The executable is MOSAIC.EXE.

Create an Internet group for Windows. Within that group, create a program item for your TCP/IP stack. The working directory you specify in the Properties dialog should be the directory in which you place all of the files associated with the stack you happen to be using.

Create a program item for Mosaic that specifies MOSAIC.EXE, and for the working directory specify MOSAIC2.

If you have other Internet utilities that you intend to use (Eudora or HGopher, for example) do the same and create program items for each of them. (Cello and WinWeb, if you decide to use them instead of Mosaic, may be installed the same way.) All of the Windows utilities have their own icons embedded in their executable files, and when you create a program item for a utility, its icon will be displayed automatically.

Mosaic's INI File

Unlike your TCP/IP stack, which is generally configured entirely through dialogs, Mosaic takes almost all of its configuration information from a very large INI file stored in your WINDOWS subdirectory. This file is MOSAIC.INI, and it is one of the files stored in the MOSAIC.ZIP file you downloaded from NCSA. The first time it is run, Mosaic will copy MOSAIC.INI from your MOSAIC2 subdirectory into the Windows directory for you. You don't have to copy it there yourself. Each time you run Mosaic, it reads its INI file and configures itself "on the fly" from information in that file.

Ordinarily, you won't have to fool with MOSAIC.INI yourself. If you have some experience manipulating INI files, you might consider printing out MOSAIC.INI and reading it over. The most important fact about MOSAIC.INI is that all of its menus are stored there, and when you edit one of Mosaic's menus (as you will when you add an item to a hotlist, as we'll explain shortly), your changes will be immediately written back to MOSAIC.INI.

Launching Mosaic to Your Home Page

Running Mosaic is no more difficult than running any Windows program: You double-click on it. Before you do that, however, your TCP/IP stack must have logged into your provider's host system. *Without the TCP/IP stack, Mosaic is connected to nothing and can do nothing.* Run your TCP/IP stack, and do whatever must be done (typically, run a login script) that makes the stack dial into your Internet host and create a SLIP or PPP connection. Typically, your TCP/IP stack program is minimized once it logs in successfully, and remains as an icon in the icon bar at the bottom of your Windows screen.

With your TCP/IP stack logged in and ready to go, run Mosaic. Mosaic will run perfectly well in a Window, but we almost always run it zoomed, so that it occupies the full screen.

In its default configuration, Mosaic when executed will immediately go out onto the Internet and retrieve what we call its *home page*. A home page is just the Web page that Mosaic reaches for when you first run it. There's nothing special about a Web page that makes it a home page. You can define any Web page to be the home page for your personal copy of Mosaic.

If you obtained your copy of Mosaic from your Internet provider, the provider may have configured the copy of Mosaic you receive to fetch the provider's home page when you launch Mosaic. This is fairly natural;

when you run Mosaic, the first thing you'll see is your provider's page, which might contain announcements of new services, changes in dialup numbers, or useful things like that.

If you went out and retrieved Mosaic over the Net direct from NCSA, you will instead see NCSA's home page, which is shown below.

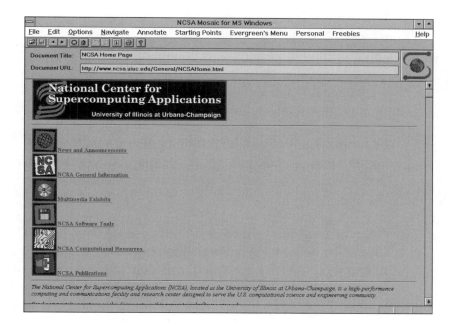

You may not want to wait several seconds for *anybody's* home page to load when you run Mosaic. We got that way after awhile; although we check into our provider's home page every so often to see if any important bulletins are there, we quickly found that nothing much changed from day to day.

What we did was change Mosaic's configuration so that it does not automatically go out and fetch a home page when you run it. When run, Mosaic simply presented us with a blank screen, and we could then choose a destination from one of the menus. This works well for us and may save you a little time on startup, especially if you're using a relatively slow connection.

Doing this requires that you edit MOSAIC.INI. This isn't difficult, since you won't have to hunt all over the INI file for things to change. Use Windows Notepad and load MOSAIC.INI. The first few lines in one of our copies of the file look like this:

```
[Main]
E-mail="someone@libre.com"
Autoload Home Page=no
Home Page=http://maple.libre.com/evergreen.html
Display Inline Images=yes
Grey Background=yes
Fancy Rules=yes
Round List Bullets=yes
Current Hotlist=Personal
```

(Your precise data will be different, of course.) Note the item Autoload Home Page. The default value is "yes." As you see, this one is set to "no." When set to "no," Mosaic will not load any home page when first run.

Note the third line, which defines the Home Page item. The one shown here is the home page belonging to our provider. You may edit this field to specify any Web page you like as your home page. Keep in mind that you can have a home page even if it doesn't load automatically. When you press the Home button in Mosaic's toolbar, the URL specified in the "Home Page=" item in MOSAIC.INI will be loaded.

One note: Don't edit MOSAIC.INI while Mosaic is actually running. Change it before you run Mosaic, or your changes may not be reflected in your Mosaic session. Mosaic reads the entire MOSAIC.INI file when it executes, and may not read the file again during that session.

Choosing a Destination from a Menu

Many people look upon Mosaic as a means of intellectual transportation, in that they think of loading a Web page as "going somewhere." It's a useful point of view, because the Web spans the world, and there is a

certain amount of effort that must go on behind the scenes to "get" anywhere on the Web. So we'll speak here of Web "destinations" when in
fact the pages we "travel to" with Mosaic come to us instead.

The easiest way to choose a destination on the Web is from one of Mosaic's
menus. Your copy of Mosaic will almost certainly come configured with
one or more menus of World Wide Web pages to which you can travel,
just by selecting them. Below you'll see one of our personal copies of
Mosaic as it looks when we first run it. (Remember, we don't load any
home page when Mosaic first executes.) We've pulled down a menu
called Starting Points, and moved the bar to an item called *NCSA Mosaic's
"What's New" Page.*

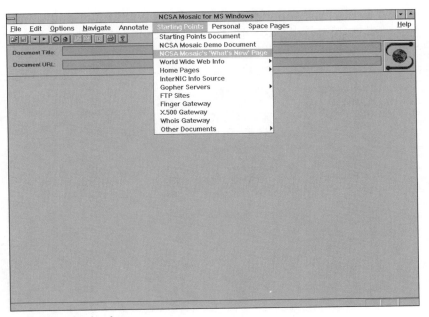

Choosing a destination

All of the items on that menu are common starting points for a Mosaic
journey. We've chosen a good starting point for Mosaic newcomers. It's
a page maintained by the NCSA and updated regularly. It summarizes
some of the best new pages to appear on the Web in recent weeks. Just
select the menu item shown, just as you would select any item on any
Windows menu.

What happens next is that Mosaic goes out on the Internet to locate and bring back the page you selected. This will take a few seconds. While it's working, notice that the globe in the Mosaic icon in the upper right corner of the screen revolves, and yellow highlights travel behind the two darker curved lines (we call them the "fishhooks") above and below the globe. This little bit of animation indicates that Mosaic is attempting to make and use a connection over the Internet. When the fishhooks are dark and the globe isn't turning, that means that Mosaic is in "standby," waiting for you to give it some command. If the yellow highlights are in the fishhooks but not moving, Internet traffic may have slowed to a standstill, or Mosaic may even have crashed. That's always a risk with software that's being actively developed.

In our case, once Mosaic retrieves NCSA's "What's New" page, you'll see something like the following screen.

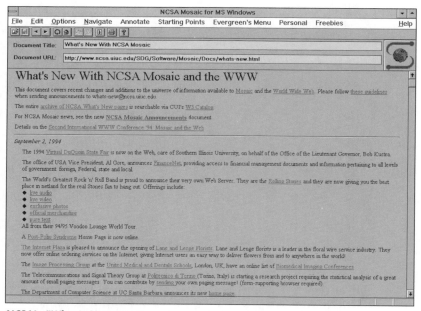

NCSA's "What's New" page

Keep in mind that this page changes regularly, so what you see will almost certainly be different from what's shown here.

If Mosaic ever seems to be taking too long to bring something back, you can abort the operation by clicking in the middle of the Mosaic globe icon. The globe will stop turning, indicating that Internet activity has been stopped. (Not all versions of Mosaic support this little trick, but the most recent ones do. This sort of difference among the many Mosaic versions currently on the street is one of the challenges of using the product.)

Traveling Mosaic's Hot Links

You'll see that a fair number of words and phrases in the "What's New" page are underlined, and on your color screen you'll see that they're displayed in blue. Any word in blue, or any image surrounded by a blue border, is a *hot link*. If you click on a hot link, you'll "go somewhere," in the grand hypertext tradition.

Try it. Bring up the "What's New" page, and pick a hot link that sounds interesting. Click *once* on the blue type for that hot link. (Double clicking a hot link may not hurt, but it may cause peculiar things to happen. One click will do it.)

The progress of your "journey" will be displayed on the status line at the bottom of the screen. After a few seconds (with a little luck and light Net traffic) your selected destination page will appear on your screen. You can scroll the page up and down with the scroll bar on the right side of the screen. There will almost certainly be more blue type or blue-framed images in the page. Click on any blue item, and you're off on another journey.

You'll find that once you get started on this stuff, you could do it all night—14.4 Kbps or not.

A very common mechanism is for a page to contain small, thumbnail images that give you some idea as to the nature of the larger images they represent. These will be rimmed in blue—and clicking on one will cause Mosaic to download the larger image from which the thumbnail was derived.

At the very end of many Web pages will be a button (actually, a simple image of a button rimmed in blue) that "returns" you to some other point. A single item on the Web may be made up of several pages that have links to one another, and that final button will take you to the main or home page of that item.

Keep in mind that this final button isn't always a path back to somewhere you've already been! You may have ridden a URL right into the middle of something interesting—and the button back may take you to another interesting place that you've never heard of. (This happens to us several times a day, it seems.) Explore! That's the way to get the most from the Web and Mosaic.

Mosaic Navigation

What you've done is actually most of what it takes to navigate around the World Wide Web using Mosaic and its friends: You choose a starting point from a menu (or enter it manually, as we'll explain a little later), go to it, and then click on a hot link to go somewhere else. Mosaic has a few other navigational features that you should be familiar with.

Going Home

First of all, at any time you can (like Dorothy) click and return home. "Home" here is your home page, if you have one defined. Defining a home page is a good idea, especially if there is one that contains hot links to most of the places you habitually go. Once you get to be more of a Mosaic expert, you can define your own home page in HTML and store it on your own hard disk. This *local* home page can be made to appear instantly as soon as you load Mosaic, and like Grand Central Station, it can be the juncture of all paths away from your machine onto the Web. (Mosaic's custom menus are an easier if not so elegant a way of doing this. We'll explain how to create custom menus later.)

To return to your home page, click on the little button on Mosaic's tool bar that has a little picture of a house on it. The home page you have defined in MOSAIC.INI will be loaded and displayed. This button is the equivalent to Mosaic's **Navigate|Home** menu item.

Reloading the Page You're Reading

There are numerous reasons for doing this, all of them having to do with the fallible nature of communications across the Internet. Sometimes an image embedded in a Web page comes down incorrectly. Sometimes, inexplicably, a page comes through part way and stops. Some of these are due to flaws in Internet itself, and others we suspect are due to flaws in the various versions of Mosaic that we have used. Either way, the way to reload the current page is to click the tool bar button that shows a loop with an arrow. (It's immediately to the left of the Home button on the tool bar.) The **Navigate|Reload** menu option has the same function. Give it a try.

Forward and Back

There are two other buttons on the tool bar that you should become familiar with. They are side by side, and each has a triangular arrow, one pointing to the left and the other pointing to the right. The arrow pointing left takes you back to the previous Web page along the path that you have been following. The arrow to the right takes you to the next Web page along the path that you've been following. The **Navigate|Forward** and **Navigate|Back** menu items are equivalent to these two buttons.

These buttons won't help you much until you've actually followed a thread through the Web a ways. If you haven't been anywhere yet, pressing **Forward** or **Back** won't take you anywhere. But if you've gone through a few hotlinks and perhaps backtracked a little, **Forward** and **Back** will allow you to retrace your steps along that path without thinking too hard about which branch you took at any particular juncture.

Entering a URL Manually

In a great many cases, you may have the URL for a particular Web page without any idea how to "get there" by way of hot links from your home page, or perhaps even any other home page listed in one of your menus. You may have been given the URL by a friend, or seen it in an E-mail message, or read about it here. There's no point-and-click way from here to there; you'll just have to enter the URL manually.

This isn't difficult. Pull down the **File|Open** URL item from the Mosaic menu. You'll see a dialog like that shown below.

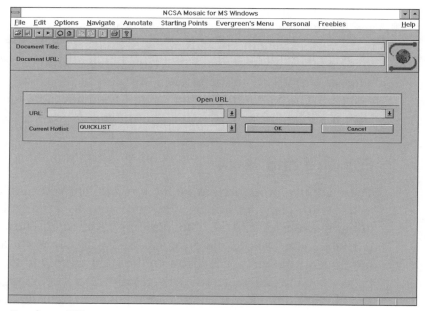

Opening a URL

Type the URL *in its entirety* into the field labeled "URL." By "in its entirety" we mean including the prefix "http://" which tells Mosaic that what you're fetching is in fact an HTML Web page. Also note that the slashes used in URLs are *forward* slashes, not the back slashes we're so used to in the DOS/Windows world.

A typical complete URL looks like the following:

http://galaxy.einet.net/galaxy.html

The prefix tells Mosaic that this is an HTML document. The part "galaxy.einet.net" tells Mosaic where the HTML document is stored on Internet; and the last part (galaxy.html) is the name of the document itself.

Another important caution: *URLs are case sensitive*. Unlike DOS where file names and path names are forced to uppercase internally before being used by your machine, the Unix world allows path names and file names to be in mixed case, and no case conversion is done. If you get the case wrong, even by one character, Mosaic will be unable to find the URL that you want.

When you click on the OK button in the dialog, Mosaic will attempt to load and display the URL. The URL we showed on the previous page is a good one, by the way. Type it in for practice, and take a look at the page it represents. The EINet company, which originated WinWeb, has a very nice page containing a host of hot links to interesting things around the world. This page, called EINet Galaxy, is a terrific example of what you'll hear referred to as a *list of links*. Many people and companies have compiled lists of Web pages that they like and present them on the Web for you to load and use as well.

Snagging a Page on Your Hotlist

Once you've found a Web page that you like (especially one with a long URL that you had to enter manually) how do you return to it quickly and easily? The answer lies in Mosaic's *hot lists*, which are nothing more than dynamically maintained menus on the Mosaic menu bar. Mosaic comes with one or two such menus by default, and your provider might add yet another for local Web resources of interest, such as those maintained by a nearby university. The Starting Points menu is such a hotlist, and it contains Web pages that Mosaic's originators at NCSA thought might be useful, especially for new Mosaic users.

Each item on a hotlist is a URL defining a Web page. You can have a fair number of hotlists, but only one of those is considered *current* at any given time. The current hotlist is the one to which you can add new items as you discover them.

Adding something to the current hotlist in Mosaic is not quite as easy as it should be. We happen to think there should be a button on the tool bar on which one push will save the Web page you're reading onto the current hotlist. Perhaps NCSA will add this feature in the future; it certainly can't be a difficult thing to do.

But we'll play it as it lays. To add a URL to the current hotlist, you have to select the **Navigate|Add Current To Hotlist** item. If you've typed in the URL for EINet Galaxy and find you like it, you can save it to the current hotlist by selecting **Navigate|Add Current To Hotlist**.

Now, the catch: *Which* hotlist?

Changing the Current Hotlist

There are actually two kinds of hotlists in Mosaic. One is called the QUICKLIST, and it is not associated with a menu on the menu bar. All other hotlists are in fact menus on the menu bar.

We'll describe how to use the QUICKLIST, but with a warning: It does *not* work correctly on many copies of Mosaic out there. Alas, QUICKLIST is Mosaic's default hotlist, and a lot of people have scratched their heads raw trying to figure out why they couldn't add a URL to QUICKLIST, when in fact they were up against a simple bug.

The **Open URL** dialog (which was displayed in the screen shot on Page 402 earlier) will tell you which hotlist is current, in the field labeled **Current hotlist**. It will probably read QUICKLIST. The QUICKLIST hotlist can be used only from the **Open URL** dialog. You can load a URL item from QUICKLIST by using the drop-down list box for the **URL** field. As explained earlier, you can type a URL into the **URL** field manually. If you click on the arrow and display the drop-down list box, what you're looking at is the QUICKLIST. Click on one of the items on the drop-down list, and Mosaic will go out and get it.

Bug Alert

That much works well on all the Mosaic versions we've tested. Where QUICKLIST often fails is in adding new items to it. You might try this on your version of Mosaic: Make sure that QUICKLIST is the current hotlist. Load a Web page that you like and select **Navigate|Add Current To Hotlist**. Then bring up the **Open URL** dialog and inspect QUICKLIST by displaying the drop-down list for the **URL** field. Is the URL for the page you added in QUICKLIST? If not, your copy of Mosaic has that bug.

Using Menus as Hotlists

We prefer to use the menus as hotlists. Adding a URL to a menu is easy enough, and works on all versions of Mosaic that we've tested. All you need to do to use a menu as your current hotlist is to bring up the **Open URL** dialog again, and drop the list box for the **Current hotlist** field. Click on the menu of your choice, and it will become the current hotlist.

As with QUICKLIST, test your newly selected hotlist: Load some Web page and then select **Navigate|Add Current To Hotlist**. The menu bar will clear and redisplay. Then bring down your chosen menu, and the page you added to it should be there on the bottom of the list of the menu's items.

You can also change the current hotlist from within the **Personal Menus** dialog, which you can bring up by selecting the **Navigate|Menu Editor...** item. We'll discuss this dialog and the way it edits menus in the next section.

Creating Multilevel Hotlist Menus

You can add items to the **Starting Points** menu, but you'll probably prefer to define one or more menus that are your own, and use them as hotlists for various projects. When you're hot on some research project, you could then define a menu just for that project, and add to it those URLs that pertain to that line of research.

Adding a Top-Level Menu

Most of Mosaic's menus are table-driven, and they can be added, deleted, or changed on the fly without having to recompile the Mosaic program. Mosaic contains its own simple menu editor, which you can invoke by selecting **Navigate|Menu Editor...** You'll see the dialog shown next:

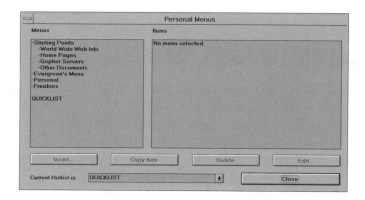

Not all of Mosaic's menus may be modified; the **File**, **Edit**, **Options**, **Navigate**, and **Annotate** menus are given and not changeable. All menus to the right of Annotate on the menu bar may, however, be changed as you desire. When you bring up the **Personal Menus** dialog, all change-able menus will be listed in the left pane labeled **Menus**.

Adding a brand new menu is easy. Notice that there is one line's worth of blank space between the last menu item (in the screen shown, "Free-bies") and the line for QUICKLIST. Click on this empty space to high-light it. Now click on the Insert button beneath the pane.

A new subdialog will appear, shown here:

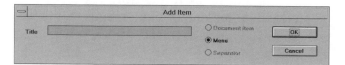

Notice that the radio button marked **Menu** is selected; this means that you will be adding a menu to the menu bar, rather than a menu item to an existing menu. Enter the name of the menu you want to add into the **Title** field, and click on **OK**. Mosaic will clear the menu bar and add a menu with that title when it redisplays all the menus.

If you intend to define several top-level menus, you should choose menu titles that are short, or you will very shortly run out of menu bar space for more menus! Better still, learn how to create menus within your menus. Here's how.

Adding Submenus to Existing Menus

Mosaic's top-level menus (like the ones you just learned how to add) may contain submenus as well as URLs. You can easily create a hierarchical menu system that can organize dozens of URLs and keep them all in easy-to-remember categories from which they can be summoned in only a few mouse clicks.

Adding a submenu to an existing menu is easy. Instead of highlighting the empty line after the name of the last top-level menu, highlight an existing menu by clicking on it. The **Add Item** dialog will again appear, ready for you to enter the name of the new submenu.

There's a hazard here, though. The dialog looks a little different this time:

Notice that you have three choices now: **Document Item, Menu**, and **Separator**. By default, the **Document Item** radio button is selected. You can add a URL to a menu this way, but that's not what we're trying to do. Instead, click on the Menu radio button. Then add the menu title as you did for the top-level menu.

You don't have to have any URLs at all in a menu. A menu can be a menu of menus only. Your **Research** menu, for example, could have submenus for **Astronomy**, **Biology**, **Music**, and **Electronics**. Furthermore, submenus may have their own submenus. Your **Astronomy** submenu could have separate submenus for planets, comets, and stars. We've set up such a multilevel **Research** menu, and its structure is shown in the **Personal Menus** dialog like this:

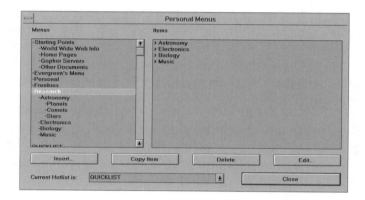

This nesting of submenus may continue to any reasonable level. However, after three or four levels it starts getting cumbersome and hard to keep straight in your head.

One unfortunate shortcoming of Mosaic's otherwise cool menu system is that you can't store and load menus to disk as disk files. Over a period of a year you might research a dozen different projects, but a dozen different menus (even if they were in some sort of nested hierarchy) would begin to clog your menu bar. After a project is done, you would then probably like to cut it from the menu and save it somehow, for possible reinsertion later on. Alas, this isn't currently possible—but if we holler loud enough, perhaps NCSA will add it to Mosaic as a new feature.

Separators

Mosaic allows you to put line separators in your menus to add an additional touch of organization. There's a bit of a trick to it, owing to the simple nature of Mosaic's menu editor: You cannot add separators after the fact, into the middle of a list of items on a menu. A separator must be added as the *last* item in a menu, and you must add items that are to display below the separator *after* the separator.

Suppose, for example, we wanted a "none of the above" submenu under **Research|Astronomy**. After adding submenus for planets, comets, and stars, we again highlighted Astronomy, then clicked the radio button for **Separator**, and then clicked on **Insert**. The separator is shown *only* in the **Items** pane, since it is an item and not a menu. After adding the separator, we added yet another submenu entitled "Odd Stuff." (This for grabbing interesting Web pages on astronomy that don't quite fit into the categories of planets, comets, or stars.)

When you get such a menu set up, it looks good and helps you keep things in order. Here's how our **Research** menu from the Mosaic menu bar looked before we added any URLs to it:

Searching the Web with Web Crawler

The Web was not designed to be indexed—it was designed to be *explored*. However, if the Web is going to be useful for much beyond entertainment, there has to be a way to find out quickly whether a desired keyword is out there somewhere. Only recently have schemes to accomplish this emerged, and while they're still a little experimental and not everything you would want them to be, they are still a whopping head start.

Our favorite so far is the Web Crawler, a fascinating word index of Web pages which you can find at:

http://www.biotech.washington.edu/WebCrawler/WebQuery.html

The Web crawler is a program that is periodically turned loose on the Web, to visit as many sites as it can reach as well as all sites linked to every site it finds. The ultimate goal is to visit and index every Web site on the planet. This isn't necessarily possible, because some Web pages aren't linked to any other, and the Web Crawler has to know that such pages exist (and where they are) before it can visit them. The Web Crawler's operators request that people send it addresses of their pages, to be added to the list of sites the Web Crawler visits.

So the Web Crawler isn't exhaustive, but it has the compensatory advantage of being *very* fast. If you ask the index a question, you get a response almost immediately. Note that the Web Crawler doesn't actually "crawl" every time you ask it a question. What you're actually doing is a simple search of the index that the Web Crawler produces. The Web Crawler goes out on its crawl every so often (how often isn't published, though we suspect it's about once a month) and takes as much time as it must to visit every page that it can. This means that your search of the index may not encompass very new Web pages, or (as explained before) isolated pages that the Web Crawler isn't aware of.

Using the Web Crawler requires Mosaic forms and buttons, which means that you must have Mosaic 2.0 to use it. The query entry screen is very simple, and is shown here:

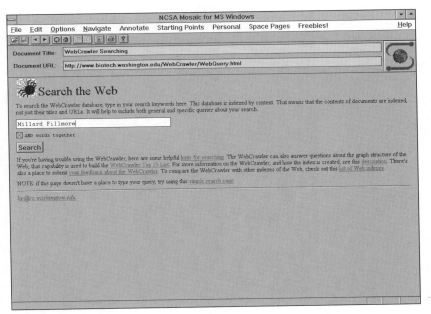

The Web Crawler

Using it is relatively simple. You type one or more words into the entry field and press the **Search** button. The index is *not* case sensitive, so you can enter everything in lowercase and not botch the search. There is a check box marked **AND words together.** This box is checked by default, and what it means is this: With the box checked, *all* of the words you type into the field must be found in each document declared a hit. If the box is cleared, a document containing *any* of the words you enter will be considered a hit. If you're looking for data on President Millard Fillmore, you should enter "Millard Fillmore" and check the **AND words together** box. Otherwise, you might find a list of documents containing references to other guys named Millard, or the Fillmore theater in San Francisco. (Poor President Fillmore has yet to be mentioned on the Web. We've checked.) If you're looking for data on dogs, cats, or mice, enter "dogs cats mice" and leave the box unchecked—but be prepared for a mountain of hits.

The next screen shot shows the result of the search we entered for the words "amateur radio" shown in the previous screen shot. It was a good search—we got dozens of hits, rather than hundreds or thousands.

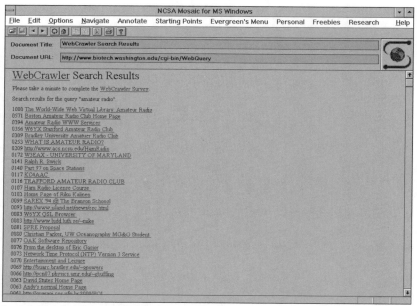

Search hits for the string "amateur radio"

Each of the hits is a hot link, and you can simply click on any of them to go out and see what you've found.

The Relevance Index

Notice the number to the left of each citation. That's a "relevance index," and is the Crawler's best guess as to how pertinent a hit is to your stated search query. The best shot is given a value of 1000, and they go down from there. A 1000 isn't considered perfect—just the best that came up, and the others are not as good. Start at the top and work down. We've found the Web Crawler's guesses to be remarkably good.

More remarkable yet is the fact that the Web Crawler runs on a simple 486 machine, rather than some massive supercomputer. Yet it indexes 40,000-plus documents and builds an index taking 50 megabytes of disk space.

Finally, something to keep in mind as you search: It's a *World* Wide Web, and some of the documents you locate will not be in English! We went searching for data on Meccano sets, an English-made construction set toy. (It's related to the old Erector Sets made in the U.S.) The Web Crawler found one citation for "meccano," but it was in a Dutch article that seemed to have nothing at all to do with toys of any sort. "Meccano" obviously means something in Dutch, but just as obviously nothing close to how we understand it in English.

Using Gopher and FTP from Inside Mosaic

What sets Mosaic apart from other Internet utilities is that it is intended to evolve into a one-stop shopping center for Mosaic services. In time, you'll use Mosaic to perform most common Internet tasks in addition to browsing the World Wide Web.

In its early stage of development, Mosaic doesn't do everything—but it does a lot, and, significantly, it provides an easy-to-use front end for both Gopher and FTP.

We don't always think of it this way, but Gopher and FTP are conceptually related. Files available for transfer via FTP are usually present in a Unix hierarchical directory of some sort. Gopher organizes "Gopherspace" into a very similar hierarchy, with menus taking the place of directories. What, in fact, is a directory but a sort of menu? The main difference is that Gopher presents a virtual hierarchy, whereas FTP directories are physical hierarchies present on a single physical machine.

Mosaic takes advantage of this similarity by presenting Gopher menus and FTP directories in basically the same way. You'll see a vertical list of items, with an icon to the left of each item. The icon indicates what sort of item it is: Image, sound file, movie, binary file, text file, and so on.

The screen shot on the next page shows a Gopher menu as Mosaic displays it. The file folder icons indicate another directory, and the page icons indicate a text file.

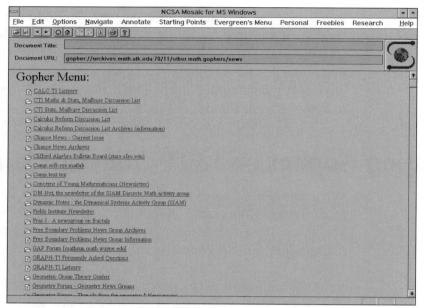

Using Gopherspace from Mosaic

Bringing Home Files with Mosaic

Bringing home a file from either gopher or an FTP site is done basically the same way from Mosaic: You check the **Options|Load To Disk** menu item and then click on the item you want. Mosaic will bring the file to your machine and store it on disk for you.

To store it on disk, of course, Mosaic needs a file name from you. Unix file names do not always map legally to DOS/Windows file names, so you have to enter a file name through a standard Windows dialog, as shown on the next page.

Mosaic will insert its best guess as to the file name you might want, and if you're downloading software or other files specifically targeted at the DOS/Windows platform, the file name will probably be legal. You might still want to change it to avoid some conflict with a file already on your system. If for that or any other reason you want to change the name, simply type over Mosaic's guess with your own file name, and click OK.

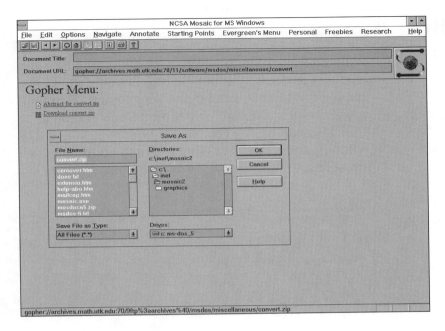

Important tip: *As soon as you download a file to disk, clear the* **Options|Load to Disk** *item!* Otherwise, any Web page you select will be downloaded as an HTML file to your disk, which probably isn't what you want to do!

Mosaic handles logging in to anonymous FTP sites for you, and in fact treats such sites as Gopher sites in terms of what it shows to you. All the same techniques apply. You can enter an FTP directory as a URL in Mosaic's Open URL dialog. Such a URL looks like this:

ftp://ftp.law.cornell.edu/pub/LII/Cello

The screen shot below is what Mosaic displays when it is logged into the above FTP directory, which contains distribution files for Cornell's Cello Web browser.

Bug Alert

All versions of Mosaic that we've used exhibit a peculiar and profoundly annoying bug: If you try to save a Gopher URL (one that begins with gopher://) to your current hotlist, Mosaic will throw a General Protection (GP) fault and dump you back to Windows. Web URLs (http://) and FTP URLs (ftp://) save to hotlists without incident.

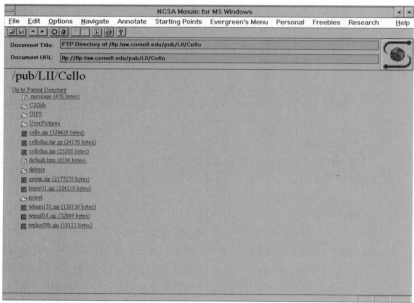

An FTP directory in Mosaic

Start Surfing!

That's the quick tour of Mosaic for the financially-challenged. There's a great deal more to Mosaic and to the World Wide Web generally than we've had time to go into here, but what's here will certainly get you started in high style for no outlay at all. Mosaic as an application still has a few bumps, but it's still mighty young as software goes, and in a year or so we think we'll find it will spread its wings and become something truly amazing.

We've scattered dozens of Mosaic free items throughout the book, but we've added a dozen more good ones on the next pages to spice up your life in the Mosaic fast lane.

The Web Hits Wall Street

Buy, buy, buy! No, wait—sell! If you want up-to-the-minute news of what's happening on Wall Street, you're not going to get it from your afternoon newspaper. Hop on the Web for free electronic quotes and graphs of the Dow Jones Industrial Average and the S&P 500. All information is delayed five minutes to satisfy the SEC, but it's definitely more current than you'll find anywhere else. You can even get historical data and graphs of stock performances over the past 25 years.

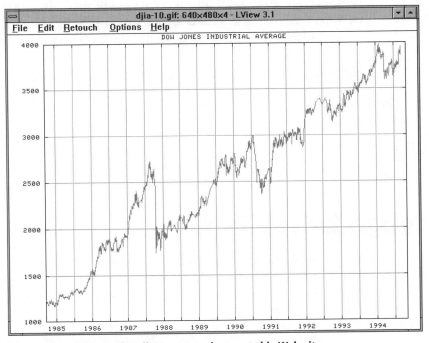

The ups and downs of Wall Street are shown at this Web site

How

Mosaic

Where

http://www.secapl.com/cgi-bin/qs

A List of Links

Electronic publications have been popping up on the Web almost as fast as they've been disappearing. Commercial newspapers especially have been experimenting with bringing their issues online, often for free but sometimes for a subscription fee. Some stick around, while others decide the effort isn't worth the payoff.

A good way to keep up with which newspapers are currently online is through the University of Florida's College of Journalism and Communications list of publications, which is actually a hotlist that you can use to select and go to your publications of choice. The list includes campus newspapers that are online as well as a list of journalism, media, and communications colleges that maintain Web servers of their own.

Note that the last portion of the URL is htm, *not* html.

How

Mosaic

Where

http://www.jou.ufl.edu/commres/webjou.htm

Through Lover's Eyes

That's the title of this one-artist exhibition by SUNY Potsdam faculty member Linda Strauss, who showcases nature art and other understated expressions of Earth presence. The images may be downloaded in either JPEG or GIF format.

TIP: As with any art exhibit on the Web, try to access the images after U.S. business hours, when net traffic has subsided a little bit. Nothing minimizes the effect of good art by having to wait interminably for it to show up!

Linda Strauss is an artist/illustrator whose work has appeared in many places, including the popular children's magazines *Cricket* and *Ladybug*.

How

Mosaic

Where

http://137.143.111.3/art/strausl/homepag.html

Financial Information

The Global Network Navigator is a great place to start if you're looking to explore all that the World Wide Web has to offer. You'll find lots of tips and resources for getting your Internet act together. There are lots of fun and helpful things to help you make the most of your Cybertravels.

Check out the Travelers' Center for help planning vacations or business trips. The Personal Finance Center teaches you how to track your finances and offers help with all things financial. You'll even find valuable information on selling your home.

Finally, connect to the *Whole Internet Catalog* to learn about the best resources available on the Internet.

How

Mosaic

Where

http://bond.edu.au/gnn/gnn.html

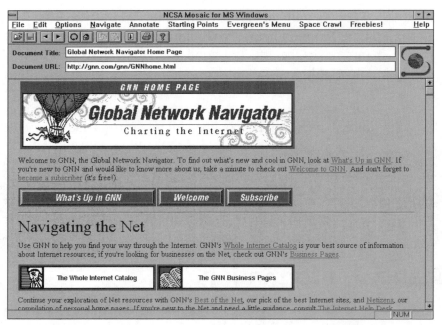

The Global Network Navigator is a great place to go for information about what's hot on the Net

A Web Browser for Macintosh

EINet (Enterprise Integration Network) has recently uploaded a freeware Web browser for the Macintosh, called MacWeb. It's just as full featured as Mosaic and Cello, but a lot easier to install and use than its rivals. EINet's parent company, Microelectronics and Computer Technology Corp. seems to be out to whet the appetite of Macintosh WWW users. The company plans to announce a commercial version of MacWeb. When that happens, there's no guarantee that the company will keep the freeware version around on the Internet. So download MacWeb and try it out while you can.

How

FTP or Mosaic

Where

ftp.einet.net (FTP) or

http://galaxy.einet.net/EINet/MacWeb/MacWebHome.html

Go To

einet/mac/macweb/macweb.latest.sea.hqx

Human Rights for the Web

Diana is the University of Cincinnati's database of hundreds of human rights documents and other legal documents, and is now available on the Web. Diana was created to "promote the creation, preservation, organization, and dissemination of primary and secondary electronic legal materials critical to human rights research," according to Taylor Fitchett, the University of Cincinatti's law library director.

Much of the database contents are documents from the U.N. and the O.A.S, although documents from several other sources are included. Putting the entire contents of Diana online for Web researches is a work in progress, so information that you expect to be there might not yet be uploaded.

How

Mosaic

Where

http://www.law.uc.edu/Diana

The TELETIMES They Are A-Changin'

Here's a theme-oriented online magazine that's as eclectic as it is interesting. Each issue focuses on a rather bland sounding theme, such as Favorite Authors or Travel, but the content itself is anything but bland. The writing style is generally professional, yet often free-wheeling— running the gamut from light and whimsical to drop-dead serious. The magazine won a "Best of the Net" award from Global Network Navigator at a recent Internet World Conference in San Jose, California.

Teletimes originates from Vancouver, Canada, so you'll sometimes find an understandable tilt towards Canadian topics, although there are plenty of articles of international interest, as the example below illustrates. You don't even need to subscribe to the publication; just go to the home page and begin browsing.

How

Mosaic

Where

http://www.wimsey.com/teletimes/teletimes_home_page.html

From one of the musically related articles available in Teletimes

Dun & Bradstreet Hits the Web

If you're in business for yourself, then you know how important it is to have an edge against your competition. Get that edge with information from Dun & Bradstreet that you can access off the World Wide Web. In addition to valuable data on economic trends, you can get lots of great business how-to's, including:

- Predicting slow payers
- Finding a job
- Managing vendors

In addition, you'll get the latest data on regional growth worldwide, industry profitability, market segment growth, and business failure statistics. Take advantage of this free educational business information and gain an advantage before your competitors do.

How
Mosaic

Where
http://www.dbisna.com

Cyberspace Middle School

"It's not just school, it's an education." With those words, sixth through ninth graders checking out Cyberspace Middle School are thrust out onto the Web to learn about all the Internet has to offer. Kids will find hundreds of links to a multitude of interesting things on the Web, like online museums located in the U.S., Australia, and Russia; study aids and research information; and links to schools around the country.

Typing was about the most high-tech class you could take back when we were in high school. Catch a ride at the Bus Stop to see what today's kids are learning. At Champaign Centennial High School in Illinois, they're teaching hypermedia and multimedia, and students developed this Web page used by other students before they head off on the Internet. Talk about your high-tech note-passing.

At some elementary-schools, kids have their own E-mail accounts they can use to communicate with each other. There are even educational resources for teachers to learn how to get the most use out of the Internet in their classrooms.

How
Mosaic

Where

http://www.scri.fsu.edu/~dennisl/CMS.html

Are You Feeling Lucky?

Spin the wheel at URouLette, "the world's first random URL generator." This program sends you to a randomly chosen Web site somewhere in Cyberspace. Where you'll end up is anybody's guess, but write us when you get there. Three random spins took us to:

- The ASTROGOF Project at Rennes' University of France, where we were treated to an awesome display of images of and from Hubble, a photo tour of the Space Shuttle, Comet Shoemaker-Levy, and animated images of eclipses and meteor showers
- Employment-related information and services for Web users from Texas A&M University
- The home page for the Green Bay Packers, with stats, trade info, history and trivia, and lots of other points of interest for "backers of the Packers"

One word of warning: If you've used the Internet for any length of time, you know you're bound to run into some offensive material from time to time. Keep that in mind as you recklessly wander the Net. By randomly accessing Web pages, you run the risk of landing somewhere less than, shall we say, tasteful.

How

Mosaic

Where

http://kuhttp.cc.ukans.edu/cwis/organizations/kucia/uroulette/uroulette.html

What Does Golf Spell Backwards?

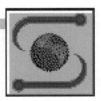

If you love golf, the 19th Hole is for you. You'll find this week's tour schedules and last week's results, rankings for the top 100 pros, the rules of golf, a great

archive of scorecards, the *Golf Digest* record book, and on and on. There are even GIFs of the hottest links, a golfer's FAQ, and a list of other great golf pages on the Web for you to check out.

How

Mosaic

Where

http://www.sdgolf.com/

Edith Cummings, golfer extraordinaire of the 1920's, downloaded from dallas.nmhu.edu

Pizza Hut Delivers!

You worked through lunch and you're so hungry you're about to eat your mouse. Maybe your're thinking about ordering a pizza but don't want to break your modem connection to make the call. Have we got news for you. If you're in an area where Pizza Hut is test marketing its new "PizzaNet," you're in luck. Order an online pizza—or pizza online—through the Web.

PizzaNet customers get product descriptions (hold the anchovies) and current specials, then place their orders. At last someone has found a practical use for the billions of dollars in research spent developing the Information Highway.

How

Mosaic

Where

http://www.pizzahut.com

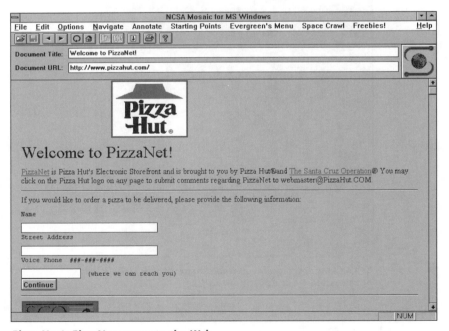

Pizza Hut's PizzaNet comes to the Web

Where to Find More Web Goodies

Where? Throughout this book! Whenever you see the Mosaic icon, you'll know that the topic refers to a Web site. And remember: you don't necessarily need Mosaic to use the World Wide Web. Any Web browser will do—Cello, MacWeb, or some other program that lets you call home (page).

FREE $TUFF

Mister, if your book was free, I'd buy it.
Comment made to the author

The Poor Man's Passport to Cyberville

The World of Free-Nets

Not everyone has the luxury of ready access to the Internet through work or school, and not everyone can afford (or wants to pay) the hourly fees charged by commercial access providers. Until recently, these Internet have-nots were left in the cold, excluded from the rapidly growing club of Internet surfers.

Enter free-nets, a grass-roots movement of community-run, volunteer-operated electronic bulletin boards designed to provide online news, entertainment, and gossip to local communities throughout the world. With access to a computer and modem, anyone can call a free-net any time of day or night to chat with neighbors, find out about upcoming community events, and learn about the people and culture that make their community special.

But most free-nets offer even more. Many have access to the Internet (most have at least some access), enabling you to take advantage of all the goodies on the Net—for *free*. If your community has a free-net, you may already have free access to the Internet and not even know it.

This section contains a list of free-nets from around the globe, although it is by no means complete. Many more are cropping up and—sadly—some are shutting down everyday, the victims of too little funding. If you don't see a free-net listed here that's in your community, contact your local library to see if they can provide more information.

California: Los Angeles Free-Net

Welcome to downtown L.A.! Now go home! Just kidding. Check out the Community Center and jump into one of the local discussions. Next you might want to check out the Media Center for stories of local and national interest. The Los Angeles Free-Net has storm alerts, travel and weather information, and an emergency network to keep you informed.

There's even access to Internet newsgroups and E-mail.

Dial

818-776-5000

Login

Select #2 at first menu

Colorado: Denver Free-Net

The Mile-High City Free-Net keeps locals informed about community happenings, educational resources, and local business. Keep in touch with other residents through local E-mail, or venture out on the Internet to chat with friends around the world.

Dial

303-270-4865

Login

guest

Florida SEFLIN Free-Net (Broward County)

The SEFLIN Free-Net includes information on local arts and entertainment, legal and financial resources, medical data, sports and recreation, and lots more. Oh yeah, you also get Internet access.

Dial

305-765-4332

Login

visitor

Florida: Tallahassee Free-Net

Tallahassee residents can check out the latest news in local government and business, as well as find out information on upcoming events in the

Tallahassee area. Users with friends and relatives in Cuba will want to access the list of names of Cuban refugees being rescued from off the coast of Florida. There's also access to Internet E-mail and discussion groups.

Dial
904-488-5056

Login
visitor

Illinois: Prairienet (Champaign-Urbana)

Users can find out about all the local happenings at the Prairienet Town Hall. You can also access the City Directory for maps and other help in getting around the Champaign-Urbana area. Looking for a special book at the library? Check out the Library and Information Center. There's also access to Internet E-mail.

Dial
217-255-9000

Login
visitor

Massachusetts: UMassK12 (Amherst)

The UMassK12 Information System BBS was created to advance education in Massachusetts schools. Its wide variety of services include computer programs and pictures you can download, an online dictionary and thesaurus, magazines, games, and a Gopher server to get you on the Internet.

Dial
413-572-5583 or 413-572-5268

Login
guest

Michigan: Almont Expression

Residents of Almont and the surrounding area will want to take advantage of all this free-net has to offer. In addition to Internet access, you'll get news and business information, sports and weather updates, and loads of newsgroups to browse. You'll also find announcements about upcoming community events and happenings, local politics and government resources, and education and health-related topics.

Dial
810-798-8290

Login
visitor

Password
visitor

Michigan: Great Lakes Free-Net (Battle Creek)

From the cereal capital of the world comes the Great Lakes Free-Net, serving Battle Creek, Kalamazoo, and other surrounding communities. Dial in for the latest news, weather, and politics, as well as business and career help, special-interest discussion groups, and E-mail to the Internet. You'll also find educational and medical resources, arts and entertainment guides, and online magazines and periodicals.

Dial
616-969-4536

Login
visitor

Michigan: Education Central (Mount Pleasant)

Education Central is the electronic communication highway for Michigan educators. Teachers can use it to exchange views and experiences,

ask questions and provide answers, expand their professional network, and discuss educational issues and policies.

Dial

517-774-3790

Login

visitor

Missouri: Columbia Online Information Network

Columbia Online Information Network (COIN) is a service to improve and expand access to community information. Use Gopher and E-mail to explore the Internet and communicate with others around the world, check out the online library for the latest newspapers and periodicals, get information about local government and politics, and learn about other services offered in the Columbia area.

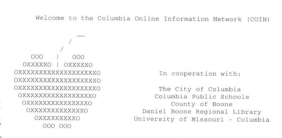

```
Welcome to the Columbia Online Information Network (COIN)

                  __
                 /
                /
   OOO   |   OOO
 OXXXXXO | OXXXXXO
OXXXXXXXXXXXXXXXXXXO          In cooperation with:
OXXXXXXXXXXXXXXXXXXO
OXXXXXXXXXXXXXXXXXXO          The City of Columbia
 OXXXXXXXXXXXXXXXXXO          Columbia Public Schools
 OXXXXXXXXXXXXXXXXO              County of Boone
  OXXXXXXXXXXXXXXO          Daniel Boone Regional Library
   OXXXXXXXXXXXO          University of Missouri - Columbia
    OOO OOO
```

Dial

314-884-7000

Login

guest

Missouri: ORION (Springfield)

The Ozarks Regional Information Online Network (ORION) offers E-mail and newsgroups of local interest, files you can download, and local, state, and federal government information. Check out the community center, which provides lots of information about local organizations, agencies, and clubs, or find the answers you're looking for in the online library's reference resources.

Dial

417-864-6100

Login

guest

Montana: Big Sky Telegraph (Dillon)

Welcome to the Big Sky Telegraph community and the online frontier! Big Sky is opening the doors to success for Montanans in the global information age by providing lots of information and resources for:

- Education
- Businesses
- Local communities

Look for government and business resources, community activities, and education-related discussions and debates.

Dial

406-683-7680

Login

bbs

New York: Buffalo Free-Net

The Buffalo Free-Net offers a great place for you to get information on local arts and cultural activities, business and employment, and government information. Are these discussions too serious?

Lighten things up a bit by discussing your hobby or favorite sport in the Hobby, Recreation, and Sports Center.

You'll even find helpful legal resources like information on the latest Supreme Court decisions and legal resources on the Internet, medical and pediatrics information, answers to your educational questions, and lots more.

Dial

716-645-3085

Login

freeport

North Dakota: SENDIT (Fargo)

Residents in the Fargo area will want to check out the educational forum for their kindergarten through twelfth graders with its links to many different educational resources. You'll also find many interesting topics at the government resource center, which provides information on the U.S. Senate and House, government bulletin boards, Gophers you can connect to, and the 1995 federal budget online.

Dial

701-237-3283

Login

bbs

Password

sendit2me

Ohio: TriState Online (Cincinnati)

TSO (TriState Online) will help answer all your business and education questions. The Business Center contains forums on:

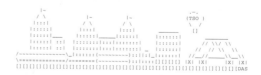

Welcome to TriState OnLine!

- Small businesses
- The construction industry

- Real estate investment
- Financial planning

Are you more interested in medical resources? The Medical Arts Center is where you can access information on a wide variety of topics and interests related to health. Doctors, hospitals, and health professionals throughout the Tri-state area have volunteered their time and expertise to answer your questions and provide articles of general interest in their individual fields. The following areas are just a few of the medical topics currently available online:

- Heart Hospital
- Children's Hospital
- Women's Health Care Center
- Burns Institute
- Special Needs
- Vet & Pet/Animals Center
- Anxiety Disorders
- Breastfeeding Resource Center
- Nurses Special Interest Group (SIG)

You'll also find E-mail and other Internet resources, access to the latest information on community happenings, online newspapers, fun and games, and science and technology resources and data.

Dial

606-781-5575

Login

visitor

Ohio: Cleveland Free-Net

Cleveland Free-Net, the one that started them all, offers an abundance of resources—both locally and on the Internet—for cyberexplorers. The Arts Building is home

to a wide variety of arts in just about every form conceivable: visual, music, performance, literary arts, and more.

Would-be gourmets and gourmands will find terrific discussion groups dedicated to cooking, dining out, planning parties, or enjoying beer and wine. Any questions? Try "Ask the Chef" and take advantage of the experience and resources of other members to help answer them. Enjoy!

Dial
216-368-3888

Login
Select #2 at first menu

Ohio: Greater Columbus Free-Net

Ohio's capital is home of the Greater Columbus Free-Net, where residents will find many interesting local and international topics to explore and enjoy. Get answers to all your medical, educational, and legal questions, find out about upcoming community events, discuss topics related to local arts and culture, and much more. Then expand your horizons by "teleporting" across the globe through one of the numerous links to the Internet.

Dial
614-292-7501

Login
guest

Ohio: Dayton Free-Net

Home of the Wright Brothers, Dayton's residents can fly (groan) through Cyberspace and check out Internet sites around the world. Those wanting to stay close to home will still find a plethora of information about their community and upcoming happenings. There's a great selection of online newspapers and magazines, medical resources and information, access to local government and educational facilities, and lots of great discussions about many different hobbies, sports, and recreational activities.

At the Science and Technology Center, you'll find many Internet resources covering a broad spectrum of interests, including:

- Earth sciences
- Life sciences
- Physical sciences
- Technological sciences
- Information on NASA

Browse the magazine rack and check out the many different electronic magazines for tips on gardening and other hobbies. There are even online versions of *The Discovery Channel Guide*, *Discover Magazine*, *Wired*, and several other popular magazines.

Dial
513-229-4373

Login
visitor

Ohio: Lorain County Free-Net

Lorain County's link to the Internet provides locals with free help with business needs, education resources, help for the disabled, and much more. You'll find answers to your health-related questions, information on local events, a library center, and a site devoted to information on natural resources and agriculture.

The Civic Center provides information on local government agencies and the histories of the various cities and townships located within Lorain County.

With businesses that run the gamut between "mom and pop" operations and international conglomerates, Lorain County has no shortage of resources to draw on for answers to your commerce-related questions.

At the Health Center, the doctor is in to help you with whatever ails you—physically or mentally. The Health Center puts members in touch with medical information and medical professionals, both locally and across the Internet.

Dial

216-366-9721

Login

guest

Ohio: Medina County Free-Net

Thomas Edison, The Wright brothers, John Glenn, John D. Rockefeller, and several presidents. There must be something in Ohio's water that produces so many great Americans. Maybe you can find out its secret on the Medina County Free-Net. While you're there, browse through the online magazines and periodicals, get some helpful medical advice, or maybe relax and catch up on some local gossip. But that's just scratching the surface. You'll find lots more to do and see here.

Dial

216-723-6732

Login

visitor

Ohio: Youngstown Free-Net

The Youngstown Free-Net offers a wide variety of resources, including local events, veterinary resources, help for small businesses, and access to legal documents. You'll find a big selection of Christian and Jewish resources as well, including:

- Bible study
- Jewish studies
- Prayer request
- News from Israel
- *Judea Magazine*
- Christian Event Center
- Traditional, liberal, and conservative Judaism
- Holocaust Documents

Byte-heads can check out the Computer Center for the latest technology and news in the computer industry, or for more general news, read *USA Today* online.

Dial

216-742-3072

Login

visitor

Ohio: Learning Village (Cleveland)

With the feel of a college campus, Cleveland's Learning Village has many resources for students and teachers alike. Try the Teacher's Lounge for discussions about topics concerning educators. The Student Lounge provides students with a forum for expressing concerns and issues. Information about college and university opportunities around the country can be obtained on College Row.

If the discussion gets too heavy, lighten up with a trip to The Cafe, where talk is more along the lines of music, entertainment, and sports.

Medical information and resources are available at The Clinic, and Internet links to over 100,000 locations worldwide are available at The Teleport.

News hounds will love the selection of newspapers and periodicals that can be found at The Newsstand. Titles include:

- *Investor Business Daily*
- *Jerusalem Post*
- *London Times*
- *Los Angeles Times*
- *USA Today*
- *Washington Post*
- *Moscow News*
- *Forbes Magazine*
- *National Review*
- *Highlights for Children*

Dial

216-247-6196

Login

visitor

Rhode Island: Providence

The Ocean State Free-Net has Gopher, Telnet, and E-mail access to the Internet, great government data, and business resources. You can also find many special interest groups to share your ideas and opinions, as well as information about special events and happenings in and around Providence.

```
Welcome to the...

        #### ####
     ## ##### ##### ##
   # #### #### #### #### #
  #### ### ### ### ### #####
 ##  #### ##      ## #### ##
######  ##          ## ######
#########            #########

 #####    ####  ##### ### ##
 #   #   ##  ##   ##   ## # ##
 #   ##  ##  ##   ##   ## # ##
 #        ## #### ##   # #  ##
 #####   ## ##  ##    ## ### 
```

The Ocean State Free-Net

Dial

401-831-4640

Login

No login or password is necessary

Texas: Rio Grande Free-Net (El Paso)

Bienvenidos! The Rio Grande Free-Net, located at El Paso Community College in El Paso, Texas, serves Juarez, Mexico, the Upper Rio Grande area of West Texas, and adjoining communities in New Mexico. Designed for both English and Spanish speakers, this free-net covers health care, news about local and surrounding communities, arts, entertainment, and government. You'll also get the latest weather and sports, as well as local business- and industry-related news.

Dial

915-775-5600

Login

visitor

Washington: Seattle

The Seattle Community Network offers forums on hot issues, people in the news, government and environmental issues affecting Washington, and health-related resources. Learn about the community life and culture of the Seattle area, upcoming events, and more. Plus, you get Internet access.

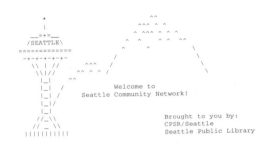

Dial

206-386-4140

Login

visitor

Washington: Tri-Cities Free-Net

Washington residents don't have to live in Seattle to get on the Internet for free. The Tri-Cities Free-Net has Internet access, plus games, news and community events information. Browse through the online library, read an online magazine, or get up-to-the-minute weather reports. You'll also find great resources for business and health, food and cooking, sports and recreation, and lots more.

Dial

509-375-1111

Login

No login ID or password is necessary

British Columbia: CIAO! Free-Net (Trail)

CIAO! offers science and technology data, local community information and services, and help from government agencies. You'll find the latest local and world news, educational resources, special interest groups on many different topics so you can discuss whatever's on your mind, and links to other free-nets.

Dial

604-368-5764

Login

guest

British Columbia: Victoria Free-Net

With the Victoria Free-Net, you get Web and Gopher access to the Internet, as well as E-mail and lots of newsgroups. If you want to stay closer to home, go to *Douglas & Yates* and "hang out with the minds of the local and global community" for discussions on issues that affect your neighborhood or the whole world.

You can also access a wide assortment of business-related resources, including:

- The Better Business Bureau of Vancouver
- The Canadian Job Bank
- *The Internet Business Journal*
- The Online Career Center

In addition, you can access many government agencies and volumes of religious texts. There's even an online medical center to discuss what ails you.

Dial

604-595-2300

Login

guest

Ontario: National Capital Free-Net (Ottawa)

French and English speakers can access the National Capital Free-Net in Ottawa. Internet access lets you recieve and send E-mail from around the globe, as well as enables you to access numerous newsgroups. Read about the latest community developments, social services, and environmental topics, plus get interesting documents and files about science, engineering, and technology.

Browsers will want to access the electronic newsstand, with copies of many interesting French and English magazines and newspapers like:

- *The Ottawa Citizen*
- *LeDroit*
- *Bulletin Amerique*
- *La presse de France / News from France* (via *Ambassade de France*)
- *Tour 'n Travel Guide* from EOTA

There's even an online boutique for you to get free-net memorabilia like T-shirts, coffee mugs, and caps.

Dial

613-564-3600

Login

guest

Finland: Finland Free-Net (Helsinki)

The Finland Free-Net offers connections in Helsinki and around the world. You can choose between English or Finnish to access the latest in news, sports, weather, and entertainment. Online resources are available for teachers and students, environmentalists, business owners, and more. Kids will enjoy World Youth News with information of interest to teens and young adults. When you're ready to check out Cyberspace, go to the Airport for Internet links worldwide.

Dial

358-929292

Login

visitor

Germany: Free-Net Erlangen-Nuernburg

Displayed in both German and English, this free-net offers sports, recreation, film reviews, and special-interest groups on many different topics. Community news and events are covered, as well as educational and government resources. Internet access is available, too.

Dial

+49-9131-85-8111

Login

gast

Index

FREE $TUFF from the Internet

B

Babylon 5, 363–64
Bach, 282
Back pain, 173–74
Back Talk: Advice for Suffering Spines, 173
Backgammon, 140, 142–43
Bailey, Covert, 164
Bank mergers, 197
Bar Mitzvah planner, 296
Barney the Dinosaur, 211–12
Baseball, 349–50, 352
Basketball, 352–53
BBS (bulletin board systems)
    CancerNet, 162
    Consumer Information Center, 13–14
    FedWorld, 157
    genealogical, 183
    legal, 267
    rail-related, 346
    Seagate, 107
Beatlemania, 290
Beer brewing supplies, 133
Bert's African Animals, 245
Books for Children, 245
Bescaby Lane Vineyards, 133
Bible
    bootup quotes, 294
    King James Bible, 299
    quiz, 300
    translations, 299
Bicycling, 370–71
Bill of Rights, 270
Binary files, 19–21, 73
Binary stars, 335
Biologist's Guide to Internet Resources, 318
Biology, 307–14
Biomedical issues, 267
BioPark, 28
Birds, 122
Bitmaps, 78
BIX, 8
Bjordahl, Hans, 213
Black History and Culture, 185
Blue Dog, 242–43
Bog (word finding game), 140
Bombings, 271
Bonds, 197–98
Bookkeeping, 68
Books and literature, 35

academic journals and newsletters, 41–42
Book of Mormon, 301
Books for Children, 245–46
children's, 326
classic works, 45
computer books, reviews of, 311
Cyber-Sleaze (music and industry), 42
electronic newsstand, 37
electronic publications, 43
electronic texts, catalog of, 36
Elements of E-text Style, 40–41
e-mail to *U.S. News and World Report*, 44
foreign, 254
Inc. Magazine, 37, 45
Internet, creators and improvers, 42–43
Moe's Books, 39
New York Times best sellers, 38
Online Book Initiative (OBI), 45
poetry, 41
Russian humanities, 39
science fiction, 46
sexual harassment, 268
Shakespeare, 38, 41
USA Today, 44
writer's resources, 40
Bookstore, 39
Boschert, Ken, DVM, 308
Brady Bill (handguns), 269
BrainCubes, 140
Breastfeeding, 178
British Broadcasting Corporation, 239
British humor, 214
British Jewish Information Network, 297
Browne, Jackson, 284
Bruce, Thomas, R., 387
Buddhism, 298
Budgeting, 202
Buffett, Jimmy, 284, 288
Bug, 405, 415–16
Bush-Clinton succession reports, 158–59
Bush, George, 209
Business and career, 47
    accounting, 64–65
    advertising products, 327
    Asian business communication, 63
    bookkeeping, 68

Career Connection's Online Information, 57
consumer news, 60
Coping with Unemployment, 56
Daily Market Report, 51
economic indicators and data, 48–49, 55
EEOC library, 268
federal government job postings, 50
flowcharting, 63–64
forms, 65–66
government agencies, 49
grant proposals workshop, 61–62
HeadsUp news service, 48
income comparisons, 59–60
incorporate online, 53
Information Researchers, 59
Internetworking guide, 52
inventory tracking, 62
invoicing, 66
laws, 49
NAFTA, 52
NC machine tool, 67–68
NetPages Internet directory, 64
Online Career Center, 57–58
overseas jobs, 49–50
sexual harassment, 268
Silicon Graphics newsletter, 55–56
stock market quote, 53–54
telephone area codes, 54
The Chronicle of Higher Learning, 56
You're Hired! interview simulator, 51
ZIP codes, 54–55
Button editors, 100–01

C

C Users' Group Library, 92
Cable TV, 364
Caffeine, 174
Caffeine Jitters: Some Safety Questions Remain, 174
CAI language, 113–14
California, University of, 238
Canada, 219, 222
    Communications Canada, 146
    Constitution, 219
    crafts and gifts, 330

Here are a few of the author's favorite E-mail messages from readers, who offer their opinions of *Free $TUFF from the Internet*. We even let Mr. Vincent include his responses, which might have been a mistake....

I just purchased the book today and cannot put it down. As a new Internet user, this is the first publication I read that I could totally understand. I am still fumbling my way around, but am learning more each day. If you have any suggestions, or are planning an update to this book, please reply —D.S.

Your wish is my Alt+Shift+Command. The next book is called FREE $TUFF *from the World Wide Web, and will be available mid-year, 1995. There are a few other titles lined up for publication soon after, but they hinge on whether I'm released from Happy Acres by then. The nurses finally let me have my computer back, and told me that next week I may even be able to have visitors.*

Your book makes sense of many confusing Internet topics. It is well organized and humorously written. I'd like to see your team tackle a book about Mosaic, including as much of the help/configuration files as possible. —Joe D.

I appreciate the comments, and have in fact recently gang-authored a book with PC Guru Jeff Duntemann and Mac Wizard Ron Pronk (their true full names) called the Mosaic EXplorer Pocket Companion. *If you're looking for my name on it, look way down at the bottom. Jeff and Ron told me it was a matter of listing the names alphabetically, though that's what they said about why I was given such a small office with no window.*

I just got your book.... This is absolutely incredible!!!!! This place [the Internet] is unlimited in getting any kind of info anyone wants to whenever!! —Duffy M.

Thanks Duffy!!!!! I know you're excited, but easy on the exclamation key!!!!! And save a little caffeine for the rest of us!!!!!

I feel that *FREE $TUFF from the Internet* will not only be helpful for education but also helpful...in personal endeavors.... I feel that there is just so much in this book that it is well worth the purchase. —R.H.

It's also guaranteed to freshen breath, whiten teeth, and generally make you more attractive to the opposite sex.

RE: "Let us know what you disliked, as well." THE INK! The stench that emanates from your book, the asthma attack it produces in people who are allergic, and the fact that it must be read contained in a sealed, metal-glass-topped box. —C. L. W.

Since FREE $TUFF *from the Internet is intended for recreational use, I guess I should have included a warning that it not be smoked, inhaled, snorted, or ingested in any way. Rest assured that this oversight will be corrected in future editions.*

Regards from Malaysia! Just a note to say I am thankful for the info you've written to enable people like me who're quite new to the Internet to surf it more easily. Do you mean that I can write to President Clinton and expect a reply? —L. H. W.

I guess that's between you and the President. All I can say is that if you are going to write him, make it fast. His address is subject to change— perhaps to something like former.president@nobody.appreciates.me.

Thanks to everyone who sent me mail. I've tried to respond to each note, but with two kids, two books I'm currently writing, and only 24 hours in a day, I may have missed someone. Thanks for the feedback!